TIDES OF BETRAYAL:
SCANDAL ON THE WAVES

by

Peter A. Antonucci

Landmark Press
Ridgefield, CT

Tides of Betrayal: Scandal on the Waves
Copyright ©2023 by Peter Antonucci.

For information on the cover illustration and design, contact Dawné
Dominque of DusktilDawn Designs.
Cover art Peter Antonucci © 2023

ISBN: 9798870321585 – paperback

If you are interested in purchasing more works of this nature, please stop
by www.peterantonuccibooks.com.

Printed in the United States of America

Dedication

To Marie Sciolino Oberacker

Acknowledgements

It seems like a lifetime ago that I was sitting in classrooms at St. David's School in Manhattan listening to my English teachers drone on about the importance of writing. Technical subjects such as grammar, sentence structure, vocabulary and their attendant quizzes were far less interesting than the street sounds outside our classroom windows.

A few years later, in Collegiate School, a different group of scholars waxed on about critical thinking, creative writing, and the analysis of classic literature.

Fast forward a few decades and legal writing became the newest challenge. Law school professors, and then law firm partners, taught me the art of effective advocacy through prose.

At relatively few points during any of the stops along that journey did I truly appreciate what I was being taught. Nor did I ever foresee myself as a novelist. But as I write this section at the outset of my third novel, my respect for those who provided me with the critical building blocks of writing has grown only more immeasurable. Without those men (yes, they were all men), I would never have mastered the skills necessary to craft the plots, subplots, and characters that live in the ensuing pages.

In the present, no one is a greater devotee and enthusiast than my wife, Tami. She has supported my thousands of keyboard hours and tolerated countless occasions when I have been unable to attend events because I "just have to finish this chapter."

My daughter, Nicole, was also a great asset as the reader and editor of early drafts of this manuscript. As a modern-day thirty-something, she made my writing less Jurassic and more *hip*.

And my son, Alex, has always been the steady hand, encouraging me to move forward to pursue my dreams, even if they involve writing fanciful tales about arrogant New York lawyers, a community with which he is only too familiar.

I am grateful to Landmark Press for their exhaustive work bringing the adventures of Eva Lampedusa and her shipmates to these pages. Everyone on the team has been remarkable and I am deeply grateful for all their hard work and assistance throughout the process.

Marci Baun was my editor *par excellence* once again. I'm profoundly indebted to her amazing attention to details, pulling my text out of the weeds, and challenging me to "make everything work together."

Dawne Dominique of DusktilDawn Designs was an excellent visionary, capturing the essence of the book in her thoughtful cover design.

Finally, this is the last episode in the *Billionaires at Sea* written trilogy. It has been a labor of love creating the characters and shenanigans that surrounded Eva Lampedusa during her nautical travels and travails. With each line of each page, I tried to weave imagination and magic into my fictional friends, without actually implicating any actual people and events whose vessels may have sailed through the waves of my life. I hope you have enjoyed their persona and exploits as much as I have enjoyed bringing them to you.

Chapter 1
Chaweng Beach Resort and Spa

Paradise had sailed through the Gulf of Thailand and was tidily moored off the coast of Koh Samui, Vietnam, by 8:30 a.m. By the time they were cleared to disembark thirty minutes later, the ship's ninety-five passengers were excited to explore the small seaside community where colorful paper lanterns hung above doorways and the people lived a simple littoral life. The early risers climbed into one of the ship's shiny white and blue tenders and motored into town.

The quaint palm-fringed destination seemed to resemble some of the smaller Vietnamese towns, like Phu Quoc, where Paradise had docked a week earlier. As was the case in many Vietnamese seaside towns the ship had just visited, Koh Samui bore a stench of raw sewage. Unfortunately for passengers aboard Paradise, the wretched stink was made even more unbearable by the September heat. The only redeeming attribute was that this town lacked the monstrous garbage trenches that had adorned each side of Phu Quoc's main roads and served as home to hundreds of scavenging rodents.

As the seafaring passengers had learned from their constant circumnavigation of the globe, the disgusting odor of rotting refuse was common in ports, especially those located in the world's lesser developed countries. And as was also the case in such ports, the main goal upon reaching shore was to leave the wharf area as quickly as possible, opting instead to explore local cultures and remote villages, and leave the reek of the dock far behind.

The ship's concierge team had arranged shuttle vans to take the ship's passengers from Koh Samui into the sleepy beach town of Bophut, about fifteen minutes from where the tenders came ashore.

The decrepit buses stopped at Fisherman's Village, a makeshift tourist trap where prototypical tourist shops peddled everything from straw bags to souvenir T-shirts and knock off versions of fine designer handbags and shoes. But the obnoxiously affluent owners of Paradise did not usually frequent such pedestrian shops. Why buy an artificial Chanel purse for $80 when the ship made regular stops in Hong Kong, Venice, New York, and Rome where women could purchase the real thing for $8,000 or more?

Representatives from the concierge team ushered their charges down the main street, if one could call it that, of Bophut. The visitors were relieved this part of Vietnam was without the legion of seemingly suicidal motorbikes that were ubiquitous throughout other parts of the country. Accordingly, they no longer had to execute Exorcist-like head swivels at every intersection.

Once they disembarked the dilapidated vans and emerged into the tropical heat, the ship's passengers were elated to call upon the   Chaweng Beach Resort and Spa. The ship's onboard social team had arranged for its passengers to enjoy unfettered access to the resort's facilities, including pool chairs and cabanas, as well as its restaurants. Those arrangements were secured by a one-time payment of $15,000 by the ship to the resort. Such practices were not at all unusual for Paradise, an owner-occupied ship that constantly circumnavigated the planet's seas.

Paradise was not a cruise ship. It was the home away from home for billionaires who wanted to avoid the paparazzi while they luxuriated in decadence. It was also home to a few legendary lotharios who spent time aboard Paradise philandering anonymously with other passengers or crew, or perhaps toting a movie star along with them for a little play time—while their wives spent time at home, or were cavorting with the local tennis pro. And they did all this while basking in unsurpassed luxury.

Paradise sailed proudly at 455 feet in length and carried only sixty luxury suites that were ostensibly to be occupied by its owners, as well as forty visitor flats available for its guests. Because of its enormous size and shiny white exterior, it could easily be mistaken for a cruise ship. Indeed, before the era of mammoth cruise ships ferrying over 7,000 passengers to and from tropical paradises, cruise ships were smaller than Paradise. It looked like a cruise ship because its physical essence *was* a cruise ship.

But Paradise was *not* a cruise ship, as its owners and staff sermonized to anyone who would listen. It was the dream of its founder, Eva Gabriella Lampedusa, a mostly-retired New York litigator who had seized the opportunity to purchase the nearly-built ship from Mitsubishi Marine and a Saudi sheik for the tidy sum of $270 million. Most of those funds had been secured by various owner-investors whom Eva had personally selected to be part of her exclusive nautical community. The overwhelming majority of owners were lawyers and business people from the New York area whom Eva had known during her decades of practicing law at Wilson Everson, a 1450-lawyer firm in Manhattan. There were a few outliers, friends of Eva's friends, but all were financially well-heeled. They had to be in order to amass the minimum net worth of $50 million before submitting a $25,000 application fee to even be considered for ownership by the owners of Paradise. If their application was deemed sufficient for consideration, the applicant next needed to secure the approval of 85% of the current owners of Paradise. Only then could they be initiated into the palace of floating opulence where almost anything was possible, and everything was expected.

Luxury suites, the trite name given to the owners' cabins, were divided into four categories—platinum, gold, silver, and bronze—depending on the extent of one's financial investment.

Prices ranged from $6 million to $30 million, excluding the one $100 million dollar platinum luxury suite owned by Lorraine Williams, one of Eva's closest friends and the wealthiest woman in Canada. Condo association fees aboard the floating bastion for the uber wealthy ranged from $30,000 to $100,000 per month, definitely not a fee structure for the faint of heart.

The Covid-19 pandemic had turned cruise ships into floating petri dishes where the newest coronavirus ran rampant. For decades, those ships had had to deal with the older strain of *ship flu*, norovirus. So Covid-19 added a layer of potentially fatal toxicity to an already fragile maritime environment. As a result, many cities or countries lobbied successfully to keep those dastardly disease carrying vessels away from their shores. Other ports understood the enormous risk visited upon them by those massive floating resorts, but concluded the financial reward that befell the local businesses outweighed those risks. Those municipalities satisfied themselves by having the passengers take Covid-19 rapid tests and walk through temperature-reading tunnels as they disembarked the ships. Many also required the ships' doctors to file daily reports concerning any passengers who exhibited symptoms of Covid-19. Aboard the ships, passengers who tested positive for Covid-19 were isolated in their cabins for as many days as the WHO or CDC recommended at the time. Even when released from quarantine, they were treated like lepers by their fellow travelers.

Shortly after one of the Chaweng Beach Resort guests complained vociferously about the ship passengers who had overrun the resort, a couple from Paradise ordered their fourth round of mojitos. Of course, they had no way of knowing about the complaint, at least not then. The Paradise travelers were just cavorting and frolicking around the hotel's quiet pool. And being anything but quiet.

The day at the Chaweng Beach Resort and Spa had started smoothly enough, with some of Paradise's owners surveying the gift shop while others walked the beach. A few couples enjoyed the resort's specialty pineapple and bacon sunrise omelets at one of Chaweng's exquisite restaurants. Most of Paradise's suite owners never felt the need to rush ashore first thing in the morning and abandon their buoyant abodes. As a result, not more than five couples from Paradise had even made it to the resort before noon. By lunchtime, everything had changed.

The Chaweng Beach Resort and Spa was a lush and picturesque location where multi-millionaires retreated to escape the chaos of their overcrowded cities in Asia, Europe, and even the United States. It featured only eleven superior beachside villas and nine deluxe beachside suites, the *cheapest* of which sprawled over 8,500 square feet and cost a fraction over $7,800 a night. Ridiculously wealthy vacationers seeking a private retreat enjoyed the resort for the privacy and luxury it provided. So, when sixty-three ship passengers from Paradise invaded the resort that afternoon, their presence did not go unnoticed.

When some of the more youthful and spirited Paradise folks first arrived at Chaweng, they headed to the main pool. Four octogenarian hotel guests had been sprawled on lounges, each reading different sections of the South China Morning Post, a Hong Kong-based, English-language newspaper owned by Alibaba. Their presence was clouded by the wretched odor being sent aloft by their massive raw-looking cigars. In addition, the air around the pool was filled with a miasma of spoiled chicken, coriander, turmeric, and braised cabbage. That was not the ambiance the Paradise posse was looking for. Nor was the slow beat of Indian classical music that whined from two tinny speakers at either end of the pool. The group was planning to set their own recreational table and the droning music, old men, and their attendant bouquet did not fit into their plans. Keen to stake out their territory for their enjoyment, they explored other opportunities in the chic resort.

Far from the main pool, the quiet pool at the Chaweng Beach Resort and Spa lived up to its name. The only discernible sounds came from indigenous birds. The air was free of cigar stench. The gentle gurgling from the fountain in the center of the pool, and the rules prohibiting radios, cell phones, or loud conversation, made the pool the most meditative location in the entire resort. Or at least it was supposed to be. But by the arrival of the noon hour, the quiet pool had been transformed into an aquatic fraternity house and all rules had been shattered.

Perhaps the quiet pool's most distinctive feature was an eight-foot-wide black quartzite shelf area *inside* the pool, only three inches below the water's surface. On that shallow sill, the hotel had positioned six stainless steel lounge chairs with grey and blue Sunbrella waterproof cushions. Those were more than enough for the resort's few guests who chose to forsake the private pools outside their individual villas, or the resort's larger community pool, for the quiet pool.

As if they were a collection of Rodney Dangerfields in Caddyshack, the Paradise contingent—some of whom were wearing cheeky thongs that could have doubled as dental floss—abruptly dragged another eight chairs into the water, splashing and shouting at each other. The mahogany chairs they towed into the pool were not designed for that purpose. Those wooden chairs were supposed to remain on the concrete patio surrounding the pool; they would rot in the salt water.

The scantily clad Paradise carousers then proceeded to order drinks and food which the attentive Chaweng Beach staff promptly delivered to their newly established, aquatic seats. It was only a matter of a few minutes before French fries, onion rings, shards of lettuce and even a few straws created a floating motif among the chairs in the shallow water. One of the Paradise owners asked a waiter to turn on some music. The surprised yet polite staff member explained that the soon-to-be revelers were in the quiet pool where music was not permitted, and voices were to be kept to a minimum. Three minutes later, it was as if that conversation had never occurred. Tim Moore, one of the Paradise suite owners, emerged from the resort's gift shop with a Sonos Bluetooth speaker with a powerful confluence of treble and bass. Within seconds, the ship's flamboyant hairstylist, Yves LeMaire had the speaker in full operational mode and Meghan Trainor's suggestive voice was roaring that it was all about the bass.

The hotel guests were aghast. Harvey Madison, a Texas father of two children he and his wife had just coaxed to sleep in their bungalow a few minutes earlier, stormed away from the pool area and directly into the general manager's office.

"What the hell's going on out there?" he asked, pointing in the general direction of the pool. "This is supposed to be some sort of fancy resort and that there is supposed to be some sort of quiet pool. Ain't nothing fancy or quiet about any of it."

"What do you mean?" the bewildered manager asked.

"The love boat just pulled up and them characters is partying all over the place. They're blasting the radio in the quiet pool, singing like it's New Year's Eve, and acting like this place is their very own frat house. Me and the missus didn't pay thirty-five grand to see a bimbo show."

"I'm so sorry Mr. Madison. I'll look into it."

"Look into it? Ain't nothing to look into. I can hear them bastards from here. Listen. Y'all hear it?"

The manager certainly could hear it. Shaggy's protestations that "It wasn't me" were so deafening the manager was gob smacked.

"Yes, Mr. Madison. I definitely hear it. I'm so sorry," he capitulated. Thinking quickly, he added, "Listen, I'd like you and Mrs. Madison to be the resort's guests at Coconut Silk tonight. Dinner's on us and I'll also comp you up to $400 on cocktails and wine. Does that sound fair?"

"With the kids?"

"With the kids."

Coconut Silk was the resort's most upscale restaurant, where bluefin tuna was plated at $125 each and Coffin Bay king oysters were priced at almost $100 per oyster. The Texan ran through the numbers in his head and calculated that the Madison family was about to enjoy a $1,000 dinner on the house. And he was able to enjoy some sort of skin carnival at the pool for the next hour or so while Mrs. Madison cajoled the kids back to sleep. For his part, the resort manager never let on that Paradise had tendered $15,000 for the privilege of using the resort's facilities, so the result of the transaction was financially beneficial to both parties.

By the time Harvey Madison returned to the quiet pool, two of the Paradise suite owners were slow dancing to Barry White in waist deep water. Unfortunately, the water was not quite deep enough to hide the man's wandering hands which the woman graciously allowed to explore the sides of her breasts.

The aquatic dancers, Donna and Don Bickford, were from Westport Connecticut. Although dancing suggestively, they were not inordinately revealing or rowdy. Donna had recently turned fifty-five and Don, a hedge fund manager in Greenwich Connecticut, was fourteen years her senior. But their grinding and kissing were not what the guests at the Chaweng Beach Resort had in mind when they had scouted out their chaise lounges at the quiet pool that morning.

One of the other suite owners, Tim Moore, the same man who had purchased the Sonos noise maker thirty minutes earlier, had taken a walk away from the group and was surreptitiously taking a few hits of dope from a vape pen he almost always carried in his tote bag when he disembarked from the ship. Drugs, and smoking of any kind, were expressly prohibited aboard Paradise.

Tim had an addiction to almost any recreational drug he could get his hands on. Originally from New Zealand, Tim met his wife, Robin, in Houston where they lived most of their adult lives. Robin had a master's degree in chemical engineering and the couple had parlayed that, and Tim's loose connections to a Mexican cartel, into a cocaine and ecstasy ring that netted them almost half a million dollars a year. Robin was not much of a presence in the party scene aboard Paradise, preferring the sanctity of her luxury suite to the bars where Tim was usually reposed.

Tim was detested as a troublemaker. He had a problem separating fantasies about other owners' daughters from the reality of seducing them. Perhaps fearing all kinds of misadventures at the resort, and knowing her husband's predilection for extramarital cavorting, Robin had opted to stay on board Paradise that day, instead enjoying the latest James Patterson novel.

After his vape pipe indulgence, Tim slinked into one of the mahogany lounge chairs that had been dragged onto the pool's shelf. It was from that seat he ogled the pool and more specifically, Donna Bickford. Donna didn't care for Tim's attention. Her husband liked it even less. Don was well aware of Tim's reputation as a womanizer, if not a pedophile. Like a few other owners aboard Paradise, Don suspected Tim was engaged in some sort of illicit activities on the ship but couldn't quite put his finger on it. Very few of the owners knew of Tim and Robin's cottage industry dealing ecstasy and cocaine, and the couple was happy to have it remain that way. They sold their product to only a few of their mega-wealthy friends aboard the ship. They didn't need to transact more business because these few contacts amounted to a regular income of hundreds of thousands of dollars.

"Hey Tim, whatcha looking at," asked Don in a menacing voice.

"Nothing really," replied Tim with the wry smile most suite owners had come to despise.

That was probably not the ideal response. Don took it to mean that Donna was not much to look at. He took offense at that.

"Then why are you staring?" He was right. During the entire verbal exchange, Tim had not once taken his eyes off the sides of Donna's breasts. The fact they had become somewhat more visible as a result of Don's fondling them made no difference in the equation as far as Don was concerned.

Tim was in some sort of a trance, probably a combination of a lack of sleep because he and Robin had an argument the previous evening, and the dope he had smoked to forget said argument. Regardless, his head remained in the same position with his eyes affixed on Donna. Don walked to the side of the pool and climbed the three concrete steps that led directly to Tim's chair.

"Dude, you need to stop staring at Donna," Don ordered, this time dispensing with any veiled politeness. Although Don was approaching seventy, he maintained an athletic physique. His presence in a bathing suit did nothing to hide the muscularity of his arms and upper body. Perhaps it was Don's words, or perhaps Tim just awoke from his stupor, but Tim's head snapped forward and he removed his gaze from the pool.

"Huh? Oh yeah. Right," Tim stammered.

Don saw the glazed look in Tim's eyes and knew he must have imbibed or inhaled something.

"Man, I don't know what you're up to, but you sure don't look good," Don responded. His calm tone reflected an almost instantaneous reversal of attitude from oppressor to buddy. "Take it easy out here in the sun, dude. It can really get to you."

Don walked away from Tim, grabbed his towel and dried himself while Donna exited the pool and joined her husband. Within minutes, while still encamped in the same chair, the same position, and with the same stupid smile on his face, Tim drifted off to sleep.

As the day waned on, the principal merrymakers from the Paradise crowd remained firmly entrenched in their seats in the shallow water of Chaweng Beach Resort's quiet pool. Yves LeMaire was the ostensible ringleader. At forty-eight years old, Yves was the social capital of Paradise. He was a spectacular stylist who had trained in Paris and worked in Beverly Hills and New York before joining a Seaborne ship as a celebrity hairstylist for a brief period. When Eva Lampedusa got word that Yves, her unequivocally favorite stylist in the world, had taken to the seas, she wanted him aboard Paradise. Period. Eva simply had to hire Yves, "at whatever the cost." As a result, Yves was paid $230,000 a year, far more than any other rank and file member of the hospitality team aboard the ship, not bad wages for a hairdresser anywhere.

Gay and proud of it, Yves was not a threat to the many male owners aboard Paradise whose wives absolutely *had* to have their hair blown out every afternoon before dinner. No, those husbands knew those suspiciously frequent sessions with Yves were as much about gossip as they were about puffing out their precious manes.

Yves was 6'1, trim, and sported a pencil-thin moustache. Even though he was past the age when most men could carry it off, Yves wore his hair in a messy quaff with a high fade. Always adorned in tight-fitting and fabulous designer clothes, Yves sought to be elegant and exotic. He pulled off both looks superbly.

Also high on Paradise's list of social butterflies, and front and center at the quiet pool, was Stephanie Holsson, the ship's Swedish golf, tennis, and bowling instructor. At 5'11, with blue eyes and platinum hair, Stephanie was more suited to the pages of Playboy than Golf Digest. She was everything a teenage boy might fantasize a Swedish golfer would look like. And more. Stephanie's smile could power Paradise's engine room and her brilliantly white teeth were a Colgate ad in waiting. But the most attractive part of Stephanie Holsson was her charismatic personality and effervescent charm. Crew members yearned to be on Stephanie's evacuation drill team or to be associated with anything she did aboard the ship. It was not unusual for her to instantly befriend someone with complete sincerity. Stephanie was always willing to dole out her time, friendship, and advice to anyone who needed it. Of course, the male owners aboard Paradise probably took a few extra golf lessons so they could inhale her smile or catch a glimpse of her gazelle-like legs or amazingly firm ass as she reached down to place a ball on the tee. Stephanie was keenly aware of that attention but never let it affect her.

At the quiet pool, Stephanie wore an Eres cornflower blue bikini that, while totally appropriate, was totally skintight against her perfectly proportioned body. Without even saying a word, Stephanie was causing more commotion at the quiet pool than any of the other people from Paradise—or than all of them combined. More than a few women caught their husbands peering over their Wall Street Journals or jumping in the pool for a dip, just to get a better view of the golf goddess in their presence.

It was somewhat unusual for the suite owners and crew aboard Paradise to socialize together. But these off-ship excursions were the exception. It was a chance for the owners to treat their favorite crew members to a bite, or a few drinks. Most crew members didn't make the cut, but those who did, like Yves and Stephanie, were always grateful to be included.

A gaggle of women, all guests of one of Paradise's British owners, were also a presence in Chaweng's quiet pool. There was nothing remarkable about any of them individually but collectively, they made quite an impression. After one or two rum drinks, their voices escalated as quickly as an elevator in a Manhattan office tower. Anxious to be heard over one another, the ladies screeched and screamed, raising their voices a magnitude of decibels every few minutes. Moreover, these five women, who were apparently celebrating someone's birthday, monopolized the waiters with their endless requests for drinks, finger food, ice cream treats, and anything else that came to mind.

As the day went on, a half dozen more Paradise owners joined the revelers at the Chaweng quiet pool. The drinks went down faster than the backside of a roller coaster loop and the volume went up just as quickly. The few Chaweng guests who decided to remain at the quiet pool looked askance at the ship people, mostly women, who were making so much noise. Their scornful looks had no effect on the merrymakers. The British women had become engaged in a detailed and thunderous discussion about their recent sexual conquests. Describing their lovers' anatomical parts and the things the men did with them, the women spared no level of detail. No element of their sexual dalliances was too intimate for them to leave out. And no amount of effort to avoid the conversation was successful for the unwilling bystanders.

At one point, three of the British women left the quiet pool. A few minutes later, they emerged from the ladies' locker room having substituted their bathing suit tops for T-shirts. Apparently, they had decided it would be entertaining to engage in a wet T-shirt contest. Standing on the black shelf inside the quiet pool, the women splashed water on each other's chests, as someone cranked the volume on the Sonos speaker to a thunderous level. It was less than five minutes after the *contest* began that two of the women, the ones with the smallest breasts, had removed their shirts and were dancing grinding their bodies against one another as the other pool occupants watched in amazement.

Stephanie Holsson had been served two double-rum punch drinks and was feeling no pain. She was also feeling mortified by the women's horrific performance. What troubled Stephanie most was the women's lack of rhythm. They were truly terrible dancers. She concluded that their inept dancing and tiny boobs rendered their entire show ill-conceived. Stephanie slithered into the pool, sauntered over to the women, and removed her own blue bikini top. Not only did she show everyone how Swedish women danced, but she made it clear that a pair of white 34 C breasts against her caramel frame trumped their white 32A breasts against equally white backgrounds. The stunning golf instructor had effectively birdied the hole while leaving the male pool-goers stroking their own putters.

Besides Mr. Madison, three other hotel guests complained to the resort's management about the histrionics at the quiet pool. Each was awarded a dinner in the hotel's restaurant that evening, but management took no steps to discipline the Paradise carousers. In addition to the handsome fee Paradise had tendered for the privilege of using the hotel's facilities, the ship's owners and guests were racking up a nearly $8,000 tab on drink and food.

One irate yet insightful resort guest returned to her villa and did some cursory online research about Paradise. Stumbling upon a year-old blog post heralding the ship's launch, she learned it was the toy of an assemblage of entitled, rich patricians who guarded their wealth and privacy with equal diligence. That was all she needed to see. With admirable technical aplomb, she posted a description of the day's events, along with a few prize photographs, on her Facebook and Instagram sites. In addition, she posted the same description on Trip Advisor, Peyton's Places, and a few other sites frequented by cruise line passengers. *If those rich bastards want to take away my solitude and quiet enjoyment*, the woman reasoned, *I'll take away their privacy.* And just like that, photos of Tim and his vape pen, Donna Bickford's skimpy top, Stephanie Holsson's exquisite almost total nudeness, and a few of the most unflattering video snippets and pictures of the loud, drunk women were set loose into cyberspace for all to see.

Chapter 2
Claude Comes Aboard

After Ko Samui, many of Paradise's *visitors* were looking forward to arriving in Bangkok and then Singapore—exciting modern cities with a real verve about them—a week later. But because Paradise's *owners* were truly world travelers. They cared less about the bright lights and big cities than about their pre-Bangkok stops in some of the less explored parts of Malaysia.

Paradise's itinerary committee had decided to bypass the always popular Kuala Lumpur in favor of some more remote destinations. As a result, Paradise's first stop in Malaysia was Kuantan, the second largest state in the country.

As the owners toured Kuantan, it became readily apparent that Malaysia was more economically advanced than the past few countries the ship had visited, especially Thailand, Cambodia, and Vietnam. Malaysia's beautifully paved roads, glass and chrome neon-studded buildings, and cutting-edge hotels would have been right at home in Chicago or Boston.

While most of the ship's luxury suite owners were excited about visiting the sultan's sprawling estate, or the Pahang art museum, Eva Lampedusa was savoring the arrival of her beau, Claude Azulai, whom she had not seen in several months. Claude was scheduled to spend two weeks aboard Paradise and Eva was looking forward to spending much of that time aboard Claude.

All her friends and colleagues on the ship and back in New York were aware of Eva's intellectual genius, legal acumen and even her unrelenting devotion to all things fitness related. But as committed and animated as Eva was in her pursuit of professional excellence, she was equally committed to her pursuit of personal pleasure and sexual satiation. And that's where Claude fit in.

Born in Cartagena to a Colombian father and Danish mother, Eva had been raised in a traditional Catholic home. Having been educated by the nuns at St. Catherine's School, Eva developed a robust respect for morality and religion. Unlike many of her classmates, both in high school, or later at Vassar College or NYU Law School, Eva eschewed promiscuity. That is not to say that she didn't like sex—she did. Very much. But Eva did not believe in random sexual encounters. Accordingly, she had neither the time nor the interest for late-night hook-ups with indiscriminate lovers.

Arousal for Eva occurred in the mind as much as the body. While she appreciated the physique of a perfectly proportioned man, or the smile of a GQ model, Eva's greatest stimulation came from making a cerebral connection with a man. Without that association, sex for Eva was simply a pleasurable, physical act, not very different from a good workout at Equinox. Emotionally disconnected sex was not enough to fulfill Eva's needs and desires. Consequently, she directed her intellectual attention towards the practice of law and her sexual attention to something more challenging and fulfilling.

Eva loved tantric sex. She had stumbled across the ancient Eastern spiritual practice of tantra in the late 1990s through a Buddhist speech coach Eva had utilized to help refine her delivery to juries. As Eva learned through her intense study of the subject, tantra was about connecting both with her partner and with her own inner being to intensify and prolong her sexual experience. As a result, Eva's sexual interactions were not so much focused on reaching climax as they were on enjoying the sensuality of the encounter. As an added benefit, Eva's lovers, if they could comprehend the practices of self-actualization and pure devotion, were treated to intimacy on a level they had never before experienced.

Claude Azulai met all Eva's criteria in a man. Educated at the University of Perpignon in France and trained as a lawyer,

Claude was serving as the attorney general of Morocco when Eva first met him. Retained by the king to study the potential effects of class action litigation in Morocco, Claude was tasked by the king to consult experienced practitioners on the subject. After having interviewed three potential candidates, all highly qualified American civil law experts, Claude quickly realized that no one was as studied or accomplished in the field of class action litigation as Eva Lampedusa. Their initial sixty-minute interview lasted just under six hours. Claude became captivated with Eva's vast knowledge of the subject matter. He was intrigued by Eva's ebullience while they discussed all the potential ramifications of allowing class actions to proceed in Morocco. As Eva spoke, she also listened, something Claude found most unusual in an American lawyer. But what impressed Claude the most was Eva's uncanny ability to convey the information in simple, unadorned terms without the need to impress him with fancy phrases, or to underscore her obviously tremendous intelligence. He knew that any substantive expert, whether in the subject of medicine, law, science, or virtually anything else, was capable of using technical phrases to show off her level of sophistication and expertise. What Claude also appreciated was that only a truly self-assured and confident authority could convey those phrases and concepts in terms easy enough for a non-technical sophisticate to understand.

Eva had become highly accomplished at presenting intricate ideas in a homespun manner during her decades of addressing juries in highly complex pharmaceutical and medical device class action cases. She well understood that if she were to simply rattle off technical phrases while cross-examining doctors and scientists, the jury would get lost somewhere along the way, possibly even nodding off to sleep. Eva saw that happen with less accomplished lawyers. She found it remarkable that some lawyers simply couldn't get over their narcissistic need to impress, even at the risk of losing the jury's attention and, subsequently, the case.

The initial attraction between these legal giants was primarily intellectual, with a heavy dose of professional respect. Even at that first meeting though, Eva's mind briefly wandered to a place of tantric awareness, aroused by Claude's legal acumen. Even more arousing was Claude's willingness to be tutored by a female lawyer, a creature that was not common among the Muslim, male-dominated culture of Morocco.

Although his legal astuteness and position as attorney general were attractive features in their own right, Claude's physical presence did not go unappreciated by Eva. An imposing 6'4", Claude also boasted a smile that manifested his authenticity. Eva found nothing more arousing that day than the way Claude appeared so sincere as his piercing green eyes rarely diverted from Eva's face when she spoke.

Claude was an Adonis. His naturally caramel complexion reminded Eva of what male models in the United States spent tens of thousands of dollars trying to achieve. In some of the photographs of Claude that Eva had viewed—yes, she researched him thoroughly before meeting him—he sported a three-or four-day beard growth, a look she adored. In other pictures, he was featured with just a touch of facial hair, jeans, and a beige cashmere sweater, a look Eva found breathtaking. When they finally met, Claude was clean shaven and had donned a navy suit, looking like he had just stepped out of a Vogue cover. He was almost *too* gorgeous, Eva thought.

Claude had done his homework on Eva too. He was impressed not only by her litigation expertise, but also by her reputation as a business strategist to her clients. Indeed, it was a combination of those factors that led Claude to fly Eva to Rabat, Morocco's capital, to discuss class action litigation.

When Eva first walked into his office, Claude was immediately struck by her grace and incomparable good looks. Eva's professional photographs portrayed her as an elegant and attractive woman. She never made public her personal social media pages that portrayed her more playful side. Eva's 5'11" frame carried her 140 pounds in perfect symmetry. With coal black hair, penetrating blue eyes, and an understated palate of makeup worn to perfection, Eva's physical appearance was also magnificent.

Two of Claude's more unique fixations when assessing a woman's physique were her calves and forearms, areas she couldn't fake, he reasoned. Eva's short sleeved white blouse and classic navy Chanel skirt provided Claude a complete view of her arms and calves, allowing him to quickly conclude that those parts of Eva's body were adroitly toned, if not muscular. But what captured Claude's attention more than anything was Eva's radiant smile. Her ivory teeth were even more dramatic against her olive complexion and black hair. And her eyes were so expressive Claude felt like he had total insight to Eva's soul, even during that first encounter.

Eva was due to spend two days in Rabat before returning to New York for a girls' Memorial Day getaway in the Hamptons. Instead, Claude whisked her away on a tour of his favorite Moroccan cities—Fes, Marrakesh, and Casablanca. It was not the government planes or limos that attracted Eva to Claude, nor was it the toadying greetings he received at every restaurant or hotel they visited. It was a combination of his intellect, personality, warmth, and sense of humor that caused Eva to spend only the first night of their stay in Fes in her own suite. After that, and later in Paris and New York, Eva spent every moment she could by Claude's side or under it, especially during those delicious evening hours. Eva later learned that her girlfriends had enjoyed a pleasant enough Memorial Day weekend, even though she never did make it back to join them.

Between litigating for her clients, mollifying her partners that she was not going to sail off the face the earth, and putting together the consortium necessary to purchase and launch Paradise, Eva was inordinately busy during her courtship with Claude. After their second night in Marrakesh, Eva concluded she did not want to date anyone else while she was seeing Claude. He held great interest for Eva, and, with all the other distractions going on in her life, Eva could scarcely afford to spread herself even more thin. As was usually the case with Eva, she wanted to focus myopically on one man to give that relationship the best opportunity to survive, if that was to be the case.

On the first morning the ship was docked in Kuantan, having not seen each other in nearly three months, Eva and Claude were happy to be reunited. Waiting for him in the reception area, Eva wore a sleeveless Etro purple, orange, and white belted midi-dress. She paced the lobby, trying to appear interested in all the goings on at the concierge desk and reception desk, and not someone who was giddily awaiting her boyfriend's arrival. She failed in her attempt to be clandestine.

When Claude finally strode aboard, sporting a picture-perfect blue blazer with brass buttons over a pink button-down shirt and khakis, Eva almost sprinted to him. Her behavior was out of character for the highly regarded founder of Paradise, but the ship's crew was glad to see that personal side of her. She embraced Claude and gave him a kiss, although nothing like the one she planned to give him in her suite as soon as possible.

As much as he was anxious to be alone with, and make love to, this woman with whom he had fallen in love, Claude was also keen for Eva to take him around the beautiful ship he'd heard so much about. The ship had been her dream, and Eva had sought Claude's input on many critical issues as she put together the financing and ownership roster for Paradise.

Similarly, Eva was as anxious to show off her ship to Claude as she was to show off Claude to all her friends. She walked his tall, handsome frame through the public areas of the 455-foot vessel, pausing to explain all the elements of it to him. They stuck their heads in all five restaurants, each of which featured a different theme or cuisine. Eva took careful pains to point out all of the crystal and brass elements of Leeward, the ship's most formal restaurant and Eva's favorite, usually open only one day every other week. They meandered through the ship's four bars, each of which was empty midday, other than the bartenders who were organizing bottles and polishing glass and wood.

"This is quite an operation. How many people do you have working on this boat?"

Eva ignored Claude's reference to a *boat*. She and the other owners preferred to think of it as a *ship* because of its gargantuan size.

"I can't be precise, but we usually sail with a crew of about 170 people. The number of crew we carry depends on our passenger load. When we're full, obviously we need more waiters and housekeepers than when we only have twenty or thirty owners aboard."

"Twenty or thirty? You'd sail this monstrosity with so few people?"

"Honey, Paradise sails every day of the year, as long as we're not visiting ports or sidelined by Covid. That's the whole point of this ship, to constantly circumnavigate the globe. So we have to plan ahead to get from port to port, sometimes spending as many as five or six days in a row at sea when we have to transverse one of the oceans. That route-plotting is critical to our operation. We can't wait until the week before making a port call to see how many people show up and then decide if or where we're going to sail. Owners and their families make plane reservations many months in advance. They need to know exactly where the ship is going to be and for how long. Barring weather, pirates, natural disasters, or some other tragedy, the ship will always be on the same course that was set by the owners a year in advance," Eva said.

"You can get this group of people to agree on something that far in advance?" Claude asked, making a mental note to double back around to asking about pirates.

During various episodes of pillow talk, Eva had regaled Claude with stories of the larger-than-life bravado, egos, and personalities that dominated Paradise's ownership roster. Based on everything Eva had told him, Claude found it difficult to believe there could be harmony around anything aboard Paradise, even something as simple as where the ship should go.

Eva walked Claude through the gyroscopic two-lane bowling alley, something he found fascinating from an engineering perspective, even if he wasn't much of a bowler.

"You mean you can bowl even while at sea? In waves?" he asked.

"Yup, the gyroscopes keep the surface of the lanes perfectly even. I have no idea how it works, but everyone wanted it, so we put it in. Honestly, people find it a novelty their first week or two aboard, and never use it again. The only regular use it gets is from guests, renters and kids of owners."

Neither Eva nor Claude had ever been married—to a person, that is. They had each been married to their respective careers and now, in their late forties, the chances of either becoming a parent was waning. The concept of *kids of owners* washed over Claude as unremarkable as the gentle folds of ankle waves in a calm bay.

Although disinterested in the bowling alley, Claude was intrigued by the tennis and golf simulator. The cavernous green room, with netting on the sides and a screen at the front, was used by owners to hone their tennis or golf games while the ship was not in port. On that day, it was outfitted as a golf studio, with a projector displaying a virtual image of the iconic Pebble Beach course on the screen at the front of the room. Although most golfing suite owners kept a set of their own clubs aboard the ship, there was also a rack of available clubs at the back of the room for those who needed them. Claude was impressed because they were not just *any* clubs; they were TaylorMade M6 irons and M6 woods, not your everyday rentals.

"How tough is it to get a reservation in here?" Claude asked.

"Not very. You just send an email to the golf pro and she reserves the time for you, up to two hours," Eva explained. "But I'll make an appointment and bring you up here if you'd like to hit. I'm not having you come up here alone." She smiled.

"Why not?"

"Because Stephanie's drop dead gorgeous, and I'm a very jealous woman," said Eva, snuggling tightly against Claude. It was not lost on Eva that this was the first time she had touched a man aboard the ship. It felt good. And, somehow, the gentle rocking of the vessel made everything seem more romantic at that moment.

Eva had come to terms with the scores of couples, and random hook ups, walking hand in hand, enjoying small talk, and sharing cocktails aboard Paradise on a daily basis. A part of Eva had longed for that intimacy since she first stepped aboard. After all, a few weeks on a cruise ship in some remote destination was almost everyone's idea of romantic. Sure, she was respected and adored aboard Paradise, but that wasn't something she could hold at night or rub against in the shower. Claude was.

"How does the tennis part of this work," Claude continued, not wanting to make any sarcastic comments about the golf pro for fear of upsetting Eva.

"You push this button," she explained while simultaneously pressing a large knob on the left wall. "And the screen goes up. You see that wall behind it? That's a deadening wall."

"What's that mean?"

"You can hit a tennis ball at it with full force and it comes back at you, but not as fast as you hit it. We'd need half a tennis court to accommodate that, but this is a ship and real estate is a premium. This works perfectly. You can play an entire match against this wall. I call it Chrissie Evert because it returns everything you hit at it."

"Kind of like you in a courtroom," responded Claude, lobbing his own volley back at Eva.

"Kind of. But I always win. Chrissie won most of the time, but not always." Again, she gave Claude a firm squeeze.

They walked through the wellness center, fitness center, and pottery studio before they arrived at the fruit market. Eva brought Claude there because she knew he would enjoy seeing it, as did all her other friends and guests who had toured Paradise with her.

"What's this?" asked Claude while picking up a mango and squeezing it to ascertain its freshness.

"It's a mango, silly."

"I mean what's this place?"

"This is our fruit market, Tutta Frutta."

Claude was aware of the phrase's meaning in Italian. He spoke six languages.

"This is crazy. How do you get fresh fruit? I mean when you're in some of those remote places you visit. Aren't you concerned about bugs or hygiene?"

"It's a complex operation. There's a whole team back in Fairfield, Connecticut, we call the Mothership. We have a procurement officer who identifies everything we'll need on the ship. Then his staff sources it based on price, availability, and delivery time. For example, when we're floating around the Med, which we'll be doing a good amount of the time, we'll order wines from France, Italy, Portugal, and countries in that region. We'll hold off on ordering wines from California, Australia, or South Africa during those periods. It just doesn't make economic sense to import wines from far away when we can get terrific wines from local vineyards. Besides, unlike fruits or vegetables, bottled wines aren't subject to bugs or disease."

"And everyone's OK with that? Not having their favorite California wines whenever they want them?" he asked, picking up a grapefruit to test its freshness.

Claude was suspicious some of the more crotchety owners wouldn't go along with being told they couldn't have something they wanted. He was right.

"Don't go looking for trouble already. You just got here," Eva teased. "But you're right, some people have to have exactly what they want, no matter what."

"And what do you do about that?"

"We get it, of course. They have to pay for it. They're also responsible for the extra shipping, duty, tariffs, and everything else that goes along with it, but they can have anything they want. Trust me, it's not worth arguing with some of the owners. They can be real pains in the ass." Eva spoke faster, keen to end that line of conversation and return to more pressing business, like getting Claude to her suite.

"Doesn't that get expensive?" Claude asked, shaking his head at the ridiculousness of it all.

"It sure does. For the same bottle of good Napa cabernet that we can get for $60 bucks while we're in the US, we'll have to pay around $200 in Europe or even $400 in other parts of the world. But, again, if they're willing to pay for it, we'll get it for them. Remember, everyone on Paradise has stupid money, money they could never spend, and their children and grandchildren could never spend. We're talking hundreds of millions, or billions, of dollars."

"Why don't you guys give some of that money to charities?" Claude raised his eyebrows. "I looked through the itinerary you sent me for this year. You visit some of the most impoverished areas of the world—places where even fresh water is at a premium. Why not give those people some of that extra wine import money?"

Claude was from the metropolitan region of Morocco, but he had spent much time in other African countries. He had witnessed the abject poverty, disease, famine, and death that were far too commonplace in parts of Africa where even the most rudimentary medical attention was unavailable. Although he had amassed a nice fortune himself, Claude never lost a sense of his roots or the destitution he had witnessed throughout Africa and the world. As a result, he was extraordinarily charitable and expected the same of people with substantial wealth. While he admired the community his friend Eva had created, he was offended by the conspicuous opulence that was an inviolable way of life among the selfish owners of Paradise.

"That's a personal decision. Many of us are involved in charitable endeavors back home. You know about my involvement with Catholic Big Sisters & Big Brothers," Eva said, reminding Claude of her charitable involvement and financial commitment. And it was true. Besides providing munificent sums of money to the organization, Eva volunteered her time generously. She was a founding member of the organization's initiative to assist young women who were daughters of battered women.

Moreover, Eva brought her charitable involvement with Catholic Big Sisters & Big Brothers to her law firm. Young associates who were hungry for courtroom experience dug into cases involving those Catholic families. Eva's litigation associates represented the women and children in court hearings. The quality of representation the families received through the pro bono services donated by Eva's firm far exceeded what they would have received through a public service outfit. These lawyers were among the nation's brightest rising stars, regularly commanding $500 an hour from paying clients.

The associates lucky enough to be selected to participate in Eva's pet program had to meet with Eva before each court appearance. She grilled them and went over their strategy and proposed approach for dealing with each case. This was time Eva took very seriously. She interrogated the aspiring trial lawyers far worse than any judge ever would. Preparation, she preached, was the cornerstone of good representation, and good representation was critical to their clients' very survival.

"I get all that. But you're special. You're different. Most of these people just write a check to some faceless organization like the Red Cross or some cancer organization. They don't ever meet the people who are hurting, who need support and caring just as much as they need money. Your rich friends on this boat never break a sweat to help anyone."

Again, ignoring Claude's reference to Paradise as a boat and not a ship, Eva responded. "I agree. But that's better than those who never give anything." Eva was tired of having to defend the wealth and largesse of her fellow owners. Every time she was interviewed about Paradise, the same issues came up—how they were spending so lavishly, that their carbon footprint was far worse than any airplane or ship at sea, that they could do much good to helping the local economies of places they visited, but never did.

"How'd we get here anyway?" Eva quipped, keen to pivot from something as controversial as the lack of philanthropic conduct by her fellow owners. "A few minutes ago, you were squeezing mangos and grapefruits. Would you rather keep discussing world poverty or can I invite you to do some mango squeezing in private?" Eva smiled at Claude and glanced down at her chest. Neither the gesture nor the invitation was lost on Claude.

A few minutes later, with the tour completed, they arrived in Eva's luxury suite. Located on the stern of the eighth deck, it was a platinum level suite, one of only two on the ship. The other belonged to Lorraine Williams, a Canadian billionaire. Lorraine had paid $100 million for hers, but not Eva. The other owners had voted to elevate Eva to a platinum level suite after she had already purchased her gold level suite at a price far exceeding market value. They recognized her outstanding financial and personal obligation to the ship's very existence, and upgrading her to the higher-level suite was their way of honoring that commitment. Besides, it cost the other owners nothing in return. In fact, they actually *made* money on the bequest because Eva was now obligated to pay condo association fees based on the higher square footage, which meant more money for the ship's coffers.

Eva's suite was elegant in its simplicity. It featured contemporary, sleek design elements in a mostly neutral, off-white palate. A glass Platner dining table surrounded by eight executive white leather side chairs filled the dining room.The living room was home to a gigantic L-shaped Albert Collection white leather sectional. Eva had had the ceiling lights removed in favor of more gentle wall sconces that provided color, mostly blue and light green, against the eggshell, bamboo-style wallpaper. She had an affinity for local artists and bought new pieces for her walls whenever she found something that could contribute to the calming influence of her maritime abode. Over the past few months, she had acquired a uniquely sculpted image of a man's head, made of white, blue, and green hand-blown Murano glass while the ship was visiting . . . Murano. She found a series of miniature hand-carved war canoes while visiting remote islanders in Papua New Guinea, and a jade impression of a godhead while in Hong Kong. Because she was so proficient at buying art, Eva would often take her *older* pieces, which had only been on the ship for a few months, and donate them to the ship's art collection, or to the otherwise artless visitor flats.

Eva's apartment had three bedrooms, as well as her study. Although she had appointed each of the bedrooms differently, they all shared a general nautical theme. The two smaller bedrooms, each of which featured queen beds, had *en suite* bathrooms as well as wall mounted thirty-four-inch Samsung televisions to complement the white end tables and desks present in each. The rooms were distinguished from each other by the way Eva had finished them, especially with regard to the lamps and artwork Eva had selected for each.

Even before she first boarded the ship, Eva had the master bathroom ripped out and replaced. At home in New York, she loved the palliative nature of her time luxuriating in her bathroom and wanted her bathroom aboard the ship to provide her with the same experience. The highlight of Eva's master bathroom aboard Paradise, besides a magnificent beige Calacatta marble countertop Eva had imported from Tuscany, was an immense soaking tub at the far end of the bathroom. Eva was aware that many people confused Calacatta marble with Carrara, its cousin from the same Carrara region of Italy, but she knew the difference. A designer had once explained to her that Calacatta marble features thick, bold veining, while Carrara marble does not. The color of this particular slab of Calacatta appealed to Eva due to its soothing white background, unique veining, and grayish color tones. As a result, Eva insisted that her tub be carved from the same Calacatta quarry as the marble that gave birth to her countertop.

Statuesque Eva enjoyed her late afternoon soaks and did not want to have to wrap her legs outside the tub or fold them under her to be able to bathe comfortably. When she designed the oversized tub, she wondered how it might accommodate a second bathing companion, a thought she fantasized about frequently.

Brass handles that matched all the brass towel racks, sink fixtures and other metallic portions of the room, were kept highly polished, revealing the shine Eva loved. In order to have all that work done in her apartment, the floors had to be reinforced, but that wasn't so difficult because the work had been done before the ship first launched. If she had needed to have that additional structural support work performed while the ship was at sea, it would have been unduly disruptive to the luxury suites below and next to hers.

By the time Eva and Claude arrived at her suite, after a stop for a quick lunch at Pasture, the ship's vegetarian restaurant, it was almost 2:30. Claude took in his surroundings and nodded in approval. Eva kicked off her Chanel flats, walked to the kitchen, and opened her Sub-Zero wine cabinet. Removing a bottle of 2009 Cristal Rose, she sashayed across the living room, aware she commanded Claude's full attention.

Seconds became minutes, and minutes meant Eva was getting excited. She had spent the past few months working assiduously to organize everything on the ship. She was also still trying to run her law firm practice group from afar. The time difference between the ship in Asia and her partners, associates, and clients in New York was killing her, often forcing Eva to participate in conference calls far past her normal waking hours. And phone sex with Claude in Morocco spun Eva's body clock completely out of whack. It had all taken a toll on her, but she was not complaining. Paradise was her dream, and she was fulfilling it. She placed the bottle next to the glasses.

"Can you think of a reason I shouldn't open this?" Eva asked while looking at the bottle she had saved specifically for this occasion.

"Can you think of a reason I shouldn't open *this*?" Claude retorted as he stood before her with his thumbs and forefingers poised adroitly atop the clasp of Eva's back-latched bra.

"Only because you didn't open *these* first," Eva said, as she put down the bottle and confidently opened the buttons of her cream-colored blouse. Eva stood in front of Claude with her blouse completely open, exposing abs that would make a teenager proud.

Instead of continuing the dance by opening the clasp of her bra as Eva had intended, Claude picked up the bottle of champagne. Eva's cut crystal champagne glasses stood at attention in front of him like good little soldiers awaiting their orders. He delicately removed the foil top, twisting the metal cage seven times, as he had been taught to do by his British governess when he was a teenager. He reached up to the company of soldiers and extracted two volunteers. After pouring a generous amount of bubbly rose into each glass, he handed Eva her glass, raised his own, and proceeded.

"To Eva Lampedusa, the woman with vision, courage, and determination like none other in the world."

"That's all? That's the way you think of me?" Eva said, pretending to pout.

"Oh, and a great piece of ass who can screw like a bunny."

"That's more like it!"

In a few minutes, the simple glass of champagne was already affecting Eva. Exhausted, she surrendered to Claude's irresistible invitation. As Eva released the tensions of the last few months, the arousal Claude elicited in her surged to the surface with the force of a King tide. Perhaps it was the effect of Claude sitting on the couch, rubbing his hand up and down her leg. If that wasn't enough, his hand, playfully straying under the lower part of her skirt, was definitely getting her attention. Like a kitten rubbing against her master, Eva leaned into Claude. She lifted her face to his and sought his mouth with hers. He did not hesitate. Within seconds, and seemingly for hours, their tongues became entangled in a sultry tango.

Eva could think of no articulable reason why the pair shouldn't retreat to the bedroom, get undressed, and get on with the business of romance. But Claude had other ideas. Eva was such a take charge person, he enjoyed seeing her out of that element. He reveled in those times she was constrained to being more submissive than dominant.

"Honey, I've been waiting months to have you on the ship. To have you in my bed. Come make love to me," Eva pleaded.

Claude smiled. He knew exactly how much Eva desired him in that moment, and he felt the same way. But foreplay was more erotic. Eva had taught him that. Anticipation was the cornerstone of her tantric sex practice. Few things excited Eva more than wanting sex and being denied, and Claude enjoyed reminding Eva of that by using Eva's own devices against her.

"You know what I'd really like?" Claude whispered. Without waiting for a reply, he continued, "I'd like you to go in the other room, take off whatever you'd like and come back here and sit next to me."

"Are you kidding me?" Eva asked. "I'm inviting you to the bedroom, virtually begging you to have your way with me right now, and you want me to do what? To undress? Into what? Something skimpy? And not even in front of you? What's that all about? What it's about is not fair, that's what it's about." Eva was noticeably slurring her speech as she unleashed a soliloquy and that caused Claude to laugh.

"Go on now," Claude chided, as he waved towards the bedroom.

Eva was too horny to argue. If she really teased him, he would be putty in her hands. But she enjoyed the art of the tease, of Claude's tease, and was curious to see what he had in mind. She was going to make love to him shortly, so she'd give him a few minutes to let him feel like he was in charge. But only a few. After that, it would be game on.

Fine, she thought to herself, *let's see if you can handle me*, as she walked into her bedroom shimmying her ass in a way she knew he would enjoy.

A few minutes later, Eva had removed her blouse and skirt, and stood proudly in only her turquoise bra and matching thong. She checked herself in the bathroom mirror and concluded, *I do look hot, dammit*. As Eva was about to head back into the living room, her bedroom door burst open. There stood Claude, stark naked, and fully erect. Before Eva's gaze could even drop to fully appreciate the amplitude of Claude's aroused manhood, he threw Eva onto the bed and climbed on top of her. Eva's lingerie had no chance of remaining on her body. Seemingly effortlessly, Claude unsnapped her bra and cradled her milky white breasts. He casually shoved Eva's thong off to one side and inserted himself into her. Eventually, that last garment, the recalcitrant thong, also found its way to Eva's carpet. Then, they were just two passionate, sweaty, naked lovers, who were excited by the fact they hadn't been intimate for weeks, combined with the knowledge they'd be together every day and night for the next month. For the next four hours, they made love, napped, and made love again.

Chapter 3
Disciplinary Matters

While Claude was aboard Paradise, the last thing Eva wanted to deal with was a disciplinary matter, but the fallout from the Chaweng Beach Resort event could no longer be overlooked. The spiteful resort guest who had spewed vitriol all over the Internet about the ship's shenanigans had caused an online sensation. Videos of the topless, bombastic elitists had gone viral.

Most of Paradise's suite owners were social media ignorant. Had that not been the case, they would have known that nearly two hundred keyboard cowboys punched away at Paradise for its owners' behavior following the initial postings. Phrases like *egotistical bastards, spoiled brats, think their shit doesn't stink,* and *hope they sink* were among the nicer comments posted to the photos of semi-topless, and then topless, hijinks of the rich and arrogant.

At 6:15 AM, Marc Romanello was not even awake when his phone rang.

"Marc, what are you going to do about the Chaweng mess?" Eva demanded.

The chairman of Paradise's board of directors, Marc was nowhere near conscious. Reflexively, he responded, "We'll have to look into it and figure out the right steps."

"There's not really much to look into. Get out of bed, open your computer, and Google *Paradise the ship.*"

"OK, will do."

"I don't mean later, I mean now," Eva said, anger dripping from her voice. "Go ahead, I'll hold."

"What's going on?" asked Marc's wife, Karen, cognizant that something was amiss, but not knowing what.

"It's nothing. I'll talk to you about it later," Marc replied as he left the bed.

"*Nothing?*" Eva screamed through the phone. "*Nothing?* Only my entire investment going to the bottom of the sea because of your golf pro's tits."

"What was that about tits?" Karen asked, sleepily. She wasn't certain what else was being said, but she knew she heard that word screamed through the phone. Marc knew better than to say anything else to Eva at that moment. She was on a rampage, and rightly so. She also had no idea that Marc was talking to Karen, and not her when he made his *nothing* comment.

Clad only in his striped Tommy John boxer briefs, Marc stumbled into his living room and opened his computer. He did as Eva instructed and was aghast to see the photos that had been posted and reposted dozens of times.

"Are you there?" Eva asked.

"I'm here."

"Well, what do you think?"

"I think . . ."

"Marc," Eva instructed impatiently, "I don't really care what you think. This is what you're going to do. Before you do anything else, you're going to email Mario and Lorraine and tell them we're meeting today at 8:00 AM. We can do it in my suite."

"But a meeting of the board requires seventy-two hours' notice according to the bylaws." Marc was proud of his knowledge of the bylaws. He had written them.

"I don't give a rat's ass what your bylaws say. This is a crisis and I'm not waiting seventy-two hours to deal with a crisis. C'mon, Marc, you know better than that. You've done enough crisis management during your career. Just do it. Now."

Although Marc and Eva were the best of friends, he knew enough to stay out of the way of a buzz saw. While Eva was still on the phone with him, Marc sent the email and reported the same to Eva.

"Good. Then I'll see you in about two hours. Oh, and please send my apologies to Karen for waking her," Eva added in a more pedestrian tone.

Marc stopped in the bathroom before walking back into the bedroom. He found Karen giggling.

"I'm glad you think something's funny. I almost got my head ripped off by Eva."

"She just sent me a text saying she wasn't talking to you about *her* tits so I needn't worry."

"I guess that's funny," Marc conceded.

"What's even funnier is she says her tits are getting plenty of attention this week from Claude."

Marc had to smile. He was familiar with Eva's tits, although his wife didn't know it. After Marc's first wife passed away, he and Eva grew quite close. They only violated the bounds of platonic friendship one weekend when Eva took him to a resort in the Berkshires. There, they blew those boundaries wide open. Eva introduced Marc to tantric sex, and Marc introduced Eva to the best oral sex she had ever experienced. Karen knew none of this.

At 8:00 AM, Marc, Lorraine Williams, and Mario Garramone showed up at Eva's luxury suite, as instructed. They were surprised to see Captain Pugliese already there. The captain rarely sat in on board meetings. The only time he was invited was when Eva or Marc intended to take some disciplinary action. The imposing Captain Pugliese would then accompany a board member to deliver the news to the offending suite owner. The captain was a brusque, 6'3" Venetian skipper who had been awarded four gold stripes on his epaulets almost twenty years ago. His admonitions were not to be taken lightly. And they weren't.

"Good morning, Captain," Marc said.

"Good morning, Mr. Romanello," the captain replied.

"Those are some rough seas out there today, aren't they?"

Captain Pugliese looked at Marc as if he were an idiot. "Yes, Mr. Romanello. We did notice that up on the bridge this morning. We've deployed the stabilizers so things should be smoothing out shortly."

"Great. I'm sure we'd all like a calm day, wouldn't we?"

Again, the captain gave Marc a gratuitous look. Marc's question needed no answer, and Pugliese knew that, if he said anything, it would be something snappy and sarcastic. Using discretion, he opted for a head nod instead.

Another unexpected presence in Eva suite was Claude. An inch taller than Pugliese, he too was a commanding figure. Whereas the captain's gravitas flowed from his white uniform, Claude's was visible through his workout shorts and tank top. When she entered the suite, Lorraine actually stopped, looked Claude up and down, and asked Eva, "Where can I get one of those?" Angry as Eva was, she still had to smile.

Marc was conflicted about Claude's presence. Marc was happily married to Karen, but sometimes he still fantasized about tantric sex with Eva. Those thoughts were especially *useful* when Karen was unable to bring him to orgasm. At moments like these, he was envious of Eva having a lover, especially the Moroccan version of Adonis. Even Marc had to admit that Claude's muscular legs and sculpted upper body were impressive. But he wouldn't.

"Everyone sit down," Eva commanded. The directors obeyed and took their seats around her dining table. Claude remained seated on the living room couch.

"Have any of you *not* seen the posts about our crew and guests at the Chaweng Resort?"

"Don't forget suite owners. Tim Moore is a suite owner," Mario reminded the woman who didn't need reminding.

"Alrighty then, since you brought it up, Mario, let's deal with Tim Moore first. He's an owner so he has a bit more standing than the crew. Still, he was an embarrassment."

"Exactly what did he do?" asked Lorraine, unfamiliar with any allegations against Moore.

"He was stoned," Marc answered.

"And he almost got in a fight with Don Bickford," Mario added.

"Wait, isn't he also the guy people on the ship have complained about because he takes pictures of their young daughters?" Lorraine asked.

"Yup. One and the same. So how shall we deal with him?" Eva asked.

"May I make a suggestion?" Captain Pugliese asked.

"Of course, Captain. In the words of King Charles, we're all ears," Eva answered.

"I don't know about his photographs or his threatening a fight. But, if he's got drugs on the ship, let me and my crew investigate that. You all know we have a zero-tolerance policy. If we catch him with drugs, that would make your jobs a lot easier, I suspect."

"Easier, and more difficult at the same time," said Eva. "But I can't argue with your logic. Besides, if we're going to discipline people every time they raise their voice, we might as well convene a meeting every morning. Yelling at a quiet pool is not the same as drug smuggling. It's the latter allegation that could give us a place to hang our hat. Speaking of that encounter, do we need to do

46

anything about Don Bickford? After all, he's the one who threatened to beat the crap out of Tim."

"I would have done the same thing," added Mario. "The guy was defending his wife."

"I can't argue with you there," said Marc.

"Good, I'm glad we dispensed with those two. Now, onto the crew. Let's start with Yves," said Eva. "Apparently, he's the one who turned up the radio and was the real rabble rouser."

Marc, Mario, and Lorraine looked at Eva intently. Eva was incredibly fond of Yves and everyone knew it. For her to single out Yves signaled true disappointment. It also underscored Eva's objectivity. Marc sensed his friend's discomfort and jumped to her aid.

"Yves did turn the radio up. And I'm told he was the ringleader. But it was Tim who bought the radio. The British women were the ones dancing in their T-shirts. Yves didn't do any of that."

"Wet T-shirts. Let's not forget that," the ever elegant Lorraine added.

"Fair points," Eva accepted, grateful for the lifeline. She was hoping someone would articulate a reason why Yves' behavior hadn't been so terrible. Marc and Lorraine may have just presented enough collateral reasons to avoid disciplining her world's favorite hair stylist.

"If you ask me, the guy's too light in the loafers, and we should keep an eye on him," Captain Pugliese added.

"*No one* asked you," Eva shot back. "And don't you ever speak like that about him, or anyone else again. Not on *my* ship."

Eva had referred to *her* ship during a disagreement with Pugliese a few months earlier. When Eva first uttered it, the captain tried to correct her. He explained that he was the master of the vessel, the one in charge.

"You raise two hundred and twenty million dollars and you can be the master of whatever vessel you like. Until then, this is *my* ship and you work for *me*," she had said, staring down the captain.

"That leaves us with the British guests who were causing all the T-shirt ruckus," Eva said, anxious to pivot away from Yves without so much as a slap on the wrist.

"Don't forget Stephanie Holsson," Lorraine reminded her.

"Oh, I won't. Marc here is going to deal with her," Eva said, throwing Marc a glance that was simultaneously wicked and salacious.

"Whose guests were those women?" Mario asked.

"They were guests of Mr. Scantello," Captain Pugliese reported.

Carmine Scantello, a sixty-five-year-old widower from Palm Beach via Brooklyn, was a former Green Beret and friend to most other suite owners. Carmine enjoyed being surrounded by beautiful women. He was not much to look at, but he always had a harem, leaving women to wonder whether the attraction was his anatomy or his investment account.

"How long will they be aboard, Captain?" Eva inquired.

"I believe they disembark the second day in Kuantan."

"Fine, that's tomorrow. Let's leave them alone. But please have a serious chat with Carmine and let him know that we expect his guests to conform to the same standards of behavior we expect of everyone else aboard Paradise."

"That leaves us with the lovely Ms. Holsson. How would you like to handle her?" Eva asked Marc, keenly aware of her double entendre.

"That's a hard one," Marc said.

"A hard one? Let's look at that. She came to the pool, wearing a skimpy bikini I couldn't imagine on a nineteen-year-old. Then she took her shirt off. Bounced her bare chest off the other women as if she was auditioning for some sort of porn film. I don't see what's so hard about that. The only thing hard were the men who witnessed it." Eva scolded.

"I agree. Taking her top off was probably not the best idea," Marc said.

"I saw the videos and I thought that was the highlight of the day," said a voice across the room. They all turned to see Claude slipping on his sneakers and grinning.

"Have you been watching those videos?" shouted an irate Eva.

"No, honey. Why would I do that when I have you to look at?"

The level of Claude's crassness was not lost on anyone, least of all Eva. If anyone was betting on the odds Claude would be having sex with Eva later that day, the house was laying twenty to one against it.

"Anyway, what do you propose to do about that, Marc?" Eva asked.

"*Me*? Why me? You've been running this entire meeting. What do *you* propose to do about it?"

Topless Stephanie was a hot topic, in more ways than one. Marc was a regular at the golf simulator, and he appreciated Stephanie's expert professional tutelage. And her tits.

"Well, you spend more time in the golf simulator with Stephanie than anyone else in this room. Presumably, you've gotten to know Stephanie . . . on a personal level."

It was impossible for any of the assembled to miss Eva's veiled suggestion that Marc may have been doing more than playing golf with Stephanie Holsson. That was simply not true, and Eva knew it, but she was a buzz saw in its highest gear. The anger of the day was causing her to lash out at everyone. From the moment he answered the phone at 6:15 that morning, Marc knew Eva was on a rampage. As a result of their years of friendship, he knew better than to try to tame the beast when she became savage.

Eva was a nine handicap, eight strokes better than Marc. She probably spent more time in the simulator perfecting her swing than anyone else on the ship. But Eva did it at night when no one was around. When all the other couples were holding hands in the pub room, or strolling about town, Eva whacked golf balls to release her tension. On occasion, she asked Stephanie for pointers. And, on occasion, they even sat together for a few minutes and shared a bit of girl talk. But they were never great friends. There was just something about Stephanie that earned her too many points on Eva's Baywatch chart.

"We're telling Yves to tone it down and advising Carmine to cool things with his female guests. It seems reasonable to say something similar to Stephanie," Marc suggested.

"Yves bought a fucking radio. That's it. And Carmine is a suite owner, one of us," Eva screamed. "Stephanie is an employee. She showed up looking like Carmen Electra in the first place. Then she morphed into Paris Hilton, or whichever Kardashian it was who got naked on video."

"That was different. Hilton and Kardashian had sex on tape. Stephanie didn't. And Tim bought the radio, not Yves. Besides, it was Kim," Marc corrected.

"Kim what?"

"Kim Kardashian who got naked."

"Be serious, Marc. She might as well have had sex with the way she was grinding herself into those other ladies. Topless! I say we fire her. Now. I mean, as soon as we get to the next port."

"Eva, you're getting a little aggressive," Marc said.

"No, I'm getting *very* aggressive. You don't seem to grasp the seriousness of what went on."

"We're supposed to be a community here. A family. We all have transgressions once in a while. Stephanie has been a model employee. This is one indiscretion," Marc pleaded.

"A model employee? Oh, she's a model, all right. A Playboy model." Eve paused and allowed herself to catch a breath.

"What do you propose, Marc?" she continued.

"Let me talk to her. I'll convey the seriousness of what happened. We can document it in her employment file as a violation. A warning. Whatever you want to call it. But the crew all love her and most of the suite owners love her as well."

"I'm sure the men do," Lorraine piped up.

Eva looked down the table at Captain Pugliese. The wise man simply shrugged his shoulders and held his hands out, palms facing upwards. He wasn't getting in the middle of that mess.

"Let's not throw her off the ship for getting a little wild," Marc continued.

Eva held her tongue. "OK. But she's your problem now. Tell her whatever you want. But be sure to tell her that, if she even comes close to doing something like that again, she's gone."

"I hear you, Eva. Consider it done."

"Good. Then let's move on and enjoy our day," said Eva, signaling an end to the meeting. As they all stood, Eva continued in a calmer voice.

"I don't mean to sound like a stick in the mud. I like having fun, and that's why we're all here, but each one of these improprieties has consequences. Look what happened at Chaweng Beach. We're the laughingstock of the Internet. That all could have been avoided. And should have been. C'mon, guys, I'm no prude. I've got a wild side too. But you don't see me doing that stuff out there."

"In here's a different story, though," Claude added, looking like the Cheshire cat.

"You, Mr. Azulai, are in for a rude awakening. If you think for a minute that anything wild is going to happen to you tonight, you're sadly mistaken."

"Hey, Claude, want to head up to the simulator with me and take a golf lesson? Stephanie's usually free at this time of the morning," Marc teased.

"Very funny. You know what? You're an asshole, Marc. A total asshole," Eva said.

"If you even set foot in that simulator, hers will be the only breasts you'll be seeing as long as you're on this ship," Eva directed at Claude.

Smart man that he was, Claude laced up his running shoes, said goodbye to those who hadn't left yet, and headed downstairs to the fitness center.

Chapter 4
Spa Day
Yves Shares a Secret

Before Paradise arrived in Bangkok, the concierge team arranged for a handful of owners to be whisked by private boat up the Chao Phraya River to the Royal Barge Museum. If one was willing to endure the unendurably foul smell of sewage and gasoline that escorted visitors along the river, the views down the small klongs, or canals, provided a fascinating glimpse into Bangkok's culture. The museum itself housed over a dozen magnificent, gold-gilded boats, most of which are over 250 years old and are used only once a year during the first full moon of November to celebrate the end of the rainy season.

There were scores of other attractions to visit and things to do in Bangkok, but because owners of Paradise were so used to traveling to the most exotic and remote cities in the world, many of them had no interest in immersing themselves in every port. Moreover, because the seas had been so rough over the past thirty-six hours, many of the owners did not venture far from their bedrooms. It was at times like these that the majority of owners opted to binge their favorite Netflix series.

During the two days of vomit-inducing swells through the Gulf of Thailand, all the wellness center activities such as Pilates, Body Pump, and Barre classes had to be cancelled. In addition, many of the spa treatments such as acupuncture or straight razor shaves had also been scratched. Holding a razor to a man's throat in twelve foot seas was tantamount to some of the torture techniques expressly forbidden by the Geneva Convention. When the seas calmed, it was no surprise the switchboards in the spa and wellness center lit up like a Christmas tree with owners and guests frantic to make up for the time they'd lost.

Yves LeMaire was the most sought after employee in the spa, beloved as much by his fellow crew members as by the owners. A hair stylist par excellence, Yves was always in great demand, often as much for his access to ship gossip as for his styling talents. Women were as enthralled with his delightful French accent as they were with his coloring and styling talents or his uncanny knowledge about all things going on about the ship.

Among Yves' most regular and favorite clients were Eva Lampedusa and Karen Romanello, Marc's wife. Both women trusted Yves completely and consequently, they felt free to talk openly with him. Because Eva was the founder and deputy chair of the vessel, and Karen was married to the chair, both women had a good sense of what was going on in the boardroom and among the owners generally. But, even with their presumed knowledge on most ship-related issues, there was scarcely a week when Yves did not inform them of something they knew nothing about. That was because everyone trusted Yves, and, when he did repeat gossip, he always did it without attribution. Moreover, Yves knew who he could share his secrets with and who would betray his confidence.

"Will you and Mr. Romanello be dining on the ship or ashore tonight?" Yves asked as he was applying strips of foil to Karen's hair. It was an absolute requirement that crew members address all owners by their surnames. It became such a habit that the crew followed that practice even below deck, never mentioning an owner by his first name. When one of the new crew members slipped and used an owner's first name, he immediately received a few awkward glances from the other crew members present.

"There's a cute little restaurant named Mazzaro that Marc and I have been to before, "Karen responded. "They make the best pad thai in all of Bangkok. We're looking forward to trying it again. What are you up to?"

"I'm going out with Dawn," Yves answered, referring to one of the aestheticians aboard Paradise. "It's her birthday, and a bunch of us are taking her out for dinner."

"That sounds fun. I was hoping we'd be able to enjoy a quiet dinner, but I think Marc invited Mario and maybe someone else to join us. I get the sense they'll be talking a lot of board business, which means I'll probably need a few extra glasses of wine."

Karen accepted that as the wife of the chairman of the board, she had to endure these business dinners, but that didn't make her enjoy them.

"I hear Mrs. Hirschfeld has an *interesting* dinner guest tonight," said Yves.

"Oh, no, that guy—Craig McDougal?" Karen asked in a shocked manner, and then laughed. "No, no, Yves. You're wrong on this one. He's a friend of Harris's, not Becky's at all. Becky just has her name attached to him on the ship's manifest. I don't even think she really knows who he is. So you see, my friend, you really *don't* know everything," Karen said gleefully, believing she knew more about a ship social issue than Yves, which would have been extraordinarily rare. Yves smiled contentedly as he continued to twist foil strips into Karen's hair.

Harris Hirschfeld had been one of the original suite owners aboard Paradise. In addition, he had been a member of the board of directors until he was caught in a multi-faceted embezzlement scheme and was forced to resign that post, sell his suite to his wife, and never return to the ship again.

Yves' silence gave Karen pause. Her discomfort forced her to break the silence.

"I'm serious. You think there's something between Becky and Harris's friend? You couldn't be more wrong," Karen repeated.

"I never said anything about Mr. McDougal. You did."

"Oh, really? You said she's going to be with an *interesting dinner guest*. If you didn't mean McDougal, what'd you mean by that?"

Yves looked both ways to make sure no one could hear them. The closest person to them in the spa was an elderly female owner whose feet were soaking in a pedicure tub, and the whirr of the motor rendered everyone else incapable of hearing what Yves was about to share.

Yves leaned over Karen's left shoulder as he applied another foil strip.

"You know that Elaine and Ms. Hirschfeld are friends, don't you?"

"Elaine? You mean Elaine Dwyer? Our Entertainment Director? Not particularly. I mean, I know they shop together occasionally."

"Well, tonight, they're having a lovely dinner at Le Normandie together. Alone." Karen looked in the mirror and saw Yves' sly grin behind her.

Karen knew of the restaurant but had never been there herself. Located in Bangkok's Mandarin Oriental hotel, Le Normandie was reputed to be one of the most romantic restaurants in all of Thailand.

"I've heard that's a great place," said Karen hesitatingly, not exactly knowing where the conversation was going, or what Yves was trying to get at. "It's supposed to be one of the most time-honored, traditional places in all of Thailand."

"Yes, it is," said Yves with a knowing smile.

Now it was Karen's turn to look from side to side to see if anybody could hear them. Still clueless, she cocked her head back.

"What are you getting at, Yves?"

"You remember what happened in Venice when the two of them went to Harry's bar together, don't you?"

Karen had no idea what Yves was talking about. The puzzled look on her face told him so.

"Wait, you mean to tell me that you never heard what happened in Venice?" queried Yves, ensnared between feeling guilty he had let the cat out of the bag and gleeful he was sharing some juicy gossip Karen didn't know. He had heard the story from Candy Podeski, who was Elaine's closest friend among the crew.

"No, Yves, I have no idea what you're talking about. But now that you've started to spill some beans, you can't stop there. Let's hear it."

Whenever Yves was caught off guard, his faux innocent grin and *mon dieu* expression gave him away. This was no exception.

"Well," he began, pausing for dramatic effect. "Apparently, there was one afternoon, or perhaps it was an evening, when the two ladies went sightseeing together and rode in a gondola. Then, they went to Harry's Bar for a drink—you know those famous bellinis that were invented there. I'm not exactly sure of all the details, but they ended up in the ladies' room together. You didn't hear it from me, but let's just say that Ms. Hirschfeld was able to relieve any pent up sexual frustration she may have had."

"What?" Karen screamed, drawing immediate attention from virtually everyone in the spa. She stared at Yves, looking for some indication of truthfulness. He just smiled and nodded gently.

"You're telling me that Becky and Elaine had sex?" Karen gasped, in a voice more than a few decibels above a whisper.

"You didn't hear that from me," Yves said.

"In a ladies' room? In a bar? Like sex sex?" the prudish Karen asked with a strong suggestion of unbelievability. A proper woman from northern Michigan who always demonstrated more maturity than her peers, Karen was having difficulty comprehending that her friend, Becky Hirschfeld, was gay. Moreover, Becky had had sex with Elaine Dwyer in the ladies' room of a bar? Why hadn't Karen heard about this before now?

"I'm just saying . . ." Yves said.

Yves was in his element at times like these, when he was able to shock his clients and friends with nuggets of golden truths he knew they would find unbelievable. He tossed back his head, raised his hands, and gave Karen a most effeminate giggle. Yves could envision the wheels turning in Karen's prudish mind as she was trying to imagine two women she knew having sex in a bathroom. The more Karen was having a tough time with the whole concept, the more tickled Yves became. As Karen blushed and squirmed uncomfortably in her seat, Yves couldn't help but provide a few details, only to tease his friend all the more.

"From what I understand they never got fully undressed. And they didn't have toys or anything."

"*Toys*? Who brings sex toys to a restaurant?"

"I said they *didn't* have them," Yves clarified.

"But who even *thinks* about having sex toys in a restaurant?" Karen asked, astonished.

Karen tried her best to remain stone-faced, to no avail. She had to get out of there, out of that chair, and out of the spa. She had to confront Becky. No wait, she couldn't. Becky was a friend. What would she say to her anyway? *"Hi Becky, I hear that you've become a lesbian and have been having sex with Elaine Dwyer? In a restaurant."* No, she wasn't going to do that. For a moment, she thought about telling Marc. But exactly what was she going to tell him? This was one of those secrets that had to remain with her.

It had been another good spa day with her friend Yves. Not only had he colored Karen's hair perfectly, but he had irreversibly colored her opinion of two of Karen's fellow shipmates—Becky Hirschfeld and Elaine Dwyer.

At dinner that night, Karen and Marc were joined by Eva, as well as Mario and Janice Garramone. Karen was glad for the female companionship. Eva was the lifeblood of the ship and Karen enjoyed spending time around her. Besides, they were both lawyers. Karen had been the general counsel of Estée Lauder while Eva was busy building her formidable litigation practice at Wilson Emerson, only a few blocks away from Karen's own office. Though the two women had never crossed paths professionally, they had both admired each other's careers through the New York legal periodicals. Even though board business was the primary discussion topic throughout dinner, Karen, Eva, and Janice were able to spend some girl time planning a three-day expedition off the ship to do some power shopping once Paradise got to Singapore.

Notwithstanding the myriad topics discussed at dinner, and the truly amazing Pla Kla Kong, deep fried crispy cutlets of sea bass with Thai herbs served with a spicy seafood sauce, Karen could not erase the vision Yves had so adroitly placed in her mind. Could he have been wrong? Was this just another of the dozens of untrue stories that floated through Paradise every month? After all, Becky was still with Harris at the time of this supposed lesbian encounter. Karen had spent a fair amount of time with Elaine since Venice and there had never been even a glimmer of a homosexual comment or indication between them. Karen downed her third glass of Ruffino chianti and just smiled.

Chapter 5
The Finances of Paradise

On occasion, lucky guests of the super wealthy were permitted to sail aboard Paradise. It was often joked that the only thing better than being an owner aboard Paradise was being a friend of an owner aboard Paradise. Even though these guests were not subject to the same rigorous financial background investigations as potential luxury suite owners, they did have to endure a more than rudimentary background check.

Owners of luxury suites aboard Paradise were fanatical about their security and privacy. They did not want an undercover reporter, or anyone else who might reveal secrets about the ship and its owners, to be allowed aboard. Traditional criminal background checks were not enough to vet potential guests. Paradise kept on retainer a detective agency that specialized in identifying issues and threats beyond what was available in formal government filings. Specifically, they scoured the Internet with particular focus on social media such as Facebook, Instagram, Twitter, and Snapchat, although the mostly aging crowd aboard Paradise would more likely have confused Snapchat with some form of circus snack. When a questionable post by a potential guest was identified, the owner sponsoring the guest was made aware of the issue, with a copy of the notice going to the chairman and deputy chairman of the board. Often, these issues were easily explained away, but at least one potential guest had been denied passage on Paradise as a result of a right wing thread he was leading on Facebook.

Once they were permitted aboard Paradise, guests were treated like royalty. In fact, there were special apartments made available exclusively for their use. These apartments, known as visitor flats, were often the same size as the bronze or silver level luxury suites that owners paid anywhere from $10 million to $30 million to acquire. Even though guests had to pay $4,000 a night to sail aboard the ship, that was far less than the $30,000 to $100,000 a month the owners had to pay as condo association dues.

If the guests then decided they really wanted to become members of the Paradise community, they had to pony up the $25,000 application fee, tender a $300,000 deposit on their condo association fees, and have their names circulated to all the owners so they could acquire the necessary approval of the entire community. So far, in Paradise's young life, no potential suite purchaser had been denied ownership for failure to meet the 85% approval threshold. Rather, that was a precautionary safeguard Marc Romanello had devised in case an applicant met all the other financial criteria but was deemed "unacceptable" by much of the community. He had in mind such miscreants as Bernie Madoff, Jeffrey Epstein, or others who clearly fit all the financial requirements, but were not the type of owners the board considered acceptable for Paradise.

One of the reasons guests were treated so well was because the ship still had over sixteen luxury suites available for sale. The financial burden of carrying those unsold units was on the shoulders of the owners of all the other luxury suites. They had to make up for the shortfall in revenue that was a direct result of not being able to book condo association fees that would have flowed from those suites. Conversely, every time a new luxury suite was sold, that resulted in a reduction of condo association fees paid by all the owners. In the happy event that all the luxury suites sold out, the ship still had an inventory of those visitor flats it could offer for sale.

There was one more financial consideration that loomed in the back of the minds of the Paradise directors, especially Eva, who had organized and arranged funding for the acquisition of Paradise. While the Saudi sheikh had been made whole on the funds his son had put down as an initial deposit on the ship, Mitsubishi Marine, the builder of the ship, still held a promissory note for the $120 million. That was the amount the owners of Paradise owed for the completion of the building of the vessel. To be more precise, it was *Eva* who owed the money. At the time the deal was structured, Mitsubishi's lawyers were clear they did not want to chase thirty or forty people for money due Mitsubishi in the event of a default. Instead, the closing documents were drafted such that Eva was singularly responsible for owing the remainder of the $120 million.

Eva had not accepted that burden blindly. It was during that period of frenetic negotiations that Eva reached out to her closest and wealthiest friends and invited them to buy luxury suites aboard her floating utopia. It was only after she had secured commitments sufficient to satisfy all her debt obligation that Eva signed the contract. Indeed, her financial professionals would never have let her sign the deal without the downstream commitments confirmed in the form of legally binding purchase agreements for the suites. But, if the remaining luxury suites did not sell, or, if a few of the existing owners failed to remain current with their condo association fees, the entire fragile financial nature of the enterprise could be in jeopardy. Not only would Eva lose the ship, but she would be subject to professional ridicule and scorn if she was forced to crawl back to New York to try to revive what had been one of the most remarkable legal careers in Manhattan. The fall of the mighty almost always provided people with glee, and the papers plenty to write about.

Chapter 6
Craig McDougal Visits the Ship

After a relaxing day at sea, Captain Paulo Pugliese effortlessly glided Paradise into her berth in Bangkok harbor. Owners aboard Paradise loved visiting cities like Bangkok where they could explore the matrimony of traditional Asian culture and the influence of millennial music and art that combined to make Bangkok such a popular tourist attraction.

Once the ship was safely moored, one of the duly approved guests who had been thoroughly vetted by Paradise's investigative agency, boarded the ship. Craig McDougal was a jolly Scotsman with a fondness for whiskey and women. The whiskey he drank was not expensive, but what it ended up costing him with women and their lawyers more than made up for that. At 68 years old, Craig believed he had the vitality of someone thirty years his junior, and he looked like he did. He kept in shape, ate well, and played four rounds of golf every week as long as the weather in Edinboro would allow. He viewed his whiskey and cigarettes as foils against weight gain, ignoring the more serious health maladies they could eventually inflict upon him.

Craig had originally been invited aboard Paradise by the now deposed Harris Hirschfeld. When Harris sold his luxury suite to his wife, Becky, Becky felt obligated to honor the invitation Harris had extended to Craig. Harris and Craig became acquainted almost 30 years earlier when a London barrister recommended Harris to represent Craig in an arbitration between Craig's Scottish oil exploration company and Exxon over rights to drill in the North Sea. Well, it really wasn't Craig's company. He was just a member of the lucky sperm club. His father had started the company. Craig just ran it into the ground. Almost. And that's where Harris came in.

Harris used his financial acumen to sell some junk bonds in order to save the company.

Craig's business turned out to be Harris's first multimillion-dollar client and the two men remained close over the ensuing decades. Not a year passed when they didn't see each other at least once or twice, with Craig visiting the Hirschfelds in New York, or Harris and Becky joining Craig in Scotland.

Becky stopped making the trips to Scotland after about ten years once she learned about Craig's true character. Craig had been accused of bringing one of his nieces to his home after a family wedding, while Craig's wife was in the hospital. Becky was sickened by what she heard. No one ever learned with certainty what occurred that evening, but the local newspaper reported that Craig, who was then 59 years old, had sex with the precocious teenager in his own marital bed before having his driver return the young lass to her home. The incident was only discovered when the girl's father stumbled upon a text message from Craig extolling the fun they had enjoyed and pleading with her not to mention it to her mother, Craig's sister. The father became enraged. Rather than involving the authorities or doing anything that could bring the incident to the attention of the media, he decided to handle things himself. At breakneck speed, he drove the six miles to Craig's home, rang the bell, and proceeded to pummel Craig mercilessly with a cricket bat for almost ten minutes. Craig sustained fractures to both orbital sockets, his nose, jaw, and many of the fingers he had raised in a failed attempt to break the impact of the blows. Although the goal had been to keep the matter private, that had not happened. When someone as esteemed and highly visible as Craig McDougal appeared in public with broken bones about his face and scarcely an inch of skin that was not black and blue, questions were raised. Initially, Craig tried to play it off as having been in a car accident.

However, the local police, who were not very fond of Craig due to his endless drunken episodes, debunked that story quickly. It didn't take long for word to circulate around town that Craig had indeed been beaten to a pulp by his brother-in-law after he'd forced himself on the man's fifteen-year-old daughter.

For years, Harris pleaded with Becky not to believe all the rumors she heard about Craig. A reserved woman who didn't fancy a confrontation where it could be avoided, Becky decided to just remove herself from any further contact with the Craig McDougal. The only reason she assented to allowing Craig to come aboard Paradise was because Harris had begged and pleaded with her not to embarrass him in front of Craig. Instead of telling Craig he'd been expelled from the ship, Harris had concocted a fanciful tale to explain his absence during Craig's visit. Harris even offered to fly Becky home privately after Craig's visit, if she would allow Craig to be her guest aboard Paradise, in name only. Of course, Craig would be relegated to one of the visitor flats. It was beyond even the most remote consideration that he would be allowed to stay in Becky's gold level luxury suite. Even if Harris had not been kicked off the ship and he and Becky remained together, there was still no way Becky was going to permit Craig to stay in their guest bedroom—or anywhere near her.

"Welcome to Paradise," offered Candy Podeski, the ship's perky Sales Manager. Because Paradise hosted so few visitors every month, it was Candy's job to meet and greet each one individually. Over the course of their stay on the ship, each guest was given a personalized tour of the ship as each guest was to be treated as a prospective new owner. Indeed, because management had elected to eschew traditional marketing channels, several of the new owners of luxury suites had come to the ship by virtue of the visitor flat program.

The sales process for luxury suites was sleek and sophisticated, yet almost invisible. Before joining Paradise, Candy had worked as a sales manager at the Four Seasons Residence Clubs where she convinced wealthy and pampered luxury travelers to buy into the lifestyle presented by those Four Seasons offerings. Her job aboard Paradise was not much different.

Without wanting to appear outwardly sexist, the management aboard Paradise realized the importance of curve appeal in a sales director. While Candy was highly qualified for the position and came with excellent recommendations, her outward appearance didn't do anything to hurt her hiring prospects. A former college softball pitcher at the University of Tennessee, Candy maintained her honeyed and convincing Nashville accent. At thirty-five years old, Candy was naturally radiant and possessed one of the most beautiful smiles imaginable framing Crest-perfect teeth. Candy's obsessive compulsion with fitness yielded a remarkably athletic body. And she was not uncomfortable displaying her ample cleavage, especially around male potential owners. For her thirtieth birthday, Candy had treated herself to two elastomer silicone implants, and she wore them like trophies. Their effect was not lost on Craig.

"Hi, I'm Craig McDougal," he said, not realizing it was Candy's job to know exactly who he was.

"Yes, you're a guest of the Hirschfeld's. We've been expecting you." Candy was diplomatic, referring to the Hirschfeld's generally and neither Harris nor Becky by name due to the delicate situation. Thanks to the background work prepared by the ship's investigator, Candy already had a reasonable approximation of Craig's net worth, annual reported income, and general financial profile.

It would have been useless for Candy to spend any appreciable amount of time with any guest or potential owner who did not meet the $50 million net worth minimum required for ownership. On occasion, however, she strayed from these guidelines and entertained male visitors simply because she found them attractive. Candy was not asexual, and she couldn't very well sleep with the married owners aboard the ship.

The ship's investigators had made Candy aware of Craig's reputation and his night of bruise-inducing incestuous pedophilia. Even without that tidbit of information, she had no interest in having anything physical to do with him. But, showing a little flash of leg or side boob sometimes made the difference between selling a suite and not closing the deal, and Candy was not above displaying those apparent enhancements.

"At some point, I'd love to show you around the ship, but I know you must be exhausted after such a long trip. For now, let me show you to your visitor flat just as soon as we get you checked in."

Candy was intimately aware of the details of Craig's trip, as she had to be about the details relative to any prospective owner. She knew his trip was almost sixteen hours long and involved two Emirates flights, Glasgow to Dubai and Dubai to Bangkok. She never knew what little detail might just convert a visitor into an owner, so she prepared herself thoroughly.

While Candy may have looked like an airhead version of a southern cheerleader, she was anything but. A European history scholar in college, Candy possessed an uncanny ability to absorb and retain details. In her position selling multi-million-dollar luxury suites to some of the most sophisticated people in the world, that talent served her well.

Candy escorted Craig to the reception desk where the attendant dutifully produced a leather folio with all the information and details pertinent to Craig's voyage. Besides the key card to his visitor flat, the dossier contained information about evacuation drills, instruction on how to log onto the Internet, a map of the ship, and a list of frequently asked questions.

"I know that's a lot of material for you to absorb but you don't really need to look at any of it today. Let's get you up to your flat now. You can have a look through it once you're rested. Besides, that's what I'm here for: to answer any questions and help you any way I can," Candy said, sporting her always effervescent smile.

As if out of nowhere, two bellmen appeared alongside Candy. One handed Craig a glass of champagne and a cold washcloth drizzled with lavender for him to refresh his hands and face. The other hoisted Craig's bags onto a cart and headed off towards Craig's visitor flat. As was always her custom when first-time visitors boarded Paradise, Candy accompanied the guest and the bellmen to the flat. Once inside, Candy walked Craig through the apartment, showing him the location of the washer and dryer units, dishwasher, microwave, and refrigerator, all of which were elegantly hidden behind white birch paneling.

"Wow, this place really does have everything, doesn't it," asked Craig who had expected elegance but was overwhelmed by the opulence of it. Candy walked Craig through the smart living room and dining room before escorting him into both bedrooms, one of which was understandably larger than the other. Craig was taken aback by the size of the rain shower and soaking tub in the master bathroom.

"Do all the flats have bathrooms setups like this?"

"Oh, no. In the owners' luxury suites, many of the bathrooms have been totally redone to reflect the owner's taste and style. In fact, a few of the owners combined both of their bathrooms into one, creating a pseudo spa effect in their own suite. Three of the suite owners have even installed saunas in their suites."

"And they can do that?"

"Yup. They can do whatever they like. They just have to submit their plans to our marine technical team eight months before any work is scheduled to begin and get the plans approved."

"This is amazing! Harris said this ship was remarkable, but I had no idea what to expect."

"Mr. McDougal, why don't you get settled, order some food, and have a good night's rest. Tomorrow, I can take you around the ship and show you all the common areas. I think you'll be very impressed. And if you like, I can show you a couple of the luxury suites. I'm not trying to sell you anything, but if you like this flat, you'll be blown away by the bigger, more ornate ones. It'll be fun for you to see them, even if it's just for your own entertainment."

Like hell Candy wasn't trying to sell anything. She was Paradise's sales director, after all. That was her job. She wasn't a tour guide or ship historian.

Craig was smitten. He was equally fascinated by the promise of seeing more exquisite apartments and the potential of getting a chance to see those marvelous implants he couldn't stop staring at.

"If there's nothing else I can show you, I'll let you get your rest and I'll stop by to check on you tomorrow," Candy said. She gave him a playful wink as she exited Craig's apartment.

An hour later, after only two whiskeys, Craig's fantasies of the lovely Candy Podeski had begun. There was plenty more Craig wanted Candy to show him, but that was only going to happen in his dreams—at least tonight.

Chapter 7
Board Meeting About Election

Four days after leaving Bangkok, Paradise was due to arrive in Singapore. It was during these days at sea that most of the ship's business got done, and this week was no exception. In his capacity as the chairman of Paradise's board of directors, Marc Romanello had convened a meeting of the ship's board.

Paradise's board was comprised entirely of luxury suite owners. Several of them had prior corporate board experience while others did not. All the suite owners were successful, intelligent people who had interfaced with their own respective boards of directors while they ran their multi-million-dollar businesses. As a result, most of them fancied themselves more than competent to serve as corporate directors. In reality, many were egotistical blowhards without a clue about corporate governance. Although those owners had established boards of directors for their own companies, most of the members of those boards were their relatives, accountants, or friends who were paid handsomely to nod their heads in agreement with whatever was being presented. At home, no one challenged anything that was presented for fear of being deposed from their highly coveted board seats. On Paradise, however, it seemed that most every decision made by the board was met with a tsunami of suspicion and opposition.

Although there were several items on the agenda, the most important was the election of a new director for Paradise. The opening had come about as the result of Harris Hirschfeld's embezzlement scandal. General counsel Marcia Coleman had retained an outside law firm to look into Harris's putative wrongdoing. The investigation was a sensitive one as the ship did not want to risk adverse publicity. Marc, Eva, and the other members of the board understood how embarrassing it would be if word leaked out that these successful billionaires had been bamboozled by one of their own. The entire situation was made even more difficult because Harris was a prestigious litigator in a major New York law firm. And the same Marcia Coleman who was tasked with investigating Harris had been his prized associate before he recommended her for the job of Paradise's general counsel.

The board was thankful that when Harris was confronted by the entire board and presented with irrefutable evidence of his misdeeds, he did not contest the findings. Marcia and her team had done an extraordinary job of marshaling the evidence in a way that defied rebuttal. Besides, Harris had convinced himself that his clients in New York couldn't live without him. Accordingly, his narcissism led him to conclude that he could not spend months at a time on the ship and the purchase of the suite had been a poor decision. He resigned from the board and left the ship under cover of darkness, selling the apartment to Becky as he calculated she would receive a lot more than that in the inevitable divorce proceedings.

It surprised many of the other owners that Becky had not only decided to remain an owner aboard Paradise, but to run for the board. The directors had not publicly shared the reasons Harris resigned from the board and transferred the ownership of his luxury suite to his wife. But there were no secrets aboard Paradise and rumors traveled faster than the wind over the bow.

For years before they bought their luxury suite aboard Paradise, Harris and Becky had been experiencing marital woes. That dissonance was made even more intense when Becky discovered that one of Harris's young associates at the firm aborted a child Harris had fathered. Harris and Becky had stayed together but Becky had no further sexual interest in Harris.

Becky was an attractive woman who had modeled for L'Oréal during her late teen years. Although Becky was most comfortable wearing jeans and a ponytail, she was a glamorous multi-millionaire in her own right thanks to a tremendous inheritance from her father. Throughout her marriage to Harris, Becky kept in shape, largely by taking Soul Cycle and Pilates classes at least four days a week. With her tiny 5'2" frame, Becky couldn't afford to carry much excess weight so she never did. Nor did she allow her face to wrinkle or her breasts to droop. During all those years as a model, Becky had learned dozens of beauty secrets she neither forgot nor abandoned. As a result, the skin surrounding her stimulating blue eyes remained virtually flawless. And what she couldn't control through exercise or beauty secrets, Becky left to Dr. Stephanie Cooperman, her favorite Manhattan plastic surgeon. At fifty, fourteen years younger than her oafish spouse, Becky was not about to throw in the towel and be reduced to attending garden parties in the Hamptons while the other wives whispered behind her back.

Becky was also a doer. In New York, Becky sat on the board of directors of the Alzheimer's Association and the Metropolitan Opera. Her sound judgement and counsel were often sought by some of her fellow board members who had far more corporate experience and were pillars of New York business. Becky was admired because she did not seek the limelight the other board members so highly coveted. So when Becky decided to run for Harris's vacated seat on Paradise's board of directors, she came to the process with well-deserved gravitas.

The couple had originally found their way to Paradise through Harris' long-standing professional acquaintance with Eva. Over time, Becky came to enjoy her time on the ship even more than Harris. She made several girlfriends and enjoyed the unassuming camaraderie they shared.

There was something else that made Becky want to remain aboard Paradise. Six months earlier, while the ship was in Venice, she had enjoyed a lovely day of sightseeing, courtesy of a handsome gondolier. Her companion that day had been Elaine Dwyer, the ship's thirty-eight year-old Entertainment Director. Elaine and Becky had forged a friendship the very first time Becky stepped foot on the ship. The afternoon in Venice was just one of many times the two women went ashore together to escape ship politics, work stress, and all the other pettiness that surrounded so many of the boasting billionaires aboard Paradise.

It was on that memorable day in Venice, while Elaine and Becky found themselves sipping cocktails inside Harry's Bar, engrossed in each other's conversations and personal travails, that the relationship realized a new level. Through a series of unorchestrated events, Becky and Elaine found themselves alone in the restaurant's ladies' room where they shared a passionate kiss and intimate embrace before gently exploring each other's bodies. Before things got too out of hand, the ladies were interrupted by a knock on the door. But Becky simply could not let go of the tingling that had come to grow inside her since that day. On many evenings, after a few cocktails, Becky fantasized about what might have happened if they hadn't been interrupted in that bathroom.

Her ill-fated husband, Harris, had gotten himself into trouble on the ship by virtue of his arrogance, greed, and criminal conduct. That was not going to define Becky's existence on the ship or purloin her ability to travel and explore the world with her good friends. And perhaps explore a part of herself she never knew existed.

Many of the owners aboard Paradise supported Becky's candidacy to ascend to Harris's vacant position on the board. Becky was steeped in major board experience, something that was not common even around the multi-millionaire owners of Paradise. Many of her fellow owners were enamored of Becky's easy going and affable personality, especially admirable considering all that was going on in her personal life. Her supporters noted that Becky was a conciliator who would be effective without being overpowering inside the boardroom.

Other owners opposed Becky's candidacy, primarily on the grounds that as Harris's wife, she had to have known of the fraud and illegal schemes he utilized to embezzle money from his fellow owners. A small but vocal minority, often referred to as The Gripers, embarked upon a whisper campaign to undermine Becky's credibility. They repeated every story and innuendo about Becky, and when they were lacking for fodder, they created rumors out of whole cloth. Thankfully, they knew nothing about Becky's dalliance with Elaine Dwyer or Becky's candidacy would have been sunk, and Elaine fired.

The board convened in the conference room adjacent to Captain Pugliese's cabin. The room looked like the board room of any investment bank, replete with wires, six wall-mounted television screens, and cameras on either end of the room for video hook-ups with the ground-based staff back in Connecticut. On that day, however, only the four directors were present. All the directors were privately in support of Becky's candidacy. But two, Marc and Eva, were lawyers, and they counseled their colleagues that existing directors should not have a material influence on the election of new directors.

"Once we were elected as directors, our roles became to act in the best interest of the entire community. We're not supposed to assert our personal will on any issue, especially the election of future directors," Eva explained.

"But Becky would provide harmony in the boardroom. That could help us achieve solidarity, something we should be striving to achieve," argued Mario Garramone, one of the other board members. "The Gripers are growing more restless. Lior, Oliver, and their buddies are out to cause trouble and if they can get a board seat, they'll try to drive a wedge among us."

Lior Perlmutter and Oliver Rasmussen were two of the original owners who, together with a few of their crotchety cronies, were disparagingly referred to as the Gripers. They were the bane of Marc Romanello's existence on the ship. In the few months they were all shipboard, Marc had almost come to blows with Lior on several occasions. Lior was a malevolent little instigator and Marc was never one to back down from a confrontation.

"Solidarity is a fine aspiration, but the more important role of a board is to vet all the issues roundly and reach a consensus decision. I would never support a candidate just because she'd agree with whatever we wanted to do. Besides, that wouldn't be responsible for her, or any of us, to do," Eva said.

"With all the type-A, overly assertive owners we have on this ship, wouldn't it be nice to have a passive voice in the boardroom?" Mario countered.

"Sure, it would be nice," Eva said. "But it would be irresponsible for us to campaign for it. If that's what the community wants, they can elect Becky. Obviously, that would be fine with me too. I'm just saying that we shouldn't impose our will or influence the votes of the other owners." Mario began to interrupt, but Eva continued before Mario could get started.

"Let me make two other points. Becky's a strong candidate, perhaps the strongest one running, so I'm not concerned about her not getting elected. And, second, don't believe for a minute that Becky would be so passive in the boardroom. There's a reason so many people in New York seek her advice and support. Becky's a lot more than a pretty face."

No one had said that Becky was just a pretty face, but Mario was smart enough not to take Eva's bait. He left that point alone.

The fourth person in the room sat quietly listening to this debate, not showing her hand either way. Besides Marc, Eva, and Mario, Lorraine Williams was the other director aboard Paradise.

Lorraine had been friends with Eva for nearly two decades. The owner of a paperboard factory and mill in Canada, Lorraine originally met Eva when Eva represented Lorraine's company in a multi-million-dollar litigation in the United States. When Lorraine inherited the business from her father, it was worth $20 million dollars. She had the business acumen and good sense to expand the company's business lines and attendant valuation to over $2 billion dollars. Lorraine didn't achieve that level of success by making rash decisions or not listening to her advisers, and Eva was her most respected counselor.

The two women had nurtured a close friendship over the years and when it came time for Eva to raise the funds necessary to buy Paradise, Lorraine was her largest single investor, fronting $100 million. That handsome check bought Lorraine the finest platinum level luxury suite on Paradise.

As she sat in the boardroom listening to the dialogue between Eva and Mario, Lorraine remained silent. She appreciated everything Eva said about needing to remain neutral, but she was also a savvy enough businesswoman to appreciate the value of listening to both sides of a discussion. Months earlier, Mario had impressed Lorraine with the way he'd uncovered, investigated, and handled the whole situation with Harris. His contention that board harmony would be helpful also resonated with Lorraine. On balance, Lorraine was pleased to be a member of such a thoughtful board.

"We can speculate all we like, but our role now is to convene an election and send out ballots to the owners," said Marc, trying to direct the dialogue back to a place of productivity. "Eva's right, it's up to all the owners to decide who sits in the fifth seat in this room. It's not our decision."

With a sigh, Mario agreed, representing a strategic retreat from his earlier position.

"How soon can we hold the election?" asked Eva.

Although the entire initiative to acquire Paradise was her idea, Eva decided early to abdicate the role of board chairman to Marc. Marc was retired and willing to take on the role, whereas Eva still maintained her law practice in New York, at least on a part-time basis. Eva served as deputy chairperson of the board and had the support and respect of every one of the owners, most of whom had been her friends for years before the Paradise opportunity even presented itself. As the author of Paradise's bylaws, Marc had the greatest familiarity with all the ship's rules.

"The bylaws provide that we must give thirty days' notice. It's September twentieth now so why don't we schedule the election for October twenty-first? I'll get on the phone with Marcia in the morning so I can figure out how we send out the ballots and all that kind of stuff. But can we please agree that we won't try to influence the election at all?"

The other directors nodded. When the ship first launched, the five initial directors had been elected by consensus at the owner's first general meeting. Eva and Marc had privately lobbied the other three, Harris, Mario, and Lorraine, to serve, and they had all agreed. What lay ahead was its first potentially contested election.

Before the meeting adjourned, the directors addressed some mundane issues related to the operation of the ship. They decided against advertising Paradise's luxury suites on social media, a small change was made to the itinerary, they approved the purchase of some new equipment for the medical center, and they passed a mission statement that would hang prominently in the ship's main hall and crew quarters. But the overarching issue that concerned each of them was the direction the leadership of the ship might take as a result of the election of a new director. That, they all recognized, could be the single most transformative event in the life of the young vessel.

Chapter 8
Elaine & Becky Make Plans for Singapore

Yves was right. Elaine Dwyer and Becky Hirschfeld enjoyed a sensational dinner at Le Normandie in Bangkok, and, just as Yves had told Karen, Le Normandie was one of Bangkok's most romantic restaurants. They were dressed to the nines when they went out in Bangkok, though not quite knowing exactly why. Their bathroom encounter in Venice had been brief, albeit powerfully sexual and both ladies wondered what would come of it. Surely, they wouldn't be making any kind of a scene in Le Normandie. Would they?

Any consideration of a public display of affection was immediately squelched when Cindy Miller and Mario and Janice Garramone waved to them from the other side of the restaurant. Cindy was one of the few single female owners aboard Paradise. Her alcoholic and clinically depressed husband had committed suicide a few years earlier and Cindy, along with her daughter, Chelsea, had moved from Seattle to Miami so Cindy could return to her family and childhood friends. She bought her luxury suite aboard Paradise to escape the judgmental eyes that followed her on land. She hadn't killed the guy, he'd done it himself. But people were quick to judge. To speculate. To gossip.

Cindy was adored by the other owners aboard Paradise. She was a kind person who sent handwritten notes just because. Sometimes, Cindy even left thumb drives in other suite owners' mailboxes with a playlist, recipe, or tour suggestion she thought appropriate for the countries they were visiting. Although she was not in the golf pro's universe of gorgeous, Cindy was equally well-liked and adored aboard the ship.

Janice Garramone, Cindy's closest friend aboard the ship, lived in the shadow of her husband, Mario, a banker. But Janice was a force in her own right. After graduating from Boston College, she kicked around in various banking jobs for a while before joining Citigroup where she enjoyed a meteoric rise to managing director. Then one day, Janice turned in her banker card for a mommy card and decided to stay home and raise the couples' two children. A fitness freak, she loved Soul Cycle, golf, and pickleball. Her attention to detail throughout her exercise routines rivaled her attention to detail while at Citigroup. The results were obvious in Janice's captivating physique. Her Jennifer Anniston looks didn't diminish the attention she garnered either. But her husband was a philanderer and Janice had learned painful details about his dalliances with at least one young woman, a junior banker at Mario's New York Savings & Guaranty. When Janice threatened to leave him, Mario wept, apologized, and swore he would never see the woman again. And he didn't—for about two weeks.

Mario's affair with the junior banker kept raging ahead at full force. At one point, Mario even had the unbridled hubris to bring the woman, Melanie Hunter, aboard Paradise. That visited its own set of problems on Mario. While aboard the ship, Mario and Melanie ran into Paradise's general counsel, Marcia Coleman. As general counsel, Marcia had reviewed and investigated all the owners' applications and background information. In that capacity, she was keenly aware that Mario was married to Janice.

Marcia had also happened to be Melanie's roommate when the two of them lived in New York. When Mario and Melanie ran into Marcia in one of the bars aboard Paradise, Mario was paralyzed. He had no clue what to say or how to explain away the situation. There really was no logical explanation and, standing in front of each other, they all knew it. The entire situation was unbearably uncomfortable. That was the last time Mario would have Melanie aboard Paradise—until the next time.

But uncomfortable and unusual situations such as these were not unique aboard Paradise. Everyone had their own collection of skeletons and once in a while, a closet would pop open and bones would come rattling out.

In Le Normandie, Elaine and Becky both waved politely after being acknowledged by Cindy and the Garramones.

"You don't think they're wondering why we're here together, do you?" asked Becky.

"Because we're having dinner maybe?" Elaine said sarcastically. "Why would they care? We're friends. Everyone knows we're friends."

"Yes, but do you think they know about what happened in Venice?"

"How could they? I didn't tell anyone, did you?" Elaine was lying. She had told Candy Podeski and that's all it took. Candy told Yves and it was anyone's guess how many people Yves, or even Candy herself, had told. Candy did enjoy her drugs and when high, she couldn't always be positive what she said, or to whom.

"No, of course not. What was I going to tell them? That I made out with you in the bathroom? Are you crazy?" Becky added.

"You could tell them that you also felt me up, or that you kissed my nipples. Or you could tell them how I slid my hand under your skirt," said Elaine as she winked in a way she made sure couldn't be seen by the restaurant's other diners.

"Shhh," Becky admonished as she looked around furtively, fearful their conversation could be overheard. "Are you *crazy*? What if someone hears you?"

"No one's going to hear me," Elaine said, smiling. She was right. The restaurant was bustling with clanging glasses, clinking silverware, and clumsy conversations.

The food at Le Normandie was every bit as extraordinary as advertised. Dinner was delicious and the company delightful. Cindy Miller even joined the ladies for an after-dinner drink once Mario and Janice headed back to the ship. Eventually, all three ladies walked back to the ship together.

Two weeks later, on the eve of docking in Singapore, Becky stopped by Elaine's office. Becky looked adorably casual in her khaki shorts and white blouse. Her hair was tied in a French braid. Elaine was wearing her Paradise uniform shirt and navy trousers and busily banging away on her keyboard.

"Do you have any plans for when we arrive in Singapore," Becky asked.

Elaine stopped typing and looked up. "I'm swamped most every day. I've been working nonstop with the concierge service to put together a bunch of really wonderful events for all the suite owners."

As Paradise's Entertainment Director, Elaine was responsible for booking the onboard entertainment as well as coordinating off-ship events with the concierge staff.

"Oh, that's too bad, I was hoping we could carve out some time to do something together," Becky said. Elaine was glad to learn that Becky's interest in her had not waned.

"Wanna make plans for another dinner ashore?" Elaine suggested. "I'm free most nights after 8 o'clock, and Singapore is kind of a late city. Maybe we could try Jinhonten."

"What's Jinhonten?" Becky asked.

"Singapore has tons of Omakase restaurants, but Jinhonten is supposed to be the best."

Becky looked downward and her lower lip dropped almost undetectably. "If it's so good, I suppose that's where everyone else from the ship will be going while we're there."

Peter Antonucci

Sensing Becky's concern, Elaine rolled her chair back from her desk and clasped her hands behind her head involuntarily emphasizing breasts that needed no emphasis. She gave Becky her complete attention. "I'm sure they will. Why? Are you afraid of people seeing us together?"

Becky wasn't afraid at all. She wasn't afraid of much of anything. She just wanted to spend some alone time with Elaine, even though she had no idea what that meant or where it might take them.

"Elaine," Becky paused, fondling a snow globe from Elaine's desk and still unsure of precisely what she wanted to ask. "What the hell are we doing?"

"What do you mean?" Elaine asked, as she slid her chair sideways from her desk and stood.

Becky closed the door behind her. "I mean *what* are we doing? Are we going to sneak around in various cities, grabbing nice dinners here and there. Are we going to get drunk and rehash what happened in Venice?"

"What do *you* want to happen?" Elaine came around the oversized desk to speak to Becky more intimately.

"I don't know," Becky said as she continued to fidget with the snow globe. "That's the thing. I really don't know. I've thought about that night a hundred times. It was very special, almost magical. Part of me wants to just leave it there. Embrace it and move forward. Part of me wants to pretend it never happened. And part of me is curious about what would've happened if that lady hadn't banged on the door and interrupted us." She looked up at Elaine, almost pleading for answers.

"Well, that's honest. It also covers the gamut of options," Elaine said with a warm smile. "I know this whole thing is new to you. And you know I enjoy women as much as I enjoy men. But the most important thing is that *you're* comfortable. Comfortable with whatever happens between us." Elaine took Becky's hand in hers and squeezed it.

"No," Becky corrected. "The most important thing is that we remain friends. I could really use a good friend on the ship and you're the best one I have."

"What's the deal with Harris?" Elaine asked, tossing her luscious hair around nervously, unsure how Becky would answer.

"Harris is an asshole. You know that. He'll never set foot on Paradise again. After he got caught embezzling money from the ship's coffers, he's not welcome. Not by the board nor by any of the other suite owners. And certainly not by me." Becky blinked uncomfortably as she shared that truth.

"Not by the crew either, you'll be pleased to know. Almost everyone below deck thought he was smarmy." Elaine reflected on what she had just said. "Sorry, he is still your husband after all. I shouldn't be saying that."

"He won't be for much longer. And I've said much worse about him," Becky assured her.

In that moment, Becky appreciated Elaine more than ever.

Although Elaine was more than ten years younger than Becky, there was something Becky found maternal about her sincerity. Simultaneously, there was something undefinably amatory about her presence. Perhaps it was the brownness of her eyes or the way the layers of her auburn hair caressed her neck. Becky never forgot that when she first encountered Elaine, she was reminded of a younger version of Tina Louise, Ginger from Gilligan's Island. When she told that to Elaine, Elaine laughed. "That's funny. When I first saw you I thought of Kristin Chenoweth."

"Elaine, I'm floundering here. I need some direction. Where are we supposed to go with this?"

"We're not *supposed* to go anywhere. We *can* go wherever we want to go," Elaine said, reaching out to hold Becky's other hand as well.

"Where do *we* want to go with it then?" Becky asked.

"Where do *you* want to go with it is the better question?" Elaine asked, her eyes betraying her desire for Becky to squeeze her hands back.

"I don't know. I really don't know. I've never thought of having a woman as a lover before, but there's something about being with you that just feels so right and comfortable." Becky did as Elaine had hoped and squeezed Elaine's hands tightly.

Elaine laughed as she breathed with relief. "So I'm like an old pair of Chanel flats?"

"No, not at all," Becky said, concerned she had insulted her friend. "I love spending time with you." The gentle rock of the majestic vessel brought Becky even closer to Elaine. She leaned forward and kissed Elaine gently on the right cheek. "But I feel like I have to sneak into your office so no one sees us. Or find a restaurant ashore and hope no one else from the ship is there." Elaine's computer pinged, signaling an incoming email. She ignored it.

"Wait a minute," Elaine said. "We were friends for many months before our little dalliance in Venice. We used to walk around the ship together and share our respective grievances, yours with Harris and mine with Paradise's management. There's no reason we can't continue that relationship in public."

"I know, I know. That's not really what I meant. It came out awkward. I just wish we could spend a few hours together with a bottle of wine. Just us. No interruptions." She shuddered briefly, empowered by her bluntness. Then she kissed Elaine on the other cheek.

"We can, silly lady. Do I have to remind you that you own a twenty-million-dollar luxury suite only three floors above where we're standing now. And sixty-five feet closer to the bow?"

"Sixty-five feet? Wow, how do you know that? Have you studied every schematic of the ship?" Becky asked.

"No." Elaine's expression gracefully morphed from amused to serious. "If you really want to know, I pace off the distance from the elevator to your door every time I have to be on your floor. Or every time I *choose* to be on your floor," Elaine added with a smile.

Becky laughed. "That all sounds great, but have you forgotten that crew aren't allowed to visit owners' suites unless they are there for a delivery or service?"

"Oh, I'd be there for service, alright. To service you and for you to service me." Elaine let go of Becky's hands and pulled her close.

Becky's ventricles may as well have exploded because it appeared that all her blood had rushed to her face.

"Shhh," she admonished, even though they were behind a closed door in Elaine's office.

"What are you afraid of now?" Elaine asked. "That somebody could be listening through the air conditioning vent?"

Becky looked around Elaine's office. She was a bit dismayed by the coldness of its walls and the lack of personal touch other than a few desktop artifacts. "It's just . . . it's just habit. I can't talk about those things the way you can."

"So let's not talk about it. Let's do it. I'll bring a bottle of wine to your suite any night. You just tell me when, and I'll be there."

"But you can't. I'm more scared for your job than you are apparently. Besides, I'm running for the board. That's all I would need, another scandal. As it is, I'm trying to overcome the Hirschfeld name thanks to my bastard of a husband. Just imagine if some of the Gripers got wind of this—of you and me doing . . . whatever it is we're doing."

Becky's breathing was beginning to take on a staccato tempo. She put her arms around Elaine and held her close, as much for security as for intimacy.

"You're cute when you get riled up, Becky. Don't worry about getting caught. I know what I'm doing," said Elaine.

"You've done this before?" Becky asked, punctuated with a pang of jealousy.

"We're not talking about what I've done before. We're talking about what you and I *will* do. That's all that matters."

"Oh shit, I totally forgot," Becky said, letting go of Elaine and allowing her hands to flop to her sides. The possibility of being alone with Elaine snapped Becky's mind back to reality. "Harris's buddy, Craig McDougal is aboard the ship now."

"I know. I saw his name on the manifest," Elaine said as she took a step back. "A few of the crew thought he'd be staying in your suite. I dare say I was glad to learn that's not the case." Elaine exhaled ever so subtly, evincing her relief that Becky was not actually entertaining the notorious womanizer.

"In *my* suite? Are you kidding me? If it were up to me, that bastard wouldn't even be on the boat." Becky suddenly looked cross. "His antics make Harris look like a saint. He's almost as bad as Tim Moore, the way he looks at underage girls. Heck, he doesn't just look at them, he's actually been caught with them. There's no way in hell he'd be staying in my suite," Becky said, her forceful pronunciation underscoring the animus she felt towards Craig.

"So why'd you mention him?" Elaine asked, as she retreated so she was standing behind her desk once again. She shot a glance at her computer screen to see what she'd been missing.

"I dunno. It just came into my mind. That's all. Like what if somehow he found out about us and he told Harris? Just imagine how that would play out in my divorce case." Becky rolled her eyes. "Harris has been a philandering whore for all these years and I've been such a goody two shoes. I've got so much on him and he has nothing on me. There *is* nothing on me. Now, just as I'm getting ready to file divorce, he finds out that I'm fooling around with a woman. Wouldn't that look great to a judge?" Becky's entire change of mood was visible as she crossed her arms with almost dramatic flair. Elaine could almost swear she was able to hear Becky grind her teeth.

"Really, are you fooling around with me? That's music to my ears," Elaine joked, trying to lighten the mood.

"I'm not kidding, Elaine. No matter what, I don't think it's a good idea for you to come to my suite at night."

"Is that really what it is? Or are you scared about what might happen?"

Elaine was dead right. Becky was frightened. She may have fantasized about what it would be like to be with Elaine, but her fantasies never actually crossed into the realm of sexuality. Kissing, or even hugging, was one thing. Even dancing could be justified. But more than that? Becky didn't even know what they did. Lesbians. Or women who liked to be with women.

Elaine walked back around to the front of her desk and sat in the guest chair next to Becky. Her crisp white blouse and pearls made her look simultaneously matronly and alluring. She reached out with her left hand and gently put two fingers under Becky's chin. Becky sat up straight, as if taking a clue.

"You don't have to do anything you don't want to do. But you owe it to yourself to see what might happen, what might be there."

Becky sat stunned, numb and excited.

Peter Antonucci

Elaine continued. "No pressure. You tell me when and I'll come visit you. Honestly, no pressure."

Elaine rose and stood above Becky. Her Coco Mademoiselle perfume filled Becky's olfactory senses with orange and jasmine. Elaine planted a gentle kiss directly atop Becky's ponytail. Becky was afraid to look up. She was afraid her face would be directly between Elaine's ample breasts. And she was afraid of being afraid.

Chapter 9
Financial Concerns

Eva remained concerned that too many luxury suites were still unsold. When the finance committee set its initial budget projections for Paradise, they had to estimate the amount of maintenance revenue that would be generated by the luxury suites. Eva was adamant they could not count on more than seventy percent of the luxury suites being purchased the first year. Now, with only fifty-five percent sold, she regretted using a number even that high. As a result, she was relentless in her admonitions to Candy Podeski that more suites had to move, and fast.

"Condo association fees are already high enough. I'm not looking forward to having to explain to my fellow owners that those fees might have to go up because you didn't sell enough suites."

"I'm doing everything I can," Candy protested.

Eva knew she was right. Candy had been doing a laudable job, but these were not inexpensive purchases. It was not so simple to conjure up another thirty or forty couples willing to shell out $10 million or more to buy a glorified cruise ship cabin. But still, Eva was frustrated because she was keenly aware of the reception she'd receive when she delivered the news at the next owners' meeting.

While the ship was still in Singapore, Eva convened a lunch meeting in the ship's Indian-Asian fusion restaurant, Lucky Seas, among the four directors—herself, Marc, Lorraine, and Mario, to address the topic. On such occasions, the Board commandeered one of the ship's otherwise closed restaurants for their private luncheon deliberations. A large round table had been isolated in the front of the room for the directors, and a rectangular table was off to one side, playing host to a variety of Asian-style snacks. On the far side of the room, almost invisible due to its plain white cover, was some sort of blackboard or easel.

"I'm glad we have a few days in port," Lorraine began. "Those last two sea nights became quite challenging for my stomach. I had to take Bonine both nights and that still didn't settle things down. I didn't actually get sick, but I felt close on occasion."

"I know what you mean," Mario added. "That first night was so rough I didn't even drink the second night. There's nothing like a few martinis to really conjure up the seasickness." For Mario to admit he endured a night without a cocktail was a major concession, an unusual occurrence.

"I'm glad everyone is feeling well now then," Marc added, keen to shift directly into the purpose of the confab. "Eva has been chewing my ear off and I think she wants to share her concerns about potential financial icebergs if we don't turn things around over the next few months."

"Thanks Marc. And I'd prefer if you didn't use any iceberg analogies while we're on board." Everyone cackled. "Marc's right though, we really don't have a lot of options available to us," Eva said, diving right into what was on her mind. "The economics are simple. We either have to raise more revenue or reduce the amount we're spending."

"So let's reduce spending," Mario suggested.

"It's not that easy, Mario. Our two largest expenses are fuel and wages. A ship without fuel is no more than a barge tethered to a pier somewhere," Eva said. She stood and walked to the table where light snacks had been laid out. Marc stole an appreciative look at Eva's always firm backside, especially visible in her tight white slacks. He wondered if she was wearing a thong and if so, what color.

"So let's reduce wages," Mario said, ignorant of Marc's wandering eyes.

"Great idea," Eva said, with her back still to the table as she put a few dumplings on her plate. "Except we sold the concept of Paradise being a super luxury yacht with the best amenities and services in the world. We hired the finest, most experienced, discriminating crew we could put together. They command the highest wages on the sea. So reducing our spend is not an option."

"Yeah, but . . ."

"There are no buts, Mario," Eva said as she walked back towards the table and sat back down. "I gave people my word that this ship will blow them away in terms of the quality of hospitality they would receive. I can't go back to them now and say: *Thanks for your money, but instead of performing to the standards of the Ritz-Carlton, we're going to operate more as a Courtyard by Marriott.* That's just not going to cut it. Moreover, it's not the person I am," Eva said.

"So what can we do?" asked Mario.

"There is only one thing left to do—get some of the unsold apartments sold. I know Candy is trying her best, and she's actually doing a great job. I feel bad I'm always bitching at her about it. But she can only sell to people who visit the ship. No one's going to plop down twenty million dollars sight unseen. Even the talented Candy Podeski can't just cold call people and seduce them into parting with millions of dollars for something they've never heard of and that probably doesn't make sense to them. *We* are the ones who have friends in the same league as us. *We* are the ones who should be extending invitations to our friends, colleagues, and country club buddies to join Paradise. That's how I got all of you to buy into the concept," Eva reminded everyone. "I'm not saying we have to do Candy's job selling the suites. What I *am* saying is that we've got to get people on board who are viable candidates to buy those luxury suites. She can take it from there." When she was finished speaking, Eva poured soy sauce on her dumplings. She sat back down and began enjoying them.

"Eva, everything you're saying makes great sense. And as the person who pays the highest condo association fees on the ship, I have a vested interest in everything you're saying, in keeping fees from escalating. But why is this so exigent right now?" asked Lorraine Williams as she stood and made her way to the table Eva had just vacated. She picked up two skewers of freshly made potstickers.

"I'm sure you remember that our shipbuilder, Mitsubishi Marine, holds a reversionary interest in the ship in the form of promissory notes. If we're unable to make our monthly payments to Mitsubishi, they have the right to purchase additional shares of the ship, essentially the unsold luxury suites, at a deeply discounted rate. It's a pseudo poison pill scenario. It's possible they could become the largest shareholder of the ship and force its sale. We're nowhere near that place today, but I'm raising the issue of unsold luxury suites now to put it on our radar screen so we can avoid that type of eventuality," Eva explained.

Lorraine stopped loading potstickers on her plate. She turned and looked around the room, her grayish eyes making contact with her fellow directors. "Eva's right. We're the ones whose capital is on the line. And *we're* the ones who have friends with a lot of money. We can't rely on Candy, or any advertising we might be doing, to reach the millionaires and billionaires we're all friendly with in the first place." Lorraine's concern was not unique, but as the owner of the most expensive luxury suite on Paradise, her financial interests trumped those of all other suite owners.

"I also have an entirely different idea. That's what I wanted to roll out today for your comments and, hopefully, your approval." Eva suggested. She paused before continuing, cognizant her idea was radical and unsure what reception might befall it. She sat back in her chair, closed her eyes for a moment, took a deep breath, and began.

"I've been thinking about this for a long time. Suppose we take thirty of the unsold luxury suites out of the Candy's inventory and offer them for rental," Eva said.

"Like a hotel?" Lorraine asked.

Marc shook his head and scowled. "We already have the visitor flats."

"Yes, but the visitor flats are only for people who are visiting suite owners. And they're smaller. I'm talking about making the suites available to a broader rental population," Eva said, her widening eyes divulging her enthusiasm for the idea.

"Like Holiday Inn?" Lorraine asked in an increasingly cynical voice.

"Not like a Holiday Inn. More like a Four Seasons. But on steroids. We can make it the best hotel in the world. Not just the best cruise experience. The best *hotel* in the world," Eva said. Her voice intensified, underscoring her excitement about what she was suggesting.

"Darling," Lorraine motioned expansively with her hands, "I've stayed in the best hotels in the world. With all respect to you and Marc, Paradise is not the Oberoi Amarvilas in India, the Waldorf Astoria in the Maldives, or the Burj al Arab in Dubai. *Those* are the finest luxury hotels in the world," Lorraine said. It would have sounded obnoxious coming from anyone else, but Lorraine Williams truly had traveled the entire world, and had done it staying in nothing less than five-star accommodations.

Eva raised an eyebrow. "Yes, but we have something that makes us more unique."

"What's that?" Lorraine asked.

Eva paused before she spoke, seeking the dramatic moment she commanded so well in a courtroom. "Location, location, location. Part of what makes each of those hotel experiences so special are their locations. We can do even better." She lowered her voice to slightly above a whisper, another technique that served her well before juries. "We can go to India, the Maldives, or Dubai, without ever leaving the comfort of our five-star accommodations," Eva said.

"Go on. Let's hear more," said Marc. He had stood to help himself to food, but slowly dropped back into his chair, rapt with attention.

"First, no one would be able to rent these apartments for a night or two. The minimum stay would be a week." Eva paused and waited until everyone was silent and staring at her. She lowered her voice, almost to a whisper, before continuing. "Next, it would be expensive. *Very* expensive. I haven't sat down with our accounting team yet because I wanted to get approval from this group first. But I'm thinking of something in the neighborhood of $8,000 to $10,000 a night depending on the size of the luxury suite." Eva looked around the room for approval. Lorraine and Marc added their agreement. "We'd require a massive deposit. Not just to protect against damage, but to only attract people to whom money is really no object. The deposit would have to be around $100,000. They'd get it back, of course, but it eliminates people who could cobble together some cash just to sail for a week."

"Who's going to pay that much for a week aboard a ship?" Mario asked, the corners of his mouth barely hiding his incredulity."

"The same people who pay three or four times that amount to stay at fabulous resorts in the Caribbean. Think Tom Brady, Paris Hilton, the Kardashians, Ryan Reynolds. That kind of clientele. They pay tons more than that. They can get a nice suite here—bring their assistant or security guy or whomever they travel with," Eva explained.

"Keep going. This sounds interesting," Marc said, now glued to his seat.

"Good. I'm glad you're receptive. Here's the kicker." Eva paused again, aware she had captured everyone's attention. She thrived in the courtroom during moments like these. She stood and walked toward the front of the room where the covered easel had been positioned. Standing next to it, she continued. "We have to get an amazing review to make this really work. Not just four or even five stars. But something even higher. Bigger. Better."

"That shouldn't be difficult. There are a million reviewing platforms. If you mean something, like Orbitz, TripAdvisor, or Yelp, I'm sure we can wow those guys into giving us five stars. But what could be higher than five stars?" Mario asked.

"No, I mean a multi-page spread in Travel & Leisure or even a full page article in the New York Times. Not just a review, but an *article*. A great, big, fat, juicy article." Eva said.

"What makes you think they'd want to write about Paradise?" Mario asked.

"Why *wouldn't* they want to write about Paradise?" Eva asked, her voice now evolving into a strategic crescendo. "We'll make some noise in the media, do some press releases, maybe even a few interviews. Once we get on their radar screen, they'll just *have* to write about us. I even have a plan in mind."

"What's that?" Marc asked.

"Peyton Flynn," Eva declared, as she dramatically whisked the cover off the easel. The presentation board was creatively comprised of a series of magazine and newspaper articles all of which had yellow highlighting over the name *Peyton Flynn* wherever it appeared.

"I've heard of her. She writes reviews, right?" Mario asked.

"She doesn't just write reviews. She *is* reviews," Eva said authoritatively. "She has a website, Peyton's Places, that's picked up by all the top newspapers and travel magazines in the world. At 6:00 p.m. on the first Sunday of every month, she publishes a review of a hotel she's recently visited. She only visits the best hotels and they all clamor for a few good sound bites. If they get a great review, they see an immediate bump in their ratings and their rooms sell out for months. She has never reviewed a hotel ship. And she's never given any hotel a 100 rating. But then again, she's never seen anything like Paradise."

The directors' eyes were all fixed on the presentation board. No one said a word or made a sound until Lorraine spoke up.

"You certainly have thought this out, haven't you?" Lorraine asked.

"I have. If we can get a great review from Peyton Flynn, we'll not only fill the hotel suites immediately, but we'll likely sell most of them as well."

"That would certainly ease our financial troubles," Marc said.

"*Ease* them? It would eliminate them," Eva roared. "We'd have a waitlist of people wanting to buy suites. Probably even a market for resale."

"So how do we get this Peyton person here? Do you have a connection with her?" asked Lorraine.

"That's the thing," Eva explained. "No one knows who she

is. She travels anonymously, so hotels can't roll out their red carpet just to get good reviews."

"So how do we get her aboard?" Marc asked.

"As I said, first I wanted to get the buy-in from the board. If you guys approve the concept, I'll speak with Candy and the rest of the sales and marketing group. We'll make some noise in the popular press and try to get Peyton's attention. We also need to get guests aboard. Peyton can't exactly review a hotel that has no guests. I'm not saying we should rush into anything. We have to maintain our high levels of security, so I'll have to interface with Steve and his team as well."

Steve Draper was the ship's head of security. A Popeye-looking, hulk, Steve weighed 280 pounds. His six-foot four-inch frame was topped with the same crewcut he'd worn during his twenty years as a Marine Corps military policeman. Steve had already proved invaluable to Paradise. He had quietly handled a situation when one of the ship's bartenders engaged in sex acts with an adolescent. He'd quickly amassed statements from anyone who had seen the pair together, and just as quickly kicked the bartender off the ship when it arrived in Bari, Italy. Steve was also involved in the investigation into Harris Hirschfeld's embezzlement and self-dealing scandal, serving under the guidance of general counsel Marcia Coleman. Once again, his discretion and diplomacy proved skillful in silencing rumors and avoiding a more widespread scandal among the owners.

"I can't think of a reason why we shouldn't proceed. In fact, it sounds kind of fun," Lorraine added. "I can't wait to meet Ms. Flynn."

"That's the thing. You may never meet her. And if you do, you won't know it. She's always incognito. No one even knows what she looks like."

"Oooh. That sounds even more fun. We'll all have to be on our best behavior," Lorraine said.

"Exactly. That's even more the case for the crew. We'll have to inform them about the plan and make sure everybody knows to be at the top of their game."

"All the time," Mario added.

"Yes, all the time," Eva said. "Believe me, if we get that amazing review I envision, it'll all be worth it. Anything else we should be considering?"

After a few more minutes of discussing Eva's concept of enticing Peyton Flynn to review Paradise, Lorraine Williams added her own suggestion. "I have an idea too," she said. "It pales compared to yours, but I've been thinking of it for a while. It's a way to help Candy sell suites. Suppose we run some sort of a contest where we reward people for bringing new owners to Paradise. We could give an existing suite owner one month's forbearance on their condo association dues if they bring in a new buyer."

"I like the contest idea, but I'm not sure I want to give away free condo association dues. Especially after what Eva just said about our finances being so tight," Mario said.

"Hold on a second. I think Lorraine's onto something," Marc said. "Think of it this way. Sure we'd have to forfeit a month of condo association dues from one of our owners. But in exchange, we get a new owner. That person will be providing us with the purchase price of the condo as well as an ongoing stream of maintenance fees we weren't getting before."

Mario thought about if for a second before nodding his head in agreement. "Yeah, when you put it like that, it makes sense."

"Overall, I like the concept," Eva said. "But like so many other things, the devil will be in the details. For example, if a new owner is a friend of two or three different suite owners, which owner gets the free rent for the month?"

"We could have them share in the origination of the new owner so they each get a percentage of their condo association fee reduced," Mario suggested.

"I don't like the idea of sharing the dues reduction among several different owners," Marc added. "What about this—we establish some kind of a recruiting catalog Candy can maintain. Like a database. Whenever one of us is going to bring a potential new owner aboard Paradise, we register that person with Candy. Whoever registers the new owner first gets credit for bringing him to the ship. That seems like the simplest way to do it."

Everyone looked to Eva for approval.

"I understand what you're saying Marc, but even that system could have problems. For example, Mario and I have a lot of friends in common," Eva pointed out.

That was an understatement. Eva had been involved in a serious relationship with Mario's brother, Eduardo Garramone, years ago. The relationship only came to an end when Eva was fearful Eduardo was going to propose to her. Marriage was not something Eva wanted to embrace at that point in her life. But during those years they were together, Eva hobnobbed with Eduardo and Mario throughout the Hamptons every weekend, collecting friends like trading cards.

"Suppose Mario and I want to bring one of our mutual friends aboard the ship so he can buy a suite," Eva continued. "We would then have a race to see who could attach the guest's name to Candy's catalog first."

"No, you're not understanding me. You only get credit for the sale if you put the prospect's name on the list and the prospect comes aboard and buys a luxury suite," Marc said.

Before Marc could barely finish his thought, Eva jumped back in. "Yes, I get that. But you know what's going to happen? People are going to run to Candy's office and present her with lists of several pages containing the names of everyone they know. That way, those prospects get posted to Candy's database first. Then, if they come aboard—even as the guest of someone else—it's the person who had put the prospect on Candy's list first who gets credit. And that's the case even if the suite owner registered the prospect years earlier. I'll bet you anything Lior and Oliver are the first ones in line to do that."

Eva had met Lior Perlmutter a decade earlier when she represented him in a patent dispute. At 71 years old, Lior was a cardiologist from Bay Ridge Brooklyn. Or at least, he had been one. Immediately after medical school, Lior moved to Jupiter, Florida. He practiced cardiology for a number of years and then left medicine to try to make his mark as an entrepreneur. As he reminded anyone who would listen, he succeeded. Lior invented a series of unique stents that immediately became the gold standard in cardiac care. When his devices, with their exorbitant price tags, flew off the shelves, the major manufacturers in the industry, namely Medtronic, St. Jude Medical, and Abbott Labs approached Lior to buy his patents. In the matter of a few months, Lior found himself in the middle of a bidding war with each company offering over $100 million to buy his business. He sold the whole enterprise to Medtronic and then went about exploring other cardiac devices and doing the whole thing over again, only for a different device, and millions more.

Lior also had a reputation for being one of the cheapest suite owners, notwithstanding his immense wealth. He had already asked Eva, and then petitioned the board, for permission to rent out his luxury suite. Marc stifled that notion immediately. Marc reminded the board the ship provided visitor flats for renters to use. Those rentals would put money directly into the ship's treasury. On the other hand, Lior's idea would only put money into Lior's pocket.

After being smacked down by the board on several occasions, Lior gradually took issue with everything the board decided. He collected a few other chronic complainers who lobbied for their own interests on a regular basis. Oliver Rasmussen, a pompous South African banker, was among the most vocal of Lior's converts. Privately and publicly, they derided the board's every move. One night, while Lior was pontificating about some perceived wrong, Marc's wife, Karen, came up with the nickname, *The Gripers*, to describe Lior, Oliver, and the rest of the malcontents. Marc and Eva were amused by the phrase, and it stuck.

Oliver Rasmussen was a different type of problem for Marc and the board. He was a jolly fat bastard who was married to Heidi, his fifth wife. Among Oliver's many traits that annoyed the hell out of Marc were the fact he spit out his food whenever he ate something, purported to know everything about everything, and was wobbly drunk from his love of scotch more nights than not.

There had been a time that Oliver, who fashioned himself a guru on corporate governance issues, was diametrically opposed to Lior and everything the Gripers stood for. He was actually somewhat aligned with the board on most issues. But he was so obnoxious and overbearing, the board grew allergic to him. His every suggestion was discarded before he even finished droning on about it. When it became apparent he could wield no political power on his own, Oliver changed stripes and became closer to Lior. Together, they forged an unholy alliance.

Eva was right about Lior and Oliver. If a reward system was being offered for bringing new owners aboard Paradise, the two of them would figure out a way to game the system. But the crux of Lorraine's suggestion had struck a chord with the others in the room. She was right—they had more connections with the super wealthy than any salesperson ever could.

"I'm glad you came up with that Lorraine," Eva said. "Even if we only come up with a handful of new owners by the end of the year, that should stave off potential financial distress. It's not like we're in real financial trouble yet. I'm just trying to avert that from becoming a possibility in the future. After putting my heart and soul into this enterprise for the past two years, I don't want to lose it back to Mitsubishi Marine."

"I'm just getting used to the new sound system in my suite," Lorraine quipped. "It would be a shame to lose that now," she joked, comparing her $12,000 sound system to her $100 million luxury suite. If the woman with the most expensive luxury suite on the ship could maintain a sense of humor and laugh about what was going on, the rest of them could too.

"If you're all onboard with Lorraine's idea, I can sit down with Candy and explain it to her. Then, we can present it to the other owners at our next owners' meeting. I move that we proceed with the concept of rewarding owners who bring in new owners." Eva said.

"I think it makes sense. I second the motion." Marc added. "Any objections?"

He paused a few moments to see if anyone wanted to formally interpose an objection to Lorraine's idea. He knew he'd have to record the vote in the minutes.

"Seeing no objection, the motion is passed. Does anyone want to make a motion that we put thirty luxury suites into a rental pool and proceed with Eva's suggestion that we try to get an amazing rating, ideally from Peyton . . . what's her name?"

"Peyton Flynn," Eva reminded.

"Yes, that we try to get an amazing rating from Peyton Flynn."

Eva articulated her proposal in a formal way. Lorraine seconded the motion, and it passed unanimously.

"Fine, I'll get started on that project," Eva said, as she started gathering the few papers strewn in front of her. "I need to speak with Richard Winchester to tell him what we're doing. Then I'll meet with Candy, the housekeeping team, and Chef Rolando to alert them that we'll be starting to take renters," she said, as she was making notes in her daily planner to hold those conversations.

Rolando was the executive chef, responsible for all areas of the food and beverage operations aboard Paradise.

"Housekeeping and the restaurant team will see the most stress if we suddenly fill those empty suites. They'll need to be prepared. At the same time, I'll check in with our marketing people to get them ready. Once we make the suites available for rental, we'll have no idea when Peyton Flynn may come aboard. Everyone will have to be prepared from day one," Eva said.

"I thought this ship was exciting enough. Now, it's really going to get crazy," Mario said.

"We don't want crazy. We want busy. Full, occupied, and well-reviewed. Crazy is for Disney Cruises. We just want to stay afloat financially," Eva said.

Chapter 10
The Gripers Plot

The election to fill the seat left vacant as a result of Harris Hirschfeld's larcenous behavior and attendant ouster was a week away. As expected, Becky Hirschfeld was widely seen as the front runner. Besides being highly respected, she was the fortunate recipient of the sympathy vote due to the unfortunate activities of her husband. Moreover, political correctness ran amok on Paradise, and Becky was a woman. The other directors, Eva Lampedusa, Marc Romanello, Mario Garramone, and Lorraine Williams had agreed not to make public their preference for Becky to fill her husband's seat. But with less than a hundred suite owners aboard Paradise, there were no secrets aboard the ship. Everyone knew the existing board would love to add Becky to their ranks. She was reasonable, a good listener, and not likely to be swayed by specious arguments.

But the Gripers saw it differently. The Gripers viewed Becky as someone who would blindly follow the leads of Eva and Marc. The election of Becky to the board would surely doom the causes the Gripers sought to pursue. Lior, Oliver, and a few of the other recalcitrant ringleaders harbored the fantasy they could elect one of their own to the five-seat board and subsequently convince the rest of the suite owners to enlarge the board to seven directors. They would then try to obtain the two new board seats, giving them a significant presence in the boardroom.

Campaigning aboard Paradise was viewed as unsightly. The owners were all supposed to be friends, fellow travelers aboard the vessel enjoying their time at sea. Becky did no campaigning at all. The Gripers took the opposite approach.

The Gripers decided to put all their strength, if they had any at all, behind Oliver. They correctly reasoned that if they proffered several candidates to fill the vacant board seat, they would split the vote of dissonant owners who wanted to see new blood on the board and Becky would waltz onto the board. They incorrectly reasoned that Oliver's background as a banker and self-proclaimed political influencer in South Africa would impress enough suite owners to get him elected.

Lior, Oliver, and two of the other most ardent complainers on the ship developed a strategy in furtherance of Oliver's candidacy. They fashioned a plan whereby one of them would have lunch or dinner with each of the other suite owners. At each dinner, they planned to run through a checklist of Oliver's strengths and Becky's weaknesses.

"We have to tout Oliver's board experience," Lior explained when the group of four first met. "He was a banker and a member of the board of the University of Cape Town."

"Don't forget that I was a trusted advisor to Nelson Mandela and Bill Clinton," Oliver added. His definition of *trusted advisor* meant he had once been in their presence at a state dinner when the CEO of Oliver's bank fell ill and the bank had to round up an understudy at the last minute.

"I hate to say it, but we have to tie Becky to Harris's scandal," Lior said. "There's no way she could have been blind to his embezzlement and womanizing. We need to portray her as part of the problem, another cog in a Hirschfeld scheme of corruption."

Oliver knew more than a little something about embezzlement and womanizing. In South Africa, he was always one step ahead of the authorities when they uncovered one banking scandal or another. Quick to blame his lawyers or accountants for his own misdeeds, Oliver had somehow escaped indictment four times. He had also escaped four marriages, each divorce a result of his womanizing, and each divorce more expensive than the last.

"I agree that we can try to tag her with knowing about the embezzlement and fraud stuff, but I'd stay away from saying she knew about Harris's womanizing," Oliver said.

"Why? Everyone knows he got one of his associates pregnant a few years ago," Lior said. Upon reflection, Lior thought better of his idea. Oliver had done the same with his secretary. Twice.

"No. Let's leave that alone," Lior said emphatically.

"What about her drinking?" Oliver asked. Lior looked at him quizzically. Becky may have had a glass of wine, or even two, with dinner once in a while, but Oliver was a raging alcoholic.

"I don't think that's our best line of attack either. Let's stick with the embezzlement theme. And promote *your* strengths." Lior said.

Ever the arrogant optimist, Oliver sat a little taller and inhaled what Lior had just said.

"Yes, let's focus on my strengths. We can tell all the other owners about the time Mandela came to me to secure a loan for his famous rugby venture." Lior and the others tuned out somewhere in the middle of Oliver's story. They had heard these tales before and their only uncertainty was around how many were true. The battle to get Oliver elected to the board would be an uphill one indeed.

Chapter 11
Craig Goes Touring with Candy

The day after Craig McDougal boarded Paradise, he found an envelope under his door. Inside was a handwritten note from Candy Podeski inviting Craig to a personal tour of the ship. It was Candy's practice to write the exact same note to all guests who sailed aboard Paradise. But with single male guests, Candy ended her letter with a smiley face after her signature. It was a friendly wink, designed to catch their attention, if they hadn't already been drawn to Candy's magnetic personality and lovely physical appearance. Men were suckers for flattery, and Candy took advantage of that like a wide-open layup.

As the Sales Director, it was her responsibility to run down every potential lead. After all, guests of suite owners already had some familiarity with the concept of Paradise and were likely wealthy. Candy had quickly realized those people were her most fertile targets.

Craig harbored fantasies about being with Candy from the moment she'd met him at the ship's reception desk and walked him to his visitor flat. Her inviting smile and suggestive demeanor were incorrectly interpreted by Craig as sexual advances. His resulting fantasies had even turned physical that night, resulting in an extra sticky situation for housekeeping the next morning.

When he received Candy's note, Craig suffered from the delusion the note was an invitation for more than a tour. His simplistic way of looking at the world led him to conclude that any communication from a woman was an invitation of some sort. He also believed he was a latter-day version of Eros, desired by all women. Craig immediately telephoned Candy to accept her invitation.

"That's great," Candy said. "Why don't you swing by my office around 4:00 and we can go from there."

"Sounds perfect," Craig said.

"And if you don't have dinner plans, perhaps we can grab a bite together at Schooners," Candy offered, referring to her favorite of the ship's five restaurants. It was also her practice, and in her budget, to invite prospects to dinner.

"Sounds even better. I'll see you at 4:00."

"I'm looking forward to it," Candy lied. It was her job. She had identified Craig McDougall as a cad the moment she laid eyes on him. Even before, actually—from the moment she learned about his statutory rape of his own niece.

Craig McDougal wasn't horrible looking. But he was offensively pompous. When he first boarded Paradise, he had strutted through the ship's lobby like a peacock, like he owned the place. Candy had seen many wealthy men behave this way, enjoying some sort of ill-conceived sense of importance. These were not the type of men Candy liked, but her job was not to like men. It was to sell them multi-million-dollar luxury suites aboard Paradise, regardless of their demeanor.

That afternoon, Craig showered, brushed his teeth, rinsed his mouth with Listerine, and slapped some cheap Nautica Voyage cologne around his face and neck. He adorned himself in a too-tight, light blue Versace shirt, pleated khaki trousers, and a pair of brown loafers. His mid-sixties beer gut was not hidden by the shirt. Nor did his thinly worn beard do much to hide the scar on his left cheek, a result of the beating he had received at the hands of his fifteen-year-old sex victim's father. He boarded the elevator, checked himself out in the mirrored front wall, and sashayed down the fifth floor hall to Candy Podeski's office. Candy was on the phone, so she held up the index finger of her right hand, the sign for *I'll be with you in a minute.* She then used that same hand to extend all five fingers towards her guest chair, indicating that Craig should come into her office and have a seat.

"I'm feeling pretty confident about that. I've got my sights on a few different guys. In fact, I have a potential candidate sitting in my office right now," she said, winking at Craig. That was all Craig needed to hear. Candy was talking to Eva about potential ownership prospects aboard the ship, but the self-absorbed Scotsman had erroneously concluded Candy was talking to a girlfriend about possible love interests.

If Candy hadn't already been turned off by the reports she'd heard about Craig McDougall's behavior on land, his slimy personality clinched it for her. Like something out of a bad *Dads Gone Wild* movie, the guy stank of cheap cologne and was dressed like he was in the 1980s. *Pleated pants.* Who wore pleated pants in 2023? Candy hung up the phone. Craig saluted her.

"Captain McDougal reporting for duty."

Candy smiled, albeit painfully. She hadn't heard anything that cringeworthy since John Kerry uttered almost the same phrase when he accepted the Democratic nomination for the presidency in 2004.

"Hi Mr. McDougal. I'm so glad you're able to make it."

"I wouldn't miss this for anything," Craig said. His smile revealed a mouthful of teeth Candy judged to be somewhere between Molson and Heineken in color. It was moments like these she couldn't stand having to spend time with some of the ship's guests.

"What do you say we get started?" Candy asked, rising from her desk so she could escape the close confines of her office.

"I'm always ready to start," Craig said.

Candy had already turned her back to him so she could

grab her jacket from the hanger behind her desk. As she did so, she considered his double entendre, rolled her eyes, and promised herself she'd give him the shortest tour imaginable.

She dutifully walked Craig McDougall through the entirety of Paradise's 455 feet. They stopped at each of the ship's bars and restaurants where Candy provided a description of their function.

"This is Schooners. Although each of our restaurants carry a variety of offerings, Schooners is generally referred to as the ship's steak restaurant. As you can see, it's located on the stern and offers views off the port and starboard, as well as off the aft of the ship."

They next visited Lucky Seas, Paradise's Indian-Asian fusion restaurant before wandering into Leeward, the ship's restaurant that hosted black tie affairs.

"In Leeward, luxury suite owners sometimes host formal dinner parties where they invite dignitaries from any of the cities we may be visiting. Last week, Mrs. Williams hosted a member of Parliament who gave a talk on Britain's role in the Russia-Ukraine conflict."

Craig stared adoringly at the black and gold décor, the Swarovski crystal chandeliers, and the Steinway grand piano in the far corner of the room.

"Surely you can't have someone playing the piano when the ship is in rough seas," he said, more questioning than stating.

"Surely we do," Candy replied. "Richard Williamson is our resident pianist. We stole Richard from Viking Cruises where he worked for over seven years. Richard has been in some ridiculously rough seas. He finds playing in those conditions to be a real challenge to his talent. He makes it his personal quest never to miss a note. He also plays the fiddle at some of our parties. He's a gregarious guy who can make even the most boring evening come to life."

"Wow, I bet there have been some pretty important people in this room," Craig said.

Comments like those made Candy recoil even more. "We like to think that all our suite owners and guests are important people. Including you, Mr. McDougal."

Craig straightened a bit, thinking Candy was paying him a compliment.

"Well, back home in Scotland, I run an oil exploration business."

"I'm aware, Mr. McDougal. I'm aware. That sounds fascinating." She really had no interest in engaging in any more conversation than necessary with this Scottish blowhard. It was her job to show him around the ship and show him around the ship she would. She preferred not to spend a minute more than necessary with him.

"Let's carry on, shall we?" Candy suggested, feigning actual interest in anything Craig might utter.

"This is Tutta Frutta," Candy said. "It's our fruit market where suite owners can stop by to pick up fresh fruit or veggies. Some of our owners cook in their suites. If they can't procure fresh vegetables in local markets, they can always count on us to have them available at Tutta Frutta."

"Whatever," Craig said. "I'm not really a vegetable guy. I'm a meat and potatoes guy," he said, predictably. "In fact, I like my meat rare, tender, and tasty."

As Craig uttered those words, the corners of his mouth turned up in the style of Snidely Whiplash, Dudley Do-Right's primary antagonist. Candy winced. *And young too, I'm sure*, she wanted to blurt out. As she turned to look at him, Candy noticed that Craig's beer-colored teeth were on full display. Eyeing her like a bone-in ribeye, Craig seemed self-amused with his "rare, tender, and tasty" comment.

"So I presume you don't want to stop by Pasture, our vegetarian restaurant?" Candy questioned, almost certain of the answer.

"Nope. One of my mates in Scotland talked me into eating one of those funny burgers last year—what do you call them?"

"Beyond Meat," Candy said.

"Yes, Beyond Meat. Anyway, I didn't find it all that bad until he told me what it was. I've got to admit, the clever bastard had pulled one over on me. But don't worry, I got him back the next week."

Candy wasn't worried at all. Nor did she think she was going to escape being subjected to the rest of the story. She wasn't. It was clear Craig was on a roll, and nothing was going to stop him.

"Turns out the bloody prankster was highly allergic to shellfish. So I convinced the chef at our club to sneak some crabmeat into our stuffed flounder the next week. He turned bright red and his throat swelled up like a blowfish. They had to get him an EpiPen so he wouldn't stop breathing. So no, I don't eat fake meat, and I don't need to see Meadow."

"Pasture," Candy corrected, her head awash in disbelief over what she had just heard. "Then let's head down to the main floor of the ship." She led Craig to the elevators, keenly aware his gaze was fixed on her athletic behind. It was on days like this she wished she wore more loose-fitting skirts.

Candy was grateful an elevator arrived almost immediately so she was spared any further tales Craig may have been keen to share about his disgusting life. As the elevator descended to the fifth deck, Candy sprinted out of the car and continued her tour.

"The fifth deck is the hub of life aboard Paradise. We refer to it as Park Avenue. We have two very diverse food and beverage opportunities here," she said, strolling along the immaculately polished teak planks.

"In the center of the ship we have Sheik Shack. Think of that as a coffee or sandwich place, kind of like a deli on shore. You can grab a bagel or egg sandwich in the morning, or something more robust for lunch."

"Like roast beef?"

"Yes, like roast beef." Candy continued walking, glad she was arriving at the final food destination and not at all looking forward to showing Craig the fitness center, spa, or other recreational spaces where he would undoubtedly extoll her with off color comments about the women working out.

"This is Shoreline, our main bar. Many of the suite owners gather here at the end of a day of touring or shopping so they can compare notes on the day or plan their activities for the next day. We try to keep it a little more upscale than some of the other places. The dress code is strictly enforced. No jeans, shorts, or collarless shirts, and gentlemen are required to wear jackets after six o'clock."

Craig ogled the enormous offering of adult beverages displayed on glass shelves behind the attractive Norwegian bartender. He also ogled her.

"Now this is my kind of place. You can keep all that vegetarian nonsense and just plop me down right here. Can we? I mean, can we sit down and have a cocktail?"

As much as Candy might not have wanted to share a cocktail with Craig McDougal, it presented a fortuitous opportunity to forego the rest of their ship tour. From her stint selling time shares at the Four Seasons to her time selling suites on Paradise, Candy had developed an almost faultless ability to separate real potential buyers from bullshitters. From the moment she first met Craig McDougal, Candy had identified him as the latter.

"Do you know how to make a smooth vodka martini?" Craig asked the Norwegian bombshell. "I mean smooth like satin sheets after they've been turned down, if you know what I mean."

"Yes, Mr. McDougal, I can handle that," Hilde said, flashing him a brilliant smile he immediately interpreted as a proposition. It wasn't. Hilde smiled at all her customers. And Craig construed every smile as a come on. Hilde knew exactly what kind of drink Craig meant—and a lot more about him based on that unctuous comment.

"And I'll have extra olive juice in a little glass on the side. Extra dirty, you know. I'm a very dirty boy," Craig said predictably, to both Hilde's and Candy's dismay.

Candy was dying to feign an emergency phone call or concoct any excuse to have to leave Craig, but that wouldn't have been fair to Hilde and the crew always stuck up for each other. Besides, Candy had to write a report to the board on each potential purchaser, essentially advising whether they were legitimate prospects or not. While relegated to seeing this tour through to the end, Candy was praying the end would come mercifully soon.

Seated at Shoreline's perfectly polished bar, Candy conversed with Craig for over an hour with the same alternative mindset as the whirling dervishes who tilt their heads at a twenty-five-degree angle and can dance in circles for long periods of time in a semi-hypnotic state devoid of contact with reality. She barely heard a word he said as he droned on about his life, accomplishments, and friendship with Harris Hirschfeld.

To Candy's delight, more than a few suite owners sidled into Shoreline and occupied seats at the bar and at the cocktail tables around the room. Craig only diverted his gaze from Candy when someone new arrived, especially a woman. He wasn't just sizing up the women who were age appropriate. He looked them all up and down, even the eighty-four-year-old Mrs. Manfred. Several of the suite owners waved in Candy's direction and a few stopped by to introduce themselves to the likely prospect who accompanied her. Finally, Candy dialed herself back into Craig's diatribe. Craig was in the cups by then, having twice hit Hilde up for refills of his Belvedere, each request accompanied by another reference to bedding.

"So, Mr. McDougal, I know you haven't seen the entire ship yet, but I'm sure Mr. Hirschfeld must've told you quite a bit about it," Candy said, searching for a gracious ending to their intercourse.

"He sure did. So did Oliver Rasmussen," said Craig as he fixed his lecherous eyes on Hilde's backside. Candy winced when she caught Craig's too-long stare.

"I didn't know you knew Mr. Rasmussen too," Candy said, suddenly shocked back into the conversation.

"Sure do. Harris was representing my company in a dispute in London," Craig said, his craggy teeth distracting Candy from what he was saying. "I was over there for depositions, stuck for about four days. One night, Harris introduced me to Oliver who was visiting from South Africa. We all had a few dinners together, ran around, and had some good fun. Oliver and I were never as tight as I was with Harris, but we had some fun together anyway."

A few of the other suite owners glanced over at Candy and the outsider, trying to determine whether Craig was a potential purchaser, or someone Candy was flirting with. Or both.

Candy's mind was ablaze with unkind speculation as she imagined the embezzler, the oaf, and the pedophile out on the town.

"I'm sure it was smashing," she said, straining to sound as polite as possible.

"Ollie and I were both still single back then, and we loved to run around and entertain the ladies." Craig belched. He actually belched. Candy didn't know how to react, so she tried to pretend she hadn't noticed. "Harris was married to Becky, but that never really seemed to bother him, if you know what I mean," he said with a wink.

Candy knew *exactly* what that meant.

"When Harris told me he wouldn't be able to be aboard during my visit this week, I was disappointed, of course, but I figured I could run around with Oliver and his new wife, Holly."

"It's Heidi," Candy corrected. She tried to make eye contact with some of the suite owners, hopeful someone would join their conversation and she could have a lifeline, even if just a brief one. But no one did. The other owners smiled at Candy but were busy greeting each other, ordering drinks, and discussing their dinner plans.

"Holly, Heidi, whatever her name is. I can never keep up with Oliver and his conquests. He's a good mate, but I really can't see why a woman would stick around with him."

Candy wondered the same about Craig's own wife.

For the second time in as many minutes, Candy was rendered speechless. Even her eternally upbeat personality was struggling with how to respond.

"The crew all love Mr. Rasmussen," she lied. "In fact, he's running for the board of directors here aboard Paradise."

Craig continued rambling, not even acknowledging Candy's remarks. "You know, besides being friends with Harris and Oliver, I'm friends with Becky and Holly too."

Candy thought better than to correct Craig again.

"In fact, I always tease Oliver that if he ever leaves her, I'll run off with Holly."

Knowing Heidi Rasmussen as a consummate lady, Candy scoffed at the notion of her having anything to do with the blathering cad sitting next to her. But Candy's unadulterated smile did nothing to give away her disapprobation.

"Turnabout's fair play, after all," Craig continued.

"What do you mean by that?" Candy asked, almost immediately regretting she had asked the question.

"There was one time when Oliver almost made it with my wife, Esther," Craig boldly announced to the shock of two of the suite owners who were sitting on the far side of him at the bar. "Or, at least, he tried to. We were all on vacation together in Tortuga, I think it was. It was me and Esther, Harris and Becky, and Oliver and Heidi." His face lit up with an incongruous degree of pride as he realized he had correctly remembered Oliver's wife's name this time.

"Anyway, after a day at the beach, we all enjoyed some gin and tonics and got a little loose. There was an outdoor shower there, a white wooden structure. Like the ones you see on Nantucket, you know. Esther stepped into the shower and tossed her bikini top over the wall, kidding around, of course. But Oliver wasn't kidding. He stood up and removed his swim trunks. Stark naked in front of me, Harris, Heidi, and Becky. Then he walked over to the door and tried to open it. Esther screamed and pulled the door shut. She almost slammed it right on Oliver's tiny pecker. He got angry, very angry. Oliver can get like that sometimes, you know. Heidi walked over to restrain him, and he shoved her backwards, away from the shower. She would have hit her head on the concrete if she hadn't fell sideways into a hedge. Oliver didn't care. He kept pulling on the door and telling Esther she had to let him in. When she didn't, he grabbed hold of himself and started to pee under the shower wall, trying to get it on Esther's feet."

Candy was speechless. She had come across her share of crass men over the years, but this story, and the brazen way Craig related it in the presence of Paradise's suite owners, was unfathomable.

"Oh, my, that sounds appalling," Candy said.

"Appalling? It was crazy. But you can see why it would only be fair play if I had a romp with Heidi."

Third strike. Candy was out of responses. She couldn't see anything fair about any of it. Least of all that she was required to sit there listening to this incredible tale of lewdness. Even more unfair, because she was on duty, Candy was unable to indulge in a drink or two, to dull the effect of the entire engagement. For the life of her, Candy could see nothing fair or redeeming about the time she spent sitting at Shoreline with Craig McDougal. Until, that is, a week later when she learned that Oliver had withdrawn his name from consideration for the board. It seemed that many of the suite owners who were in Shoreline that day were not spared Craig's fantastical rant.

It didn't take long for news of Craig's offensive description of Oliver's Tortuga exploits to get back to The Gripers. There was nothing Oliver could do to rehabilitate his reputation after Craig's alarming revelations, and any efforts to do so would most likely be met with further embarrassment. When the board election was held a few weeks later, Becky Hirschfeld was overwhelmingly elected to replace Harris and the extant board breathed a collective sigh of relief.

Chapter 12
Intel on Peyton

One Sunday afternoon, a week after jettisoning its mooring lines from Jurong Port in Singapore, Paradise skated into its berth in Colombo, Sri Lanka. Suite owners aboard Paradise were excited about visiting Sri Lanka, the place Lonely Planet had designated as the best in the world to visit only two years earlier.

When they arrived in port, the newly constituted board of directors took a specially organized tour of Galle. Eva was hoping to start a tradition of facilitating a board outing after the election of a new director. Board cohesion would prove critical to her new venture and having the group spend the day together would be a helpful first step.

The five directors listened intently as their tour guide explained that Galle, a fishing-intensive city with a population of 100,000, was a major trading port in Sri Lanka since 125 A.D. At that time in its history, Sri Lankans trafficked in ivory, peacocks, and apes. Over the past half century, fishing became the predominant industry, as made clear by the abundance of rickety fishing boats gathered in clusters along the roadside throughout their tour.

Eva listened intently as the guide also informed them that cinnamon is the other major economic staple in Sri Lanka. In fact, seventy percent of the world's cinnamon comes from the island of Colombo. Weaving tales of pirate bounty among stories of ancient seafaring days, he told the five travelers that Portuguese mariners in the fifteenth century equated cinnamon to gold. If a seafarer was lucky enough to make it back to England with a bag of cinnamon, he would have enough money to build a beautiful home.

Shortly before sunset, as the group was touring the Pettah Market, a blocks-long collection of maddening noise and haggling that had started as a fruit and vegetable exchange and been in constant use for over 350 years, Eva received a phone call from Elaine Dwyer. Elaine had been tasked with keeping a virtual eye on Peyton Flynn and her whereabouts.

"Eva, can you talk? I've got some news for you."

"Sure, just give me a minute to break free," Eva said, shuffling away from the rest of the group. "What's up?"

"It's Sunday, and you know what that means," Elaine said.

Eva hesitated. She wondered if the ship had missed a payment to Mitsubishi Marine, or if headquarters had been unable to make payroll.

"I know it means it's the beginning of the week. What else does it mean?"

"It's the last week of the month so it's the day Peyton Flynn publishes Peyton's Places," Elaine gushed.

"Oh, that's right," Eva said. She had never really focused on the details of when Peyton published her hotel reviews but was glad that Elaine was on top of it.

"Well, you'll never believe this. She just reviewed the Oberoi Amarvilas in Agra."

The significance of that information was immediately apparent to Eva. Agra was the city in India that played host to the Taj Mahal. And India was the country immediately above Sri Lanka.

"Are you serious?" Eva fidgeted nervously, her elevated voice doing nothing to hide her excitement.

"Deadly serious. She gave them a ninety-four. Raved about the place," Elaine said.

"What's not to rave about?" Eva asked. "It's one of the most elegant hotels in the world and most of the guest rooms overlook the Taj. A ninety-four? If there's any hotel I that should get a 100, it's the Oberoi Taj. How could she find fault with it?"

"Well, she loved it. Almost every bit of it. Let me read you a quick blurb. *Constructed over 350 years ago, the Taj Mahal was commissioned by Emperor Shah Jahan as a tribute to his wife, Mumtaz Mahal, who died during childbirth. So as the Taj itself is a monument to love, the Oberoi Amarvilas is a place to share with the one you love. Its lavish interiors and sumptuous gardens create a magical place for lovers to share. The guest rooms are palatial, each one luxuriously furnished with traditional Indian fabrics and appointments, hand-crafted ornaments, and every modern amenity one might imagine. The luxury spa, magnificent ballroom, and inviting swimming pool are all enveloped by some of the most beautiful white marble one can imagine.*"

"Peyton nails it perfectly. She makes the hotel sound as divine as it is. Why on earth did she deduct six points?" Eva asked.

"The front desk staff," Elaine said.

"The front desk staff?"

"Yes. Hold on. I'll read it to you. *A hotel is only as good as those who make the wheels turn. The people who run the Oberoi property are aware of that and have hired some of the best hotel staff in the world. Without exception, they were polite, courteous, and knowledgeable about their jobs.*"

"So what the hell is she complaining about?" asked Eva, growing as anxious as she was confused.

Elaine continued. "*While the hotel earned top marks in every category, I could not overlook the two instances when front desk personnel were unable to accommodate two distinct requests. Those who have followed my reviews know that I often request an uncommon amenity that may stretch a concierge or front desk employee. That can differentiate the good hotels from the outstanding ones. And that is precisely what happened at the Taj Oberoi Amarviles. I requested a private tour guide for the Taj*" *which, I'm pleased to say, they were able to accommodate. But I also requested a Sony FE 24mm f/1.4GM lens to rent for the day. While they were able to scare up a few Nikon and other Sony lenses, they were unable to secure the specific lens I had requested. Let me be clear. I would not expect every hotel in the world to have an assortment of camera lenses. But a hotel that is located next to the Taj Mahal, and whose guests are presumed visitors to the Taj Mahal, should have the finest lenses available to a discerning client willing to pay for them."*

"Are you kidding? She dinged them over a camera lens?" Eva asked.

"Yup. Should I make sure our onboard boutique has an ample supply of camera lenses?" Elaine asked.

"No, I wouldn't worry about camera lenses," Eva said. "It's unlikely Peyton will make the same request again. But what *is* immediately intriguing is that she's in India."

"Should we talk to Captain Pugliese about rerouting Paradise so we head north into India?" Elaine asked.

"No, that's too obvious. Besides, our owners made their flight arrangements weeks and months ago. We can't just reposition the ship on a whim because a hotel reviewer might be in the area. Besides, we're heading that way after we leave Sri Lanka."

Elaine was a tad embarrassed. She had spaced out on the ship's itinerary. After leaving Galle, Paradise had one more stop in Sri Lanka before it headed north to visit the Indian cities of Cochin, Mangalore, Goa, and Mumbai.

"Yeah, I guess you're right."

"Besides, the trip from Agra to Sri Lanka is a relatively short hop. If she's gotten word about Paradise, Peyton will know how to find us."

"I know. That's what I was thinking. And why I called you as soon as I read this month's Peyton Places. Should I alert the front desk?"

"No. Let's wait until we all get back aboard. I may want to address them myself. Or with Marc. I'm not sure yet. Give me a little while to think about it, and we'll formulate a plan. But thanks so much for telling me right away. I'll tell the other board members while we're here so they'll know what's up." Thinking aloud, Eva continued, "I don't think any of them have read anything about Peyton Flynn. Except Lorraine. I'd be willing to bet she read all about Peyton after I mentioned her at the last board meeting. Anyway, thanks for the call. See you soon."

With that, Eva rejoined the rest of the group as the tour guide was wrapping up his narration. "Of course, no visit to Sri Lanka would be complete without reference to the 2004 tsunami that took 40,000 lives in a matter of an hour. With one twenty-four-foot wave, our already-distressed country was set back decades and propelled into economic turmoil. I lost three cousins that afternoon. Even though the tsunami occurred almost twenty years ago, many parts of the country have still not been able to rebuild."

As they listened, each of the five board members was visibly distressed. Becky and Lorraine even teared up a bit.

"How have things progressed since then?" Marc asked.

"They've progressed, but not well. To rebuild something that should have been built in a year, now takes five years. Our government is filthy with red tape and corruption."

Marc rolled his eyes as he met Eva's glance.

"Welcome to our world," Marc said. "If misery loves company, I can assure you things are no better in America."

"Or Canada," Lorraine chimed in.

Aboard the van on the way back to the ship, Eva shared the news about Peyton Flynn's newest post. The other board members peppered her with questions, most of which she could not answer.

"You guys have to read some of Peyton's previous reviews. Each one offers a little insight about what she might be looking for during a visit. And each one provides a clue about how she can trip up a hotel. It seems like no matter how well prepared someone is for a visit from Peyton Flynn, she always finds a few chinks in the armor. Our job is to make sure we don't have any of those chinks."

Once back aboard Paradise, Eva and Marc divided up Peyton Flynn's last four years of Peyton's Places' reviews. In addition to reviewing luxury properties, Peyton also reviewed theme parks, restaurants, and sports venues. Once they eliminated the irrelevant comparisons from the collection, the work became more manageable. They agreed to each make a list of frequently identified issues Peyton had focused on in her prior reviews. Then, they would each meet with the heads of the respective departments that might be implicated by one of the things they had identified.

As they compiled their lists, it became clear that a hotel's front desk was often the source of negative comments from Peyton Flynn. Because of that, Eva convened a meeting of the entire board and the front desk staff. That Friday afternoon, at 8:00 AM, they met in Paradise's boardroom to go over their findings and recommendations.

"You've all heard about our marketing initiative to try to get Peyton Flynn to visit Paradise and write us up in Peyton's Places, right?" Eva asked.

Heads nodded in unison.

"Well, we've been doing a little homework about Peyton Flynn to identify the things she often finds problematic at a property," said Eva as she opened a bottle of Perrier and poured it slowly down the inside of her tilted glass. "Not surprisingly, many of those topics involve front desk personnel. It's not because front desk personnel aren't good at their jobs or don't care about pleasing guests. It's simply because front desk personnel are a hotel's front line of attack when guests come to visit. If the shower is too cold, they call the front desk. If the pillows are too soft, they call the front desk. If the Internet doesn't work, they call the front desk. You guys know what I mean, right?" she asked, pausing to take a drink.

Again, all heads nodded. A few people snickered.

"Peyton's reports don't ding the hotels just because of those things. Things will always go wrong. The hotels get dinged because of the way their personnel *respond* when something goes wrong," Eva said, emphatically. "While we can't prevent against every issue, we *can* ensure that every contact with a guest is done pleasantly, respectfully, and with every possible attempt to correct a problem and enhance their visit. Even better though, we'd like to obviate the problems before they arise.

"Peyton is already on this continent and there aren't a ton of luxury properties between Agra and here." She looked around the room for effect. "We need to be on high alert in case she joins us any time over the next few days or weeks. She just published a report on the Oberoi Amarviles on Sunday. That probably means she was there a few weeks before that. Therefore, if she's still in the region, she could be here any day. She could even write about Paradise this month," she said with great enthusiasm. "So we need to think of *every* guest as a potential Peyton Flynn. We have no idea what she looks like, how tall she is, how she speaks, nothing. We don't even know her nationality. So we have to use our best efforts with every guest we welcome."

Excuse me, but isn't that what we're supposed to be doing already?" Donna Lafat asked.

Donna was a newly-promoted front desk manager who had impressed everyone from the moment she stepped aboard Paradise. Raised in Connecticut, Donna had attended the prestigious Deerfield Academy before matriculating at Cornell where she majored in hospitality services. Her manners came from her parents and Deerfield; her personality and dedication were her own. Donna also possessed an infectious smile that could disarm even the crankiest of guests. She had gained high praise from all her colleagues and managers and seemed destined for great things with Paradise or beyond.

"Yes, Donna, that is *exactly* what you're supposed to be doing every day. And I'm certain all of you are doing that with every guest interaction. But now, let's do even more. Let's step up our game. We don't know when, or how, Peyton Flynn will appear. But when she does, we have to be ready," Eva said.

The assembled had few questions but Eva had few answers. Eva had made herself clear, or as clear as she could. Essentially, the team had to get ready, without knowing what they were getting ready for.

"Okay then, let's get to work. And let's have fun doing it," Eva said, signaling the end of the meeting.

Chapter 13
New Owners Lists for Candy

The journey from Galle to Colombo was less than ten hours, but that was precisely when Candy Podeski's office became ground zero for an inevitable turf war, a war Eva had predicted only a week earlier.

After lunch, while on her way back to her luxury suite, Lorraine Williams ran into Candy Podeski in the Park Avenue hallway.

"Good afternoon, Candy. I've been meaning to stop by your office. Have we started that new referral program yet? The one where we're supposed to give you the names of prospective new owners?" Lorraine asked.

"Yes. In fact, I was just working on it this morning. I've created the template for a spreadsheet so I can keep track of everything. Why, are there any names you'd like to share with me?"

"There are. I have three candidates, if you will. I'm not sure what the process is, but if you tell me what I need to do, I'll get you whatever information you need."

"Nothing really for you to do at all," Candy replied. "If you just give me their names and addresses, phone numbers, email addresses, that sort of thing, I'll be happy to take it from there."

"Are you sure? Isn't there anything I need to do? I'm happy to do whatever I can to help."

"Don't be silly, Mrs. Williams. It's my job. I'll handle it." She paused before continuing. "Of course, you're free to do whatever you like. A personal phone call from you would never hurt the cause."

Of course it wouldn't. Lorraine Williams was one of the most prominent figures in all of Canada. A call from her would command the attention of most anyone.

"I'll do just that. Two of the gentlemen have sat on my boards for over twenty years. I see them all the time, but I've never really asked them for anything. I can call them tonight." Lorraine's eyes twinkled. "The third will be a more interesting call. He was one of my first gentleman callers when I was only seventeen. We've shared some special memories together."

"I completely understand," said Candy, smitten with Lorraine's use of *gentleman caller*, a phrase not common anymore. Candy broke into an embarrassing grin.

Lorraine sensed that Candy may have interpreted her statement as being more than what was intended.

"Oh, no, dear. Not like that. Not like Prince Harry and that girl in the stables. What was her name . . . Sasha Walpole, wasn't it?"

"Yes, I think that's right," Candy said.

"Well. it wasn't anything like that, so don't let your mind wander. We snuggled and smooched a bit, but nothing more. We've remained friends for over forty years now."

Candy was impressed that Lorraine had been able to maintain a friendship with an ex-boyfriend longer than Candy had been alive. All Candy's ex-boyfriends turned out to be stalkers, haters, or just irrelevant. If she were Taylor Swift, Candy could have written an entire song catalogue about her ex-flames.

"The old bloke went on to become a doctor. He abandoned our cold Toronto weather to go to medical school in Florida. After that, he only came back on holidays to visit his brother and mum. We've remained in touch ever since. Occasionally, when I would go to Florida, we'd get together for stone crabs and some good laughs. After my second divorce, we even had a few dates. He invited me to be his guest at the Super Bowl one year, and we had a splendid week together."

Candy leaned forward on her toes, opened her mouth into a broad smile, and asked, "And?"

"And . . . nothing materialized of it, dear. He's still sewing up people's hearts, and I didn't want him to break mine. He's such a fun guy. He'd be a great asset to Paradise."

"And to you, it seems," Candy said, grinning.

"Now you stop it, you devilish little Cupid."

Lorraine burst out laughing, drawing questioning looks from an elderly couple, also suite owners, who were passing at that moment. Candy made a sarcastic face behind their backs causing Lorraine to laugh even harder.

"I'm headed back to my suite now. I'll write up contact info for all three gentleman and bring them to you later. Hold off on calling them for about four or five days. I'd like to call them myself first and explain what's going on, what Paradise is all about, and why they simply *must* come aboard."

"That's fine. But there's no need for you to write anything formal, Mrs. Williams. You can just send me an email with all that information and that will more than suffice."

Fifteen minutes after the ladies bid each other farewell, Candy received an email with the names of the people Lorraine had promised.

Nothing involving the Gripers was ever easy aboard Paradise and the roster of prospects was no exception. Within an hour after receiving Lorraine's list, Candy circulated it to the other luxury suite owners, consistent with the board's new policy. The hope was that other owners might know the same prospects and also contact them, thereby increasing the odds the person would visit Paradise and, hopefully, eventually buy a luxury suite. It wasn't more than fifteen minutes after Lior Perlmutter received Candy's list than Candy's phone rang.

"Dr. Perlmutter. Good day. How may I help you today?"

"I know Klein. He's my prospect," Lior asserted forcefully.

Candy was caught off guard by Lior's abrupt nature and the way he began the conversation seemingly midstream. She quickly recovered and recognized Dr. Adam Klein as one of the three names Lorraine Williams had given her the day before.

"Oh, that's wonderful, Dr. Perlmutter. I'm sure Mrs. Williams would welcome your help. I know I would."

"You don't understand. He's going to be on my list. I just haven't given it to you yet," Lior said.

"Well, since he's already on Ms. Williams' list, there's no need for you to include him as well. Ms. Williams was kind enough to forward all his particulars already so we're all set when it comes to Dr. Klein. But a call to him would be terrific." Candy tried her best to maintain her cool and not tell Dr. Perlmutter what she was really thinking.

"Perhaps you didn't hear me. Dr. Klein is going to be on my list. We go to the same synagogue, and he attended my grandson's bar mitzvah. If he buys a luxury suite aboard Paradise, I want the credit, not Ms. Williams, or anyone else."

"Dr. Perlmutter, I understand. But I don't make those rules. If it were up to me, I'd love to see everyone get credit for any referrals. But the board sets the rules, and I simply abide by them. I suggest that if you don't like the system, you contact Ms. Lampedusa, or Mr. Romanello." Candy was growing impatient with Perlmutter, as most people did, but she knew she couldn't show it.

"I will. And I'll be getting you my list of potential owners shortly," he grunted, abruptly.

Just as he promised, Lior Perlmutter marched down to Candy Podeski's office an hour later, his white wavy hair knotted in a ponytail that draped down the back of his suede vest. The

Sixties may have come and gone decades ago, but Lior Perlmutter continued to dress as if Woodstock was his next port of call. Peering through his John Lennon shaped glasses, he not so politely tossed a few pages of chicken-scratched names on Candy's desk. As she picked up the torn pages of notebook paper, Candy squinted. Her lips pursed unconsciously as she struggled to make out the scripted, crossed out, and rewritten names, complete with arrows hither and yon.

"What's wrong? Can't you read it?" he whined, in his typically confrontational tone.

"I'm certain I can try," Candy said, doing her best to remain poised as she turned the pages over, miserable to realize there was writing on both sides.

"There are 335 names on my list. They're all people you should contact about Paradise. Some might buy, most might not. You never know until you try," instructed the old curmudgeon.

Candy struggled as she tried to determine any order of the names, let alone whether each had a phone number or email next to it. Aware that she might be poking a bear, Candy nevertheless asked, "Dr. Perlmutter, is there contact information for each of the names?"

"No. I don't have contact information for many of them. They're just a list of people I put together who might be interested in buying luxury suites. You wanted names. I gave you names," he barked.

Candy realized little good would come of interrogating Lior Perlmutter any further. This was an issue for the board to address. Moreover, Candy was much more comfortable dealing with Eva and the other board members, most of whom she considered friends, than she was dealing with the crusty Dr. Perlmutter.

"This is great, Dr. Perlmutter. I'll circulate these names and we'll continue to build our database of new potential owners."

Once Lior Perlmutter waddled away, Candy left her office to grab a mocha latte from Sheik Shack. More than anything, she needed to clear her head. Perlmutter and his gang of Gripers could suck the fun out of any day, and he'd just ruined Candy's afternoon.

The always engaging and usually affable Podeski was neither as she waited her turn to order a blast of caffeine infusion. Instead, she was muttering to herself as she turned Lior Perlmutter's pages sideways and upside down to try to decipher what he had scribbled.

"Whatcha got there?" Marc Romanello asked over Candy's left shoulder.

Startled, Candy folded the pages and gracefully stuffed them into the pocket of her slacks.

"Nothing really. Dr. Perlmutter gave me his list of potential prospects and I was just reviewing it."

"Oh, that's great. I'm glad to hear that people are giving you some names. Maybe that little initiative of ours will take hold, and we'll be able to sell a few more suites this quarter."

"Yes, that would be lovely," Candy said. "Ms. Williams gave me a list as well."

"Even better. I have a few names I'd like to add to your list. If you already have a bunch of names, I don't want to overwhelm you. I can only think of four or five real possibilities and I don't want to bury you with a bunch of names just for names' sake," Marc said.

Candy smiled and before she could catch herself, sputtered, "Too late for that."

"What's that mean?"

"Nothing really."

"C'mon. Out with it."

"Well, Ms. Williams gave me three names. And she walked me through exactly who they are and how she knows them. Then she gave me their telephone numbers and email addresses."

"What's wrong with that?" Marc asked.

"Nothing. But look at this," Candy said as she removed the folded pages from her pocket and handed them to Marc.

"What the hell is this?" he asked.

"That's the list Dr. Perlmutter just gave me."

"List? This is no list. This is horseshit. How can you possibly make heads or tails of this?" Marc rarely hid his disdain for Lior Perlmutter.

"That was my initial thought, but, you know me, I'll hunker down and endeavor to ascertain who these people are and how I can get a hold of them."

"That's ridiculous. Do what you can do, but don't kill yourself for him. I'm sure you'll be getting lots of names from other suite owners, and you can prioritize, however you like," Marc said. "He's a selfish idiot, and, if he can't give you a legible list, that's his problem, not yours."

"Thank you, Mr. Romanello. To be honest, I don't even know how I'm going to decipher these names so I can circulate them to the rest of the owners."

"As I said, Candy, do your best. If you have any questions, go back to Dr. Perlmutter and ask him for help. He can't just dump this pile of crap on you and expect you to figure it all out yourself."

Candy smiled, reassured that someone had her back. And not just anyone, but Marc Romanello, the chairman of Paradise's board of directors. Marc's hatred of Perlmutter was as well known among the crew as it was among the suite owners. Candy hadn't *accidentally* shared her lament with Marc. She knew exactly what she was doing.

Emboldened by a cornucopia of Marc's words and Sheik Shack caffeine, Candy returned to her office to update her slide deck on Paradise for potential investors. Working on the spread sheet of leads she'd received that morning was the last thing she wanted to do, especially if it meant having to look at Perlmutter's scrawling again. An hour later, she received an email from Marc Romanello encouraging her to *hang in there* and providing the names of the few leads he had promised. Candy breathed a sigh of relief when she saw the three names, each typed neatly and followed by email addresses, contact telephone numbers, and a sentence or two containing a few points about each person he identified.

This is why I like working here, Candy reminded herself.

Not wanting to let grass grow beneath her feet, she immediately circulated these three names to the other suite owners. Within seconds of launching her email into the universe, Candy's phone rang. When she saw the name on the display, she exhaled and slumped forward before lifting the receiver.

"Didn't you go over the list I sent you?" Dr. Perlmutter asked in an adversarial tone.

"Yes, Dr. Perlmutter, I did."

"Then why haven't you circulated that to everyone? Or did I miss it?"

"No, sir, I haven't finished going through it yet."

"But you finished Romanello's list? When did he give it to you?"

Candy knew better than to play games or be anything less than forthwith when dealing with the suite owners, especially Dr. Perlmutter.

"He just gave it to me an hour or so ago. But it was only three names, and it was neatly typed. So I wanted to circulate it as soon as possible."

"And you didn't want to circulate mine?"

"Of course, I do. I just need a little while to go through it. It's handwritten, and I need to figure out all your writing. I also need to find contact information for all the people you listed so I can reach out to them. Without that, I can't really do anything, now can I?"

As soon as she finished uttering the predicate to that sentence, Candy regretted it. She hadn't needed to add those last three words. Fortunately, Perlmutter let them slide, for whatever reason.

"Well, two of the names on Romanello's list are on mine. Claremont Burns and Henry Gerard. So you can strike them from his list. I gave them to you first. That's the rule, isn't it? Isn't that what you told me when I spoke with you about Adam Klein this morning? He was on Lorraine's list so I couldn't share credit, right? So Burns and Gerard are on my list. That means Romanello can't have them. First come, first served. That's what you said me this morning and that's what I'm holding you to."

Candy winced. She had enough real work on her plate. She didn't need to become embroiled in a pissing contest between two suite owners. A contest that wouldn't end well for her regardless of the outcome.

"I suggest you speak to Mr. Romanello. When we spoke this morning, and you asked me about Dr. Klein, I told you it was a board matter. I suggested you speak to Mr. Romanello or one of the other board members. I have to respectfully suggest the same with regard to Mr. Burns and Mr. Gerard. I'm happy to allocate credit whatever the board suggests. But, frankly, it's not my place to make that determination."

"I'll speak to Marc and straighten him out. But, in the meantime, you need to go through my list and circulate it to the other owners. And I'd be grateful if you could get that done by the end of tomorrow."

In the privacy of her office, Candy lifted her middle finger to the phone. Decrypting Lior Perlmutter's handwritten mess was not high on Candy's priority list. Neither was anything to do with Lior Perlmutter. Besides, the contacts provided to her by Lorraine Williams and Marc Romanello were real ones, contacts she intended to research and speak with once her study was completed. Unraveling Lior Perlmutter's mess was not something Candy was looking forward to doing—or thought would yield much fruit.

"I assure you I'll do my best, Dr. Perlmutter. Now I was just on my way to give a tour to a potential new owner so if you don't mind, I need to hop off." Candy was not about to give any tours. And since the only viable prospect on the ship was Craig McDougal, that was doubly true. But the ruse was foolproof and Perlmutter reluctantly huffed his assent.

After she hung up the phone, Candy looked at her watch. She knew that once the ship landed in Colombo, the suite owners would disembark, tour the city, and hopefully leave her alone for the rest of the day. Before they did that, however, she decided she needed to loop back with Marc about that conversation with Dr. Perlmutter. Marc had been supportive to Candy at Sheik Shack not long ago, and he had a vested interest in Claremont Burns and Henry Gerard, two of the three names he wanted Candy to contact. Candy called Marc and explained what had just transpired.

"That little fucker. You mean he had those names on his list? I'll be right there."

Although Marc was on his way up to the golf simulator for a session with the inimitable Stephanie Holsson, he detoured down to Candy's office to take a look at Lior's list in person.

"I don't know how you're supposed to be able to make out anything on this," Marc hissed as he turned the pages over to scour them for the two names Candy had shared. When he came upon them, he was floored.

"Not only did he include Burns and Gerard, he added Munday, Bowler, and Saporito," he exclaimed.

"And?" Candy asked, looking up at Marc.

"And . . . they're partners in the Miami office of my old law firm. It's almost like he went through the firm's online directory and added all the partners from the litigation group. First of all, most of them don't have the money to afford a luxury suite aboard Paradise. And if they did, that weaselly bastard isn't going to get credit for them. They were *my* law partners. I doubt he even knows them."

Candy laughed, sharing Marc's sense of incredulity.

"Well, I'm glad this is a board problem then and not a Candy problem," she said. "Sounds like Dr. Perlmutter is playing a game with you. When I told him he wouldn't get credit for contacting anyone Ms. Williams put on her list, I guess he wrote down some names he thought you might put on yours."

Marc was continuing to read Lior Perlmutter's list, turning a page sideways to decipher two of the lines. "Oh, my God, look at this, he has Franzetti and Goldstein on his list. Eva's going to freak out when she sees this."

"Why? Who are they?"

"They're only Eva's closest friends from her old firm, Wilson Everson, that's who they are. That stupid shit. I can see what he was thinking. By simply putting all those names on his list, he'd get credit if any of our former business colleagues bought suites. I'll bet most of the names on his list are business contacts of other suite owners. He probably doesn't even know 335 people, let alone 335 people who are qualified and financially able to buy suites aboard Paradise."

"As I said, I'm just glad that I don't have to figure this out," Candy said.

"There's nothing to figure out. I can assure you of that," Marc said as he tossed the pages back on Candy's desk.

"So what do I do with the list he sent me? He asked me to circulate it by the end of tomorrow."

"Don't do any such thing. Eva and I will handle Lior. Just sit tight."

"You're the boss," Candy said appreciatively. Eva and Marc were straight up good people, the kind of people she liked having her back.

Chapter 14
A Meeting in the Golf Simulator

Marc was angry and frustrated, and hitting golf balls into the simulator screen was exactly the outlet he needed to relieve that frustration. He proceeded as he had earlier intended and made his way to the ninth deck. When he entered the golf simulator, it was dark, so he switched on the lights. He sat at the computer behind Stephanie Holsson's wooden desk and called up the course at Pebble Beach. That was one of his favorite simulated courses because he could hit the ball freely without having to worry about losing sleeves of balls into the ocean below, as opposed to when he played the actual course and carded a score about fifteen strokes higher than his handicap would suggest.

After slamming a 235-yard drive down the center of the fairway, Marc lofted a seven iron and the ball came to rest on the front of the green, just as he had intended. He knew that was birdie territory. He two putted the ball into the simulated hole and was content with a par.

The entire time he was warming up, and then playing the first hole, Marc replayed the conversation with Candy in his mind. He knew he had to tell Eva and could think of no reason to wait. Well, the only reason might be Eva's desire for alone time with her friend Claude, but that was Eva's determination to make, not Marc's.

An accomplished golfer herself who never minded having conversations in the simulator, Eva often met Marc there to talk ship business. Recently, Eva had been staying away from the simulator because of her animus towards Stephanie Holsson after the golf pro's topless stunt at the Chaweng Beach Resort. Marc knew that.

But Stephanie was nowhere to be seen so Marc picked up the wall phone and dialed Eva's suite.

"Hey, Marc. What's up?"

"Something came up a little while ago, and I think it's important we talk it through."

From her caller display, Eva could see Marc was calling from the simulator. "Are you being serious, or do you just need a playing partner?"

"I'm totally serious. I can meet you down in your suite if you like."

"No, housekeeping hasn't been here yet, and Claude is a slob. Let me put on my sneakers, and I'll be up there in two minutes."

Two minutes later, as Marc was scrambling to make bogey out of the sand on the second hole, Eva stood in the door of the simulator wearing a light blue coverup that, Marc concluded, in all likelihood hid a swimsuit.

"If you bend your knees more, those bunker shots come out cleaner," she announced.

"Maybe I should've met you in your suite after all. The last thing I need today is a golf lesson from you," Marc said.

"I'm sure you'd rather have one from your friend. Our resident topless golf pro."

"That's not fair," Marc said, tossing a scowl in Eva's direction. "We agreed that after I talked to her about that incident, you were going to drop it."

"True. But I said, I was going to drop it with her. Not with you. And exactly why are you so sensitive about that subject? Is there something I should know? Has she been making your putter sputter?" Eva said, smiling at her own wit.

Eva's cobalt blue eyes grew large, and she swung her jet black hair over her left shoulder. Although Marc was married,

Eva had always coveted more than a passing interest in him. But apart from their one weekend retreat when Marc had been unexpectedly invited into Eva's world of tantric sex, they had kept their relationship professional.

"I can't believe you even suggested that. Maybe you're just a little concerned your beloved Claude might take up golf. That would be a fun game to watch."

"What's that?"

"You dueling with Stephanie over Claude's affections."

Eva slowly wandered deeper into the simulator, walking with a practiced femininity. "There would be no duel, I assure you. I don't fight any woman over any man. I shouldn't think I need to remind you, but I don't need to fight anybody over anything. When I set my mind to it, I get what I want."

Eva was right, and Marc knew it. Whether it was winning a case in court, convincing banks to give her a loan large enough to purchase a mega yacht, or winning the affection of any man she wanted, Eva got what she wanted. Always.

As he teed off on the third hole, Marc slammed a three wood into the barranca on the left side of the fairway.

"Shit," he exclaimed.

"Thinking of Stephanie, are you?" Eva asked with a self-satisfied grin.

"No, I'm just pissed you already got under my skin."

"Darling, I've been under your sheets as well as under your skin." Eva finally ventured all the way into the simulator and assumed her position on the well-worn suede couch on the left side of the room. Crossing her legs and arms, she was well aware of Marc's attention on her moisturized legs.

"Now, hold onto that visual of my sheets and I'll just sit here and watch you smash your next shot into the lake," Eva said, self-assuredly.

"And why would I do that?" Marc asked.

"Because you're distracted, my handsome friend," Eva said as she uncrossed her luscious legs and crossed them in the other direction. "And when you're distracted, you always screw up your swings."

Marc focused intently on the screen and pursed his lips. Determined to hit the ball perfectly to spite Eva, he gripped his club much tighter than appropriate and did precisely what Eva had presaged—hit his ball directly into the middle of the simulated lake.

"Fuck you," he mumbled as he turned around to face Eva. He leaned his golf club against the wall.

"You have Marc. And I'm guessing you've never forgotten it," she said with a lingering wink and knowing smile. "Now, what's up?" Eva asked, adroitly migrating from temptress to board colleague.

"Remember that idea Lorraine introduced at our last board meeting about establishing a database for potential new suite owners?"

"Of course. And I remember saying, I thought it could be problematic because many of us have overlapping groups of friends. I think the example I used is that Mario and I run in the same legal circles in Manhattan. So it's only logical we'd have the same group of contacts who might be interested in buying aboard Paradise."

"Well, you were right. It's turning into a mess."

"Already?" Eva was never big into *I told you so's*.

"Yup. Lorraine gave Candy a list of three people," Marc said.

"And?"

"And Lior said he knew one of the people on that list so he wanted to share in any finder's fee."

"That's not how it works. We said *first come first serve*, didn't we?"

"Yes we did. So technically Lior is out."

"So what's the problem?" Eva asked.

"Hold on. I'm getting to that. I just had to lay the groundwork so you'll know how we got there. Next, I gave Candy a list of three of my former partners I thought could be strong leads." He paused, aware he had jumbled the order of things. "Oh, wait a second. Let me get the timing right. After Lorraine gave her list to Candy, Lior gave Candy a list of 335 people."

"335 people?"

"That's right. You should've seen his list. It was a bunch of scribbles on four pages of yellow notepad. Candy showed it to me, and I couldn't figure out what the hell the guy had written. Anyway, get this. Two of the people were Claremont Burns and Henry Gerard."

"From your old law firm?" Eva asked.

"Precisely. And I don't know if you ever met them, but David Munday, Bob Bowler, and John Saporito were partners in my firm's Miami office. They were on Lior's list too."

"Why would he do that?" Eva asked.

"He obviously went online, found a firm directory, and just wrote down all those names. I'm guessing he did the same with people who worked with you, Mario, and others on the board."

"Because he knew we'd probably introduce them to Paradise eventually," Eva deduced.

"Exactly. And by putting them on his list first, he gets the referral credit if they end up buying."

"Even if he doesn't know them."

"Even if he doesn't know them," Marc affirmed. "But wait, it gets even better. He included Simon Franzetti and Mark Goldstein on his list."

"From my firm?" Eva asked incredulously.

"Exactly. Now you see what I'm talking about?"

"Let me back this up a second," Eva said. "You gave Candy a list with three names on it, and two of those names were on a list of 335 people that Lior had already given her. And that same list had Simon Franzetti and Mark Goldstein on it. Is that right?"

"Precisely," Marc said.

"So why'd you put them on your list if Lior already had them on his?"

"I didn't know anything about Lior or his stupid list," Marc exclaimed, his voice rising. "Candy hadn't posted it yet. Hell, she still hasn't untangled it. It's such a mess it'll take her weeks to figure it out. But in the meantime, he's locked down all these names. That's the crazy shit I'm talking about."

Eva uncrossed her legs and crossed them in the other direction. Marc tried hard to fight back any thoughts of Sharon Stone and hoped his hypersonic glance towards Eva's legs had gone unnoticed. It hadn't.

"I hate to remind you of this, sweetheart, but this is exactly what I warned everyone about. Of course, I never thought Lior, or anyone else for that matter, would provide hundreds of names to effectively corner the market on potential purchasers, but he figured out how to play the game and he's playing it better than you."

"It's not supposed to be a game," Marc pleaded.

"But he's made it a game and he's winning. Those are the rules and there's nothing we can really do about it now."

"Oh yes there is. I can have a little talk with him."

"And what might that look like?"

"Let's just say I'll be careful not to break his glasses this time."

Marc was referring to an incident about four months earlier when he had confronted Lior and Marc ended up punching Lior in the face. Marc never regretted what he did. But he regretted that he did it while Lior was wearing his glasses. Lior, Oliver, and the rest of The Gripers made a big deal out of that fact, and there were even discussions about removing Marc from the board.

"I love it when you get mad. You're so exciting," Eva teased. She flexed her biceps in her best Arnold Schwarzenegger imitation.

"Fuck you," said Marc.

"That's Claude's job these days. And if we're done here, I'd like to go back to my suite so he can do just that."

Eva stood and didn't make much of an effort to cinch the waist of her coverup that became slightly unfurled when she did so. Besides being a brilliant litigator and an enterprising entrepreneur, Eva was an accomplished tease around men. Once she was confident she had Marc totally distracted, she headed towards the door of the simulator.

"Good luck with whatever you do with Lior. And if you hit him, I just hope you hit it straighter and harder than you do your driver. Oh, and give my best to Karen," she added, with a wink.

Chapter 15
Elaine Visits Becky's Suite

Every day, Becky thought of myriad reasons why being alone with Elaine behind closed doors was a terrible idea. And every night, she thought of just as many reasons why she wanted to do just that. Something inside her had been awakened that night in Venice with Elaine. Becky felt she owed it to herself to see if there was anything more to it. Finally, after much consternation and deliberation, Becky Hirschfeld finally mustered the confidence to *entertain* Elaine Dwyer in her luxury suite.

Elaine was not shy about her desire to share a rendezvous with Becky. But she was always respectful, appreciating that Becky had to get comfortable with the situation and Becky had to be the one to make the affirmative decision to be together on the ship. Elaine repeatedly assured Becky they could arrange a tryst without anyone knowing about it. Although Becky was curious about how Elaine could be so confident, and what the other crew members might have been doing in secrecy, Becky blocked those thoughts from her conscious mind. Her focus was on Elaine. And on not getting caught.

The plan was set. Paradise's owners almost invariably disembarked from the ship the first night in a new port. With the ship docking at 7:30 p.m. in Colombo, it was certain the owners and their guests would be flocking to some of the best restaurants in Sri Lanka's capital city. Scrolling through the concierge team's database, Elaine learned that the owners of the three other suites on Becky's hallway had dinner reservations in town. When Elaine called Becky to tell her that, Becky was relieved. She was also relieved when she opened her door at the appointed time that evening, 8:15, and Elaine was the only one in the hallway. Becky rushed Elaine inside and shut the door, as if wild animals would charge into the suite if she left the door open any longer than absolutely necessary.

Besides being nervous about the entire encounter, Becky had also been perplexed about what to wear. *What did lesbians wear on a first date*, she wondered. Not surprisingly, she didn't ponder the question too long. Becky exuded self-confidence and knew what looked good on her and what didn't. She wore a pair of form-fitting white Missoni slacks and a multi-colored Pucci blouse. Without much fanfare, she selected a gold braid necklace. She reached for her bottle of Jo Malone Pomegranate Noir but thought better of it. She decided to forego perfume. *Who wears perfume to sit in her own apartment?* She wanted to exude cool assurance, even if she was burning with anxiety inside.

By contrast, Elaine appeared as tranquil and self-possessed as she felt when she stepped into Becky's suite. While butterflies had taken flight in Becky's stomach, Elaine owned a calm confidence, a trait that rarely abandoned her.

"You look lovely tonight. And so relaxed," Elaine said as she admired Becky's ensemble and gently stroked Becky's hair. "I'm glad to see that."

"Well I'm not. I'm nervous as a cat," Becky confessed.

"Nervous? What's there to be nervous about? We're just two friends having a drink together." Elaine winked.

"Maybe I won't be so nervous after I have that drink," Becky said as she slid her bare feet over the white Berber carpet and headed to the wet bar located just to the left of the full-length sliding glass doors that led to Becky's balcony.

Before she followed Becky, Elaine took the opportunity to survey the apartment, inhaling Becky's taste in furniture, art, and all the small appointments Becky had gathered during her time aboard Paradise visiting exotic countries.

"You've been in here before, haven't you," Becky asked.

"Yes, but only to meet with Harris and have him sign some papers. You'll be happy to know that when that happened, I was the nervous one. I don't know what it was about that husband of yours that made me so uncomfortable, but I was always nervous around him."

"Me too sometimes. And that's one of the reasons he's my almost ex-husband. That, and the fact he embezzled all that money from the ship."

Elaine had no interest in discussing Harris any further.

"I've never really had the chance to see your entire apartment. It's marvelous. I love what you've done with all the animal figurines."

Collecting small glass sculptures was the only nod Becky gave toward being a tourist. Whenever the ship visited a new port, Becky tried to find a small glass ornament that embodied something indigenous to the area. As a result, she had three shelves full of glass tortoises, elephants, emu, oryx, hippos, rhinos, fish, and birds. They were all backlit with a hidden device that changed the color of the illumination every fifteen seconds, imparting a sense of movement to the shelf.

"What are you drinking?" Elaine asked as she made her way over to the wet bar.

"Anything with lots of alcohol in it," Becky answered.

"Because you're nervous?"

"Damn straight. And not afraid to admit it. At least not to you."

"Why?" Elaine asked. "What's there to be nervous about? We've already kissed. Even groped each other a bit," she reminded Becky.

Like a schoolteacher reprimanding her fourth graders, Becky put her index finger to her lips and closed her eyes, the universal signal for silence.

Elaine laughed.

"What are you afraid of? Who do you possibly think can hear us?"

"I don't know. I just don't like it when you talk about it."

"But it's OK to do it?" Elaine asked with a grin.

"I guess so," said Becky sheepishly.

Elaine took a step towards Becky, leaned forward and kissed her. Even though it was on the mouth, it was a gentle kiss, not the passionate fury they had shared in the ladies' room at Harry's Bar in Venice. Becky wrapped her arms around Elaine and held her closely, Becky's head buried alongside the taller woman's neck. The embrace lasted longer than Elaine expected and Elaine could almost swear she felt a slight tremble in Becky's grasp. It was at that moment she appreciated the fear Becky was experiencing. Elaine pulled away, put her hands on Becky's shoulders, and looked her in the eye.

"You know I value our friendship more than anything else. If any of this makes you uncomfortable, I'd rather forget about any further sexual contact than jeopardize that," Elaine said.

"No, don't be silly. Please don't leave," Becky pleaded, small beads of water forming in the inside corners of her eyes. The phrase *further sexual contact* resonated in her head. "I love having you here. I've wanted to be alone with you for a long time. I mean truly alone. Like this. Not in your office. Not walking through town. Not somewhere where we have to look over our shoulders. I mean here— where we can sit, talk, share, and just be girlfriends, not owner and . . . whatever your formal title is."

"Entertainment Director," Elaine reminded her.

"Whatever. If we met on land, we'd be fast friends." Becky paused as frustration built inside her. "I hate the class structure that governs this ship. I hate that because you're an employee on this stupid ship, we can't do the same here."

"We can. We are," Elaine corrected her.

"Yes . . . but no. You had to sneak up here when no one's around. Crew can't hang out in the owners' suites. It's against the rules. We both know that. It's almost like it's against the rules for us to be friends."

"We *are* friends," Elaine said. "If we weren't friends, I wouldn't be here. And not just because I shouldn't be here. I don't know about you, but I don't hang out with people who aren't my friends."

Becky smiled at that. "I guess you're right."

Elaine leaned forward and gave Becky another kiss. On the mouth again. A bit longer than the last one. But still not passionate or sexual.

"Now, what kind of poison are you pouring and where's mine?" Elaine asked.

"Grey Goose. On ice. With a splash of lemon perhaps."

"Nice. I love Grey Goose. Might you have vermouth and olive juice? I'd absolutely love a martini," Elaine said.

"Elaine, I just want to get the alcohol down my throat right now to get rid of these nerves. I'm not screwing around with anything else," Becky said with a twinkle. When Becky flashed her smile, she displayed the same stunning elegance she possessed during her days as a L'Oreal model decades earlier. Her cobalt blue eyes and natural blonde hair tied back in a ponytail conjured up images of a Beach Boys love interest.

"Sold. I'll have the same," Elaine conceded. "Grey Goose on ice it is. Screw the olive juice."

Becky smiled and turned her attention back to the wet bar. Both ladies were momentarily distracted by the screaming siren of a police car chasing two boys on motorcycles through the port.

When the drinks were poured into a pair of delicately cut crystal highball glasses Becky had picked up on Murano, Elaine raised hers and proposed a toast.

"To friendship."

"Yes, to friendship. And whatever else it brings," Becky added with a wink.

"My, my, aren't we getting a tad forward? And the vodka hasn't even gone down yet," Elaine kidded.

"What the hell. I've always wanted to know what it's all about. You've opened my eyes in a way I never thought any woman would."

"What *what's* all about?"

"The whole woman with woman thing."

"What about it?" Elaine prodded, well aware she was making Becky blush.

"You know. What you do and stuff."

"What *stuff*?" Elaine continued.

"Oh, shut up," Becky cackled as she threw most of the vodka down her throat. She tipped another small helping of vodka into her glass before turning to the Bose speaker system across the other side of the living room.

"Alexa, play Melissa Etheridge," Becky instructed.

Elaine snickered. "You're even playing lesbian music, eh?"

"I *knew* you were going to say that. I love her music. I don't care if she's gay or not."

"I'm just making notes for myself," Elaine teased.

Having seen Becky refill her own glass, Elaine did the same before walking over to join Becky. Becky thought it was classy how

Elaine was wearing a high-neck white blouse over a black skirt. Like Becky, she was wearing pearls, but Elaine's were more of the choker variety, not the twenty-eight inch opera length Becky favored and which were dangling attractively on her bosom.

"Would you like something to eat?" Becky asked.

"I don't suppose you're going to call room service and have Herman or one of the guys come up here and serve us?" Elaine quipped.

"Don't be silly. Do you think I'm an idiot? I stopped at Sheik Shack this afternoon and picked up some brie, gorgonzola, and blue cheese. I know I have crackers around here somewhere," she said as she rummaged through a cabinet above the microwave.

Elaine stood behind Becky and admired the firmness of her undulating globes as Becky hunted for the crackers. As she continued to focus her gaze on Becky's posterior, Elaine found herself identifying the shape and blue shading of Becky's thong through Becky's white slacks. She dared not say anything for fear of making Becky even more uncomfortable.

When Becky turned back to Elaine, crackers in hand, she caught Elaine in somewhat of a trance, her eyes still fixated downwards.

"What are you looking at?" Becky asked uncomfortably, just as Elaine had feared.

Elaine rewarded her with a grin.

"Is it bad? Am I fat?" Becky asked self-consciously.

"Fat? I wish I had an ass like yours. So does everyone else, for that matter."

"What do you mean everyone else? Do you all sit around downstairs talking about owners' asses?"

"Not at all. There aren't that many we'd talk about if we did. I can assure you of that."

Becky straightened up, grateful for the compliment.

"I was blessed with a small frame. I have my parents to thank for that. But I've worked at the rest of it all my life. I train four days a week and watch what I eat," she continued, almost nervously. "It's easier now that Harris isn't around. He had the worst eating habits, and I found myself starting to eat the same crap he did. I could have easily become a vegetarian. I would have never missed meat at all. But, with Harris, we had to have steak, pork chops, or some other kind of meat five nights a week. And when we didn't, it was pasta, pizza, or some other equally unhealthy collection of fat."

"Whatever you're doing is working for you. And it's working for me too!"

"Really? Are you being serious? I don't look fat?"

Elaine took a step towards Becky and reached around her backside, planting each hand firmly on Becky's ass.

"You don't look fat, and you don't feel fat," Elaine proclaimed as she gave Becky's bottom an approving squeeze.

Becky looked up at Elaine who leaned forward and opened her mouth for Becky. This kiss was vastly different from the two they had enjoyed a few minutes earlier. It began to approach the level of passion they had shared in Venice. Their arms wrapped firmly around one another, they kissed for what felt like minutes. Their hands wandered up and down each other's bodies, with no body parts off limits.

Elaine adroitly unbuttoned the top two buttons of Becky's blouse, stopping to admire Becky's pearls, but focusing even more on the tops of Becky's breasts. She reached down below Becky's pearls and assiduously continued her work until all Becky's buttons had been opened. Becky's firm stomach was totally exposed. The only things between Elaine and Becky's breasts were a light blue lace bra and an elevated sense of expectation.

"This is no fair. I can't open yours at all," Becky pouted, bemoaning the fact Elaine's blouse opened from the back.

"Sure you can," Elaine volunteered as she turned her back to Becky. "Go ahead, get on with it."

At first, Becky placed her hands on Elaine's shoulders. She caressed them and fondled Elaine's shoulder blades and neck. As Becky's hands drifted south to unbutton Elaine's blouse, her hands fumbled. She was beginning to appreciate the reality of being almost topless with another woman. A woman she liked. A woman who liked women. A woman she was undressing.

As she peeled open Elaine's blouse, Becky was struck by the milky whiteness of Elaine's back, free of blemishes, freckles, or any other imperfections. She wanted to reach around and feel Elaine's breasts, but she lacked the courage.

When Elaine realized her blouse was completely undone, she casually slipped out of it before turning around to face Becky. Before Becky could even fathom what was happening, Elaine reached behind her back, unfastened her bra, and laid it on Becky's kitchen counter. Becky was stunned. Elaine's breasts were larger than Becky's but because she was over a dozen years younger, and childless, they still possessed the ripeness Becky's children had sucked from her own breasts years earlier. Like a skilled teacher, Elaine took Becky's hands and placed them on her breasts. Although frightened, Becky was fascinated. She gently embraced Elaine's breasts and couldn't look anywhere else. Elaine removed Becky's bra and began rubbing Becky's breasts with the delicate touch of a surgeon. Becky twitched as Elaine's fingers rolled over her nipples. Sensing Becky's intensity, Elaine broke the ice.

"I guess we don't need that brie, do we?"

"I guess not," Becky answered breathlessly.

Elaine took Becky's hand and led her into the living room while Becky's heart pounded like a steel drum at a beach bonfire. They sat on the couch, both topless, both aroused, and both wondering what might happen next. As they continued to kiss and fondle each other, their bodies became wrapped in a tangled and uncomfortable mess.

"If we're going to do this, let's be comfortable," Becky said as she stood and led Elaine through a door frame on the right side of the living room that led into the master bedroom.

"What do you mean by *this*?" Elaine asked coquettishly.

"Don't be coy. You're the teacher. I've never done this before. Remember? C'mon now, before I lose my nerve."

Elaine smiled and squeezed Becky's hand. As they entered the master bedroom, Elaine was amazed by the ornate embroidery and finery that adorned the entire room. Becky tugged down the comforter and lay on her back, clad only in her white pants. Elaine removed her own skirt before joining her. The two friends embraced and kissed, once again allowing their hands to roam freely, although this time unencumbered by clothes, except for Becky's slacks, and Elaine's thong. And neither of those garments remained on very long.

When Becky kicked her slacks off and removed her underwear, Elaine was startled by the near perfection of Becky's body. Not only was she impeccably proportioned, but Becky's creamy skin was the same silky texture as goat's milk. Moreover, below her eyes, there was not a hair anywhere on Becky's body. None. That Becky was completely and freshly waxed, was curious to Elaine. She couldn't imagine that Becky had had the nerve to go to the ship's spa to have the hair removed from her nether regions. But she couldn't imagine Becky trusting a salon in Sri Lanka to have the work performed either. Heck, for that matter, Elaine couldn't imagine Becky being totally waxed period. Elaine surmised that Becky had done it for her, in contemplation of their evening together. And that made Elaine tingle.

Becky was engrossed by Elaine's voluptuousness. Though by no means zaftig, Elaine's was more full-bodied than her smaller bedmate. There was something almost cherubic about Elaine's figure, but in an alluringly sexual way. The ripeness of her breasts, hips, and buttocks all gave Becky plenty to hold, squeeze, and explore.

Unlike Elaine, Becky had never touched a naked woman before. With childlike curiosity, and an attendant degree of timidity, Becky explored Elaine's body with her fingers. Elaine, on the other hand, lacked Becky's inexperience and diffidence. She firmly embraced all of Becky's smooth body, spending a disproportionate amount of time in Becky's most personal places. As Becky's playlist meandered across a litany of gentle music, the two women meandered across each other's bodies for hours.

Chapter 16
Lori Bracker Checks In

An elegant woman in her early forties leisurely strode to Paradise's reception desk. Smartly dressed in khaki shorts and a yellow silk blouse, she adroitly placed her Birkin bag on the counter.

"Good afternoon," Donna Lafat said.

"Good afternoon. Mrs. Lori Bracker checking in. With my husband Jack, and daughter Hannah."

Tagging along behind Mrs. Bracker was an equally impressive looking man, holding hands with the young lady who'd just been identified as their daughter.

"Yes, of course, Mrs. Bracker. We've been expecting you," Donna said as she'd been trained to greet all Paradise's guests. When a woman referred to herself as *Mrs.*, the staff was encouraged to use the same salutation, eschewing the more contemporary *Ms.* in favor of whatever the guest wanted.

"We've prepared a little welcome packet for you. It includes ship rules, evacuation instructions, information about our Internet, and a host of other valuable information. I know it's a lot to digest, but feel free to take your time with it. If you have any questions, you can always call me, or anyone else at the reception desk, and we'll be happy to help you."

"That sounds marvelous. And I have one little request. Is it possible to get a suite upgrade? We're here to celebrate our daughter's sixteenth birthday and we'd like to make the trip as special as possible."

Donna's antenna perked up like a Doberman's ears. Room upgrades were a common request made by Peyton Flynn. She didn't always get them, but she always wrote about how the various hotels reacted to the requests.

"I think we can arrange that," Donna answered. "Let me just check with my manager." She ducked into the front desk manager's office and together they quickly reviewed the ship's manifest. It was evident there were plenty of available suites larger than what the Brackers had booked.

"It would be our pleasure to accommodate you and your family, Mrs. Bracker," Donna reverted to the potential Peyton Flynn. "And what day is your daughter's birthday? Paradise's owners would like to do something special for her."

"That's so sweet of you. Her birthday is next Saturday, but please don't do anything extravagant. You know how sixteen-year-old girls can be. It was like pulling teeth getting her to come along with us. If we embarrass her, she might not talk to us until she graduates from college."

"I fully understand," Donna said with a knowing smile. "I have two nieces at home, and they would be mortified if my sister did anything to embarrass them. In the meantime, please don't hesitate to contact us with any questions. Anything at all."

"Thank you so much. I'm sure all will be wonderful." Mrs. Bracker said. She turned to her husband who was busy pointing out all the highlights of the enormous entrance hall to the couple's daughter. With practiced stealth, Marlon the handsome Filipino bellman, placed the couple's three suitcases on a trolley and invited them to follow him to the ship's elevator. As soon as the family was out of sight, Donna sprinted across the lobby and into Elaine's office to explain what had just happened.

"Good job, Donna. Sounds like you handled it perfectly. It also sounds like she fits the bill of what Peyton Flynn might look like." That observation was a bit imprudent as no one actually knew what Peyton Flynn looked like, but the ship's staff was uber sensitive about any female guest in her thirties or forties who made special requests upon check in. Elaine opened the Brackers' folio on her computer and banged a few notes into their file. Lori Bracker was the first guest aboard Paradise who Elaine was going to try to investigate. If she was Peyton Flynn, Elaine was going to make damn sure she got the best treatment Paradise had to offer.

Chapter 17
Marc Confronts Lior

After his conversation with Eva, Marc didn't even wait an hour before confronting Lior Perlmutter about Lior's mass name submission to Candy Podeski. They were in line for afternoon lattes at Sheik Shack when Marc ran into him.

"Hey there, Lior, I've been meaning to talk to you."

Cowering, Lior replied, "Oh, sure, about what?"

"About that list of 500 names you gave to Candy. Are you kidding me?" Marc asked, doing nothing to hide his hostility.

"Why? What's wrong with that? I identified a bunch of people who might be candidates and I gave her the names."

"A *bunch*? 500 is more than a *bunch*."

"It wasn't 500. Besides, no one ever said there was a limit on the number of names I could put on my list."

"And no one ever said there's a limit on the number of complementary cookies you can eat after dinner. But there's a rule of reason most people follow. It's called common sense."

"I used my common sense. I sat down and came up with a list of people no one else had given to Candy. That's *exactly* what we're supposed to be doing if we're going to sell suites aboard this damn ship."

"Not *exactly* correct," Marc said, his sarcasm unmuted. "Two of the names on your list were also on the list I gave Candy."

"Yes, but as I understand it, my list was submitted first."

"Your list is a bunch of chicken scratch that no one can even read," Marc said, his voice beginning to escalate. "How is Candy supposed to make sense of what you gave her?"

161

"No one said there are points for penmanship," Lior whined. "Look, I gave her my list. I played by the rules. If you think I played better than you, so be it."

"Not so be it. That's not the way it works around here, you little bastard. We have to respect one another. And, even if you don't respect anyone as an individual, I'm the chairman of the board of this ship, so you'd better respect me."

His voice now having risen to a boisterous level, Marc was attracting the attention of other owners and crew members in the area. He continued, albeit in a slightly more subdued tone. This time, he leaned into Lior, over whom he towered by at least five inches.

"I bet you don't even know most of the people on your own list. In fact, I bet you don't know 450 of them. You just searched whatever you searched on the Internet and scribbled those names down on a sheet of paper."

"So, what if I did? There's no rule against that."

"I make the rules. And I'm going to make a rule that says your list is disqualified."

"You can't do that," Lior said.

"I can. And I just did."

Although those who were overhearing the conversation were able to detect the hostile nature of the exchange between Marc and Lior, they were unable to ascertain the actual words being spoken.

"There's no rule that says we can't impeach you as chairman," Lior said as he struggled to find his masculinity.

"And there's no rule that says I can't tell your wife about some of the dalliances we both know you've had on this ship," Marc replied, making a direct threat about Lior's inappropriate use of his manhood with Monique, one of the waitresses at Sheik Shack. That issue had been elevated to the board of directors a few months earlier when one of the other suite owners saw Lior speaking forcefully to Monique one morning. During an urgent human resources interview, Monique confessed that she had been to Lior's suite on two occasions and they'd had sex. Apparently, Lior was not content to leave it at that and had continued to push Monique for more trysts. The board decided not to terminate Monique on grounds of violating her employment agreement for fear she would sue Paradise and its owners for sexual harassment. Such a suit would bring public embarrassment to the entire enterprise, something no one was keen to experience. The board also agreed to keep Lior's behavior confidential on the condition he never propositioned a crew member again.

"Listen, you give Candy a real list of potential buyers and I'll let it slide," Marc said, trying to sound solicitous. "But I'm gonna ask you how you know each and every one of the people on your list. And, if you don't know all of them—every single one—the entire list will be disqualified."

"What if I don't agree?"

"I'm not asking you to agree. I'm *telling* you what we're doing here, Lior. If you don't like it, I really don't care. Not one iota."

Marc stepped out of the line and walked towards the elevator at the bow of the ship. Although no one was sure exactly what had just transpired between the two known adversaries, one thing was clear—Marc had humiliated Lior. Lior looked like a wounded goose as he kept his gaze focused on his ridiculous looking sneakers, waiting for his turn to order.

Chapter 18
Harrison Marshall Checks In

After checking in at Paradise's reception desk and asking a barrage of questions about upcoming events, Harrison Marshall was directed to Elaine Dwyer's desk.

"I hear you're the person I should speak to about reservations," Harrison said.

"Well, I'm the ship's Entertainment Director. If you'd like to make restaurant reservations, I can walk you over to the concierge's desk. They'll be only too happy to help you."

"No, not restaurant reservations. I'd like to make some golf reservations. I understand Paradise plays at the best local courses when it travels."

"Yes, we do. Our golf instructor, Stephanie Holsson, makes those arrangements months in advance."

"Oh, so there's no way I could get on a course here in Colombo, or in the ship's next ports of call?"

"Of course you can, Mr. Marshall. Ms. Holsson always makes reservations for a large group, usually more players than have expressed interest. That way she always has room for unexpected golfers, like yourself."

"That's terrific. How can I get in touch with her?"

"No need," said Elaine as she punched away at her keyboard. "I've just sent her a message on The Skipper. You should expect to hear from her within the hour."

"The Skipper?" Harrison asked.

"Oh, I'm sorry. The Skipper is our internal intranet system. It's how we all communicate with one another."

"Splendid, it sounds like you've got everything covered. I'll look forward to hearing from her. And thanks again for your assistance. You've been most helpful."

Sure as clockwork, the phone in Harrison's visitor flat rang only a few minutes after he'd finished unpacking his suitcase.

"Mr. Marshall? This is Stephanie Holsson, Paradise's golf and tennis manager."

"Wow, that was fast. Thanks for calling." Harrison was marginally impressed with his ability to answer what looked like a complicated telephone set.

"I understand you'd like to play golf with us while you're aboard." Before Harrison could even answer, Stephanie continued. "I see that you'll be sailing with us for two weeks. So you'd be able to join us in Cochin, Goa, and Mumbai. I've already got tee times set in each of those cities."

"That's amazing. How do you arrange all that so far in advance?" Harrison was still looking at the telephone console, trying to decipher the meaning of all the buttons and icons.

"We have to. You're a golfer, so you'd know. We can't exactly roll up to a golf course with twelve or sixteen golfers and say we'd like tee times. It all needs to be coordinated months in advance. It's really not as complicated as you'd think. Paradise's itineraries are fixed almost a year ahead. Once I get the itinerary, I do my research, find the best courses in the area, and try to get reservations."

"Do you always get on the best courses?" Harrison asked, sinking into a large white leather chair and surveying the view from his generous window.

"We try. Our suite owners want the finest of everything, and it's up to our team to make it happen. In fact, and I don't know if you are up to it after such a long trip, but I happen to have reservations for eight golfers at the Royal Colombo Golf Club tomorrow morning, and we only have six players so far," Stephanie said as she scoured her computer screen to be sure there hadn't been any late additions to the tee sheet. "It's a private club, but one of our suite owners has a connection through a reciprocity agreement with his club in France so he was able to get us tee times. It's the oldest course in Sri Lanka and it was founded in the 1800s, but I've never played it so I can't vouch for it. Would you like to join us?"

Harrison stretched his legs and yawned. "I'd love to, but I'm afraid I'm exhausted. I flew in from California, and it's been a long day for me. Do you mind if I stop by the simulator the following day?"

"Not at all. That's absolutely fine. And have a good rest. I know how those long trips can wear you out."

"Thanks. I'll see you then."

"Great. I look forward to meeting you."

As Harrison was getting ready to hang up, another thought sprang to his mind. "Oh, one more question, if you don't mind. I brought my golf shoes, hats, balls, and things like that. But I didn't bother to lug my clubs with me. Do the courses in this part of the world have rentals?"

"I'm not sure, but we do," Stephanie said as she looked around the simulator trying to remember where she had put the extra clubs. "We carry a half dozen extra bags of TaylorMade irons. And if you don't like what we have, I can call the courses and see what they might have available."

"That would be awesome," Harrison answered. "Would it be possible for me to stop by and see the TaylorMade clubs on board? I'm kind of a TaylorMade guy so that might work out perfectly," he said, suddenly a bit more enthusiastic than he had been a few minutes earlier.

"Of course it would. Or would you like me to bring them

to your visitor flat?" Stephanie offered. She knew she'd stored the extra clubs somewhere out of the way but couldn't quite remember exactly where. She knew she'd soon find them though.

"No, that's quite all right. If I'm coming up to the simulator, I can just check them out then. Have a great outing tomorrow and I'll see you the next day," Harrison said.

"Cheers, and good night," said Stephanie.

"And the same," Harrison replied.

Chapter 19
Ginger Tarpley Checks In

As the ship continued to welcome its last tranche of guests before dinner, Ms. Ginger Tarpley from Birmingham Alabama confidently strolled through Paradise's lobby and sauntered up to the reception desk.

"My name is Tarpley. Ginger Tarpley," the effervescent Alabamian said. "Don't call me Ginger Bennett either. Bennett was my married name, and I flushed that terrible name out of my life right after I flushed that scoundrel out of my house." Without even the briefest pause, she continued. "Anyhow, I'm traveling with Mother and we've been on planes for a week, so it seems. We had to fly from Birmingham to Atlanta, Atlanta to London, London to Dubai, and then Dubai to here. Colombo. Which, by the way, Mother keeps calling Columbus."

The diminutive and radiant older woman by Ginger's side flashed an adorable smile and shrugged her shoulders.

Just when it seemed like Ginger needed to come up for a big breath of air, she didn't. She continued her narrative in a penetrating and shrill southern drawl that caught the attention of Donna Lafat and the other two ladies at the reception desk.

Ginger stood erect and slammed her hands against her hips in dramatic fashion. "And let me tell y'all something else. This wasn't exactly Delta Air Lines we were on. Oh, sure it was on the first two flights. But then they put us on some Etihad or something like that. They should have named it Etiharem. The stewardesses were so beautiful, weren't they, Mother?" Ginger said, more than asked. She was not about to let Mother, or anyone else, steal her spotlight. "But their pants were so tight I could see their religion. And there were so many of them. I'm telling y'all, they could all have been models. It didn't do much for my ego, that's for sure," the pleasantly plump southerner continued.

Ginger's mother stood obediently beside her, obviously afraid to get caught in the blades of her daughter's windmill.

"Then we had to fly on Air Sri Lanka or whatever they call it. And the food? Oh, my goodness. You should've seen the food they were serving. Garbage. Just garbage," Ginger said, waving her arms through the air. By this point, two of the other women at the reception desk had stopped plugging away at their keyboards and gave Ginger their undivided attention. "I wouldn't have fed that to our cattle dogs. And I was hungry. I was so hungry I could've eaten the north end of a south-bound goat. By the way, they eat goats here, don't they? That's some Indian kind of dish? Some kebab thing? Well, Mother and I don't eat goats. No monkeys or bats or dogs or any of whatever other crazy things these people eat."

Donna Lafat started to answer, but, before her mouth could make a sound, Ginger Tarpley had wound up and was preparing to deliver her next pitch.

"So anyway. We landed, and that was a miracle in and of itself. We collected all our bags and tried to get a taxi. Well, let me tell you, it wasn't easy. Wait, I'm almost done now," Ginger added, fearing she was losing her audience, but she wasn't. Donna and the other two women behind the desk continued to be riveted by Ginger's staccato performance. Even Eva Lampedusa, who was busy in conversation with the concierge on the other side of the hall, turned her head to see what the screeching was all about.

"Our travel agent told us that everyone in Sri Lanka speaks English. Obviously, he's never been to Sri Lanka. Well finally, we got an English-speaking taxi driver and that was another adventure. The boy was on his phone the entire way speaking some gibberish Mother and I couldn't make heads or tails of. And when I asked him questions—so I could learn something about Columbus or Colombo—he didn't know a damn thing about his own town. Was that boy ever stupid? I mean, he could've fallen into a barrel full of titties and come out sucking his thumb. But we got here. And that's all that matters. Mother was fuming mad the entire way, but I told her the trip would be worth it."

The senior Mrs. Tarpley continued to smile, the personification of a woman who likely hadn't been fuming mad in the past forty years.

"Well, it certainly sounds like you've had a busy journey," Donna offered. "We're thrilled to have you on board, and, I assure you, we'll take excellent care of you both."

"That's why we're here. To be pampered and taken care of, right, Mother?"

Mother remained nonplussed. She smiled sweetly, the by-product of seeing her daughter display this level of comedic performance on a regular basis for fifty plus years.

"Then you're in the right place, I assure you," Donna said.

"First things first, whom do I see to set up restaurant reservations?" Ginger asked as she looked around the room, not really certain what she was looking for. "Mother and I have never been to Sri Lanka or India, and we want to make sure we eat at safe places. I know we're not going to get grits or pulled pork, but I want to make sure we don't get maggots or giardia either." Ginger offered a condescending look. "I'm not teasing, y'all. I came here to digest the food, not spend the next day having to sit on one of your fancy toilets."

Donna did her best not to laugh, though a knowing smile escaped her lips.

"Yes, of course, Mrs. Tarpley. Our concierge has made a list of the finest restaurants in every city we'll be visiting. I'm sure she'd be glad to make reservations for you." Donna nodded to her right, where the concierge desk was stationed not more than twenty feet away.

"Marvelous. And we don't need anyone trying to fix Mother up with any eligible, handsome bachelors. She's so old she knew dirt when it was still a rock. On the other hand, if you just happen to have any Justin Timberlands walking around here, feel free to send them to my cabin."

"I will definitely do that, Mrs. Tarpley," Donna said with a faux serious smile. "And, by the way, we refer to them as visitor flats. You'll find them to be far more spacious than a cabin on a cruise line."

"Cabins, flats, whatever. Thank you for the correction," Ginger said with genuine appreciation. "I never mind being corrected. I used to be an English teacher, you know. So I'm very particular about pronunciations and mispronunciations."

"Then I should let you know that if a certain singer shows up at your visitor flat, you may want to refer to him as Justin Timberlake, not Justin Timberland."

"Honey, if Justin whatever he's called shows up at my flat, I'll refer to him as the bottom sheet."

Donna couldn't contain herself. She spat laughter across the desk and turned tomato red. As if in unison, the other two ladies howled as well. Even Mother broke into a wide smile before demurely putting her right hand over her mouth. Eva left her seat and began to stroll over to the reception desk to get a better view of the priceless encounter.

"Now, please ask your concierge lady to send me a list of restaurants and some possible times we can strap on the old feed bag."

Ginger picked up the folio Donna had laid before her, turned smartly towards the elevator, and announced, "C'mon, Mother, let's get a move on before they confuse us for a herd of turtles."

As soon as Ginger and Mother walked away, Eva made a beeline to the reception desk.

"I'm betting that's *her*," Eva said to Donna, enthusiastically.

"Who's her?"

"Peyton Flynn!" Eva's cobalt eyes were open wide as she continued to stare at Ginger and her mother make their way towards the elevator.

"You think?" asked Donna.

"Absolutely," said Eva, still transfixed on them, as if searching for some sort of signal.

"Really? That's not what I would've expected at all," Donna said, her eyebrows scrunched.

"That's precisely the point. She doesn't want you to expect her. And she doesn't want you to even suspect she is who she is. I know she travels with other people sometimes—a guy pretending to be her husband, or even kids on a few occasions. Don't be fooled by the old lady's presence. I'd be willing to bet big money the younger one is Peyton Flynn."

"Wow, if you say so," Donna responded.

"Look, we can't be certain. But I definitely think you need to march right into Elaine's office and tell her what just happened. Tell her my suspicion. Let's be sure she tracks that Ginger lady the whole time she's on board. Let's make sure she gets everything she needs. And then some."

Chapter 20
Crazy Caitlin Checks In

Among the constellation of new guests boarding Paradise, one caught everyone's attention almost immediately. That was because it didn't take long for Caitlin Cappilletti from Los Angeles to distinguish herself from the rest.

At the front desk, Donna Lafat provided the customary welcome and presented Caitlin with the Paradise folio containing all the ship's requisite information.

"What's going on?" Caitlin asked. And then, merely a second later, she responded, "Not a lot. Just checking into this ship." As anyone might have done, Donna presumed, the woman was wearing an ear piece and talking on her mobile phone.

Donna continued her welcome speech. "I know it's been a long trip. Is there anything we can do to help you get adjusted today?"

"No thank you. I'm just going to go to my cabin and rest."

"That sounds like a lovely plan," Donna said, ascertaining no need to correct Caitlin and refer to it as a visitor flat.

"What do you think I can eat around here?" Caitlin asked. And again, replied to herself, "I'm sure there are a few restaurants around here. Let's go find them."

Still confused, but wanting to be helpful, Donna volunteered, "We have two restaurants open for lunch right now, Pasture, our vegetarian restaurant in on the seventh deck. And Lucky Seas, which features more of a pan Asian theme is on eight. Of course, our deli, Sheik Shack is open twenty-four hours a day. That's somewhat of an amalgam of a coffee shop and a deli. You can get muffins and pastries, as well as sandwiches, and a few small, hot dishes."

"Thank you. I am quite famished. I think I'll try the Asian food. I don't ordinarily eat something that heavy during the middle of the day. But with the time difference and everything, I guess I can convince myself it's evening," the woman said, smiling.

"I hope I didn't lose my passport," said Caitlin. And then continued, "You put it in that big pouch on the outside of your briefcase.

Marlon, one of the bellmen, picked up Caitlin's bags and walked her to the elevator. He allowed Caitlin to enter and he pushed nine.

"Where are we going?" she asked. And then answered, "I hope he knows. I have no clue."

Marlon sensed something was amiss. But since Caitlin seemed to have begun and ended the conversation by herself, there was really nothing for him to add. Once the elevator opened, he walked her to her flat and rolled in the luggage trolley.

After showing Caitlin around her visitor flat, Marlon dutifully asked, "Is there anything else I can get for you, Ms. Cappilletti?"

"No, thank you. Everything seems to be marvelous."

As Marlon turned to leave Caitlin alone, he heard her ask, "Do you have to pee?" And then, "Definitely, as soon as that guy leaves." Marlon tilted his head in a confused fashion. He thought better of looking back at Caitlin. He had provided her all the information necessary, and she said she didn't need anything else.

When Marlon returned to the lobby, Donna was the only one at the reception desk.

"Can I tell you something weird?" he asked her.

"Sure."

"That lady I just brought to 915. Cappilletti. I think there's something wrong with her."

Donna smirked knowingly. "You mean Crazy Caitlin?"

"Yeah. Why do you call her that?" Marlon asked.

"We all just named her that because she talks to herself. Didn't you notice?"

"That's *exactly* what I wanted to tell you. She asks questions and then answers them right away. Herself. At first, I thought she was talking to me, asking me something. But she literally answered herself. And she did it a couple of times."

"I know. She did it here too. The first time she did it, I thought I misheard something. But, when she did it twice more, I knew she was a bit off."

Holly Ensign, another front desk employee, was tidying up her end of the desk and overheard their conversation. "Do you think that's her?" Holly asked Donna.

"Who?"

"You know. Peyton Flynn."

Donna turned and looked at Marlon before swiveling her head to back towards Holly. "You think? She was a weird one. That Cappilletti. Not at all what I would expect."

"Isn't that the point?" Holly asked. "Isn't that what Elaine said we should be ready for? That Peyton Flynn tries to come across as someone no one would have expected?"

Donna's thoughts became immediately apparent on her face as she broke into a slow grin. "Ya think? Holy shit, you may be right."

Holly laughed. "Hey, Donna, Crazy Caitlin must be rubbing off on you. You just did it too."

"Did what?"

"You just asked yourself a question and answered it," said Holly, bemused.

"Oh, shush. That's different. I'm not a bloody head-case. Although some of the owners around here might just turn me into one."

Donna concluded that Caitlyn Cappilletti was just weird enough that she could be Peyton Flynn. As she had been instructed to do in the case of any potential Peyton Flynn sightings, Donna marched into Elaine Dwyer's office and reported what she had observed.

"That sounds quite funny, actually," Elaine said.

"It was. Kind of. Until it got weird," Donna replied.

"Well, you're right. I'd better put her on my spreadsheet. It would be kind of wild if we tracked all the other women and missed this one." Elaine shook her head as she looked at the list of all the eccentrics who had boarded Paradise over the past few days. "This is going to be wild. Fun, but wild," she said to Donna before Donna retreated to go back to her duties.

Chapter 21
Claude Visits the Simulator

During the ship's second day in Colombo, Stephanie Holsson led a group of intrepid Paradise golfers on an outing to the Royal Colombo Golf Club. The golf was uneventful. Stephanie's main concerns were making sure the bus showed up on time, all the clubs got loaded onto the bus, everyone had what they needed for their rounds, and the bus returned the passengers and clubs to the ship. That was it. The actual playing of golf was usually a secondary concern for Stephanie, whose primary job was to see to the enjoyment of the suite owners and their guests. She assigned the foursomes herself unless certain players specifically requested being paired with others. For her part, Stephanie had a short list of players she avoided at all costs. And a few others she enjoyed playing with.

On the day the group played the Royal Colombo Club, Stephanie made sure that Claude Azulai, Eva's beau, was in her foursome. After the dust up with Eva as a result of Stephanie's topless adventures at the Chaweng Beach Resort, Stephanie wanted to do everything possible to impress her boss. Unfortunately, Claude wanted to impress Stephanie. On the course, he made more than a few comments about Stephanie's physique and the way her body moved when she swung a club. Stephanie was used to garnering indelicate attention from men and didn't think much of it until Claude proposed a few suggestive bets including neck rubs or true confessions if either scored a birdie or made a putt over forty feet. As a still-stunning former model who was often compared to Tiger Woods' ex-wife, Elin Nordegren, Stephanie had more than her share of experience batting away suggestive comments or men with overactive libidos. Claude remained a gentleman, but he also remained persistent.

On the bus ride back to the ship, he made it a point to sit next to Stephanie. That wasn't particularly unusual because playing partners often boarded the bus together given that they'd spent the day together. Nor was it unusual that he asked Stephanie for a few tips to correct some of the things she had pointed out on the course.

"Sure. I'm always happy to help. A lot of your issues relate to the way you point your right thumb at the top of your backswing." Stephanie simulated a golf grip as she lifted both hands over her right shoulder. "Listen, why don't you come up to the simulator and I can show you there. It's kind of hard to demonstrate sitting on a bus."

"Sounds like a plan. Do you mind if I come up this afternoon? Eva's planning to go shopping with Karen Romanello so I know she's not waiting for me."

"It's been a long day, but if you give me thirty minutes to freshen up, I'll be happy to meet you in the simulator," Stephanie said.

Like clockwork, Claude strolled into the golf simulator thirty-five minutes after the bus had pulled up outside Paradise and everyone had boarded the ship. Stephanie had just finished putting the golf clubs in the storage lockers and had barely finished washing her hands and face when Claude arrived.

For his part, Claude had changed into a bright yellow silk golf shirt and even smelled of cologne, something Stephanie definitely hadn't noticed on the course or on the bus. She would not have missed that stench in such close proximity.

"The needy pupil is reporting for instruction. Do with me what you will," he joked.

If Stephanie could have rolled her eyes, she would have. She had no time or interest in fulfilling this man's teacher/temptress fantasy. But she had a job to do and keeping the suite owners happy was her main focus. Keeping her own job after the stern warning she'd been issued after the Chewang Beach incident was a close second.

"Great. Why don't you grab a seven iron and come over here," she said beckoning Claude to stand in the middle of the mat.

Claude did as instructed and took a few lazy swings, as one does before seriously striking a golf ball. Stephanie stood directly across from Claude.

"Now take the club back slowly and pause at the top of your backswing," she directed.

Claude obeyed. Stephanie reached across and grabbed his wrists and gently pushed them into a more upright position.

"This is where you're going to get your power," she instructed. "Now bring these wrists straight down and release hard," she said, as she threw his wrists towards the screen at the front of the simulator.

"Ah, I get it." Claude took a few hard swings emulating what Stephanie had just shown him. "What about my hip movement?" he asked.

"What about it?"

"Am I rotating my hips properly?"

Stephanie stepped back so she could observe the totality of Claude's swing.

"It doesn't look bad to me. But I'd like to see you push your right hip forward a little more as you come through the ball."

"What do you mean?" Claude asked.

"Like this." Stephanie took a few exaggerated swings, forcing both hips to finish directly fronting the screen at the front of the room.

"Wait, I'm not positive I get the feel of that. May I?" he asked as he stood behind Stephanie and placed his hands on her hips.

Since she was already in his grasp, Stephanie didn't have a lot of say in the matter. She hated this kind of crap from men. There were some creeps who did anything possible to put their hands on her body or have her do the same to them.

"Sure. Hold on and feel the complete rotation." She took two more swings, this time with Claude behind her, his torso leaning against hers. The moment she suspected his groin was imposing even the slightest pressure against her, Stephanie politely stepped forward. She wanted no part of this guy, and certainly not that part. With all the trouble she was already in with Eva, the last thing she needed was for Eva's boyfriend to be pushing his hard-on against her.

"You try it. Just rotate completely and hold your finish."

Claude made three more swings, utilizing the instruction, Stephanie had just provided. Not wanting to belabor the lesson any further, she said, "That's it, you've got it. Now you just need to come up to the simulator sometime and practice on your own."

"You won't be here?"

"I can't promise that I will, or I won't. I have other duties aboard the ship. When I'm not in the simulator, I'm tending to whatever management asks me to do."

"Fair enough," Claude said. "Hey, I really enjoyed playing with you today in Colombo. And the lesson was very helpful. I hope we get paired up again on the next outing."

"Yes, I'd like that too," Stephanie replied, damn sure she was never going to allow that to happen.

Chapter 22
Harrison Visits the Simulator

Two days after he arrived on Paradise, Harrison Marshall grabbed a coffee at Sheik Shack and made his way to the golf simulator. Stephanie Holsson sat behind her desk arranging tee times for the following day's outing. The ship had left Colombo and was on its way to Cochin, Paradise's first stop in India.

"Stephanie?" he asked.

"Yes?" she said before looking up. When she did , she blinked twice, instantly captivated by the attractive man with Southern California written all over him in the way of blue eyes, curly, blonde hair, and unmistakable surfer boy appeal.

"Hi, I'm Harrison Marshall. We spoke on the phone the other day."

"Of course. I've been expecting you," she said as she stood and smoothed out her skirt, almost nervously. "Greetings and welcome aboard. I hope you got that much needed rest."

"Thanks. I was hoping to make it up here yesterday afternoon," he said.

She would gladly have had him in the simulator the previous afternoon, as opposed to Claude, the differently attractive, but unduly lecherous, boyfriend of her ultimate boss.

Harrison also took his measure of the woman who was now standing behind her desk. She had cheekbones that could cut glass, sapphires where her eyes should have been, and lustrous platinum blonde hair. He had encountered more than his share of Beach Boys babes during his years in Southern California, but this oceangoing beauty put them all to shame.

"Unfortunately, I got caught up with a bunch of paperwork and conference calls and wasn't able to pull away," Harrison said, his eyes darting around the room, trying to absorb all the fascinating technology that caught his gaze no matter where he looked. Then, he brought his focus back to Stephanie, undoubtedly the most fascinating thing in the room. By far.

"That doesn't sound like a lot of fun. Well, anyway, welcome to the Paradise golf simulator, the best office I've ever had," Stephanie said enthusiastically.

"I thought I worked in a great place. But when I'm there I really have to do work. Sitting up here, I wouldn't get anything done other than reduce my handicap. By a lot." Harrison's shoulders relaxed, and his smile widened as he became more comfortable standing in the presence of the seafaring Aphrodite.

"That's the whole point," she said, flashing the most dazzling smile Harrison had ever seen on a golf instructor. "What kind of work do you do?" she asked.

"I work in La Jolla, California. Land of the beautiful golf courses and even more beautiful ocean walks."

"I adore La Jolla," Stephanie said, her eyes opening wide as she conjured up memories of playing golf along Torrey Pines' iconic cliffs.

"You've been?" asked Harrison, full well knowing the answer. Any worthwhile golf pro has made the California golf circuit at least once or twice.

"Been? I play Torrey Pines every chance I get," Stephanie said, rubbing her hands together with enthusiasm.

"Which do you prefer—the north course or the south course?" Harrison asked. He took a step inside the simulator, but wanted to be sure he was still facing Stephanie. He could see golf courses anywhere, but she was a unique vision.

"The north is much harder, but I like it more." Stephanie's gaze briefly wandered to her computer as she tried to remember which of the two courses the ship had on its simulator menu.

"Me too. I feel the same way about both. Next time you find yourself out that way, you'll have to give me a call and we'll get in a round," he said, raising his hand to his ear in approximation of a telephone call.

"I wish it were that easy," Stephanie said, her shoulders slumping and the enthusiasm draining out of her face. "Every time I try to get on the courses there, I'm told the waitlist is several months." Her pout, pretend or otherwise, was enchanting.

"As I said, call me. Give me a day's notice, and we'll get on either course." At that moment, he was ready to disembark the ship with this golfing icon, fly directly to La Jolla, and wine and dine her at his favorite haunts, all with the goal of having her spend the rest of her life with him. Or at least a really pleasurable weekend.

Harrison spied the full set of TaylorMade woods and irons that were adroitly positioned on a slotted wooden rack on the wall, ostensibly to prevent them from becoming airborne when the ship hit high seas.

"I'm not on board all that long, but I promised myself I'd focus on golf while I'm here. I haven't played much the last few months, and I'd be keen to sharpen up a few areas and take a few strokes off my handicap."

"That's what I'm here for," Stephanie said. She was glad to have such a willing student. She was also glad he was so handsome.

"Let's see you hit a few balls," she said, reverting to her instructor voice.

"Remember, I need to borrow some clubs."

"Oh sure, that's right. Just grab anything you like from the rack. Probably best to start with a seven iron," she said, nodding towards the clubs on the wall rack.

"I know I'm going to sound like a real pain in the neck, but I'm a lefty."

"Not a pain at all. As I said, we do have a few rental sets, and I know we have at least two sets of left-handed clubs. Sit tight and I'll pop into the room next-door and see what I can grab."

Harrison first became aware of Stephanie's eye-catching stature when she walked out of the simulator. Although La Jolla and San Diego had their share of tall, blonde bombshells, he was not expecting to find one aboard Paradise. Certainly not as a tutor in his favorite pastime. Before Harrison could let his mind wander further about the statuesque woman who had been so lovely to him on the phone, and now in person, she returned with two left-handed seven irons.

"We have two sets for you to try. The first is our regular TaylorMade M6 series. But I also found a set of Callaways, if you prefer the way those heads look. I know some people like that look."

"No, thanks. I try to stick with TaylorMades whenever I can. I've been playing them for years." He paused. "Frankly, I'm just grateful you have left-handed clubs."

"Good. Glad to help. Now, let's see what you've got." Stephanie was careful not to let her face divulge the other meaning to what she'd just said. She would have loved to have seen what Harrison had to show, in more ways than one.

Stephanie reached into the metal pail of golf balls on the side of the room, threw a half dozen on the mat in front of Harris, and went back to her desk where she could sit and observe Harrison's shot-making skills. Harrison slammed the balls into the mat, retrieved them and repeated the action. He was just loosening up when Stephanie got up from her desk, ambled over to where he was hitting. She stood with her arms crossed, observing him. The pressure of someone watching him often unnerved Harrison.

But whenever an instructor was watching, he got doubly nervous. A woman made him even more jumpy. An attractive woman, even more so. And an attractive woman instructor . . . well, that made him slam balls erratically in a way he hadn't with the first six.

"Relax. Take a few deep breaths and relax," Stephanie said.

Embarrassed, Harrison did as Stephanie instructed, but he was still swinging at an exceedingly rapid pace.

"Slow down, man," she said. "Just be cool. We're going to be like a couple of little Fonzies here. Cool."

Harrison was stunned. He stopped hitting and looked at Stephanie.

"Did you just say 'We're going to be like a couple of little Fonzies here?'"

"Yeah, why," she asked.

"That's a Samuel L. Jackson line from *Pulp Fiction*."

"I can't believe you know that," Stephanie exclaimed, smiling and clapping her hands together. "That's my favorite movie."

"Oh, my God. Mine too," Harrison said. "But I've never heard anybody quote that line. And I never expected it to come from a woman."

Stephanie smiled. "I'm an enigma. You never know what I might say. Now, back to golf. Hit the ball straight and firm or I'm gonna get medieval on your ass."

Harrison started to howl. "Marcellus Wiley said that! In the scene when he pulled that red ball out of his mouth. One of my favorite scenes. This is hilarious. It sounds like you've memorized the entire movie."

"Most of it. I've seen it over a dozen times. Easily."

Over the course of the next hour, Harrison hit golf balls, and Stephanie provided professional tutelage. It didn't take him long to loosen up and show her his natural swing, as well as his natural character and sense of humor. They laughed, hit balls, and peppered each other with favorite lines from *Pulp Fiction*, as well as a few other Quentin Tarantino films.

At the end of the hour, he remarked, "This was great fun. Thanks so much. How often am I allowed to take lessons while I'm on the ship?"

"As often as you like. You guys have to pay some outrageous amount to be on board in those visitor flats. Because of that, everything is included. Except food and beverages, that is. They can't exactly give guests a blank check when it comes to wine. Some people enjoy those really expensive $800 bottles and Paradise would go bankrupt if it gave those away."

"That makes sense. But wait, does that mean I can have lessons every day?"

"You sure can. And I'll even buy you a drink from my personal refrigerator up here," she said, nodding to a small refrigerator located behind her desk. "The sky's the limit. You can have Coke, Diet Coke or Perrier. Just no $800 bottles," she said, smiling.

"Wow, there's no end to your generosity, is there?"

"No. I'm just a goofy character," she said.

"Just because you *are* a character, doesn't mean that you *have* character."

Stephanie jumped up and down and clapped her hands. "That was the Wolf. Winston Wolf. Right after he helped Jules and Vincent clean up all the blood in the car."

"Right you are, Stephanie. You really do know your *Pulp Fiction*. We'll have to pick this up again tomorrow morning. Do you have anything scheduled at 8:00 o'clock?" Harrison was keen to get back to the simulator as soon as possible to see if what he was sensing could really be something interesting.

"You're an early bird? I go on duty at 8:00 o'clock so that should work out just fine."

"Great. I'll see you then."

Harrison left the simulator and headed back to his visitor flat bearing a contented grin. On the way, he passed Candy Podeski and a few others in the ship's main hallway. *They sure do hire beautiful women on this ship*, he thought. Candy appeared to be leading a group of potential suite owners from what Harrison could ascertain. Marc Romanello happened to be passing by and Candy introduced Marc to the four people accompanying her. Harrison found that he was walking in the same direction as Marc so he took the opportunity to catch up with him.

"I'm sorry, but I just overheard that woman introduce you. You're the chairman of the board on Paradise, aren't you?"

"Yes, I am," Marc replied, always conscious of his role as a part-time cheerleader for the ship. "I'm Marc Romanello."

"My name is Harrison Marshall, and I'm on board for two weeks. I haven't signed up for the full tour yet, but I'd love to ask you a few questions if you have a minute."

With the ship still at sea, and nothing on his calendar for a few hours, Marc agreed to chat with Harrison. They grabbed two seats in the ship's lobby, and Harrison asked Marc a barrage of questions about the ship's operations.

"That's great. Thanks for indulging me," Harrison concluded. "It definitely sounds like I should get with Candy and schedule a proper tour of the ship."

"Yes, I think you'll enjoy that. Even though I'm the chairman, I'm the first to admit that Candy and the operations team know far more about the ship than I ever will."

They said their goodbyes and Harrison left a message for Candy to schedule a time when she could show him around the ship.

Chapter 23
Becky Visits Elaine's Office

After two days at sea, Paradise slipped gracefully into port in Cochin India, and Becky Hirschfeld slipped nervously into Elaine Dwyer's office. It was the first time the two women had been together since the evening when they had actually . . . *been together.* Elaine removed her glasses and looked up at her welcome guest.

"C'mon in and close the door," she said. Elaine's command proved unnecessary as Becky's hand never had left the doorknob; she had every intention of shutting it.

"I thought you'd be out enjoying Cochin this morning," Elaine offered.

"This isn't exactly Mumbai or the town with the Taj Mahal. What's that called again."

"Agra," Elaine said.

"Yeah, Agra. So what the hell does anyone do in Cochin anyway?" Becky asked, as she moved closer to Elaine and helped herself to a seat in one of Elaine's guest chairs.

"Don't you know? It's called the Queen of the Arabian Sea," Elaine said with a mock booming voice. "Spices, rubber, tea, rice, nutmeg, cardamon and fish are the main industries in Cochin, one of the southernmost cities in India."

"You sound like a tour guide. You must've been here before."

"At least three times. It's really the most logical port of entry for a ship coming from our direction."

"Is it worth exploring?" Becky asked, fingering one of the snow globes Elaine had lined up on her desk.

"Nope. Unless do you want to take a two-hour bus to Kerala."

"What's there?"

"Not much. But the locals in Kerala run tour boat rides on the Vembanad lake."

"Is there much to see?" Becky asked, as she shook the snow globe vigorously.

"Not really. Just a lot of canals, rice patties, and mangroves. Oh, and women doing their laundry in the river. Which is disgusting, by the way. The river, not their laundry," she was sure to correct.

"Doesn't sound like anything I should be in a hurry to see," Becky said. "What are you up to today?"

"I'm up to my ears in this Peyton Flynn guessing game," Elaine confided. "Is she coming aboard? Is she already on board? If so, who is she? We've had six new female guests check in over the past few days, and any one of them could be Peyton Flynn. Obviously, we have to be super attentive to each one. We can't make any mistakes, or Eva would have our heads. Most of them make crazy requests, and one is a certified nut-job." Elaine exhaled, her frustration with the Peyton Flynn derby obvious by her scowl.

"Nut-job?" Becky asked, resting the snow globe back in its original place.

"Yeah, we call her Crazy Caitlin. She walks around, talking to herself." Elaine shook her head as she reflected on Crazy Caitlin's antics.

Becky nodded appreciatively, understanding the pressure Elaine was under. "Actually, I think I saw her in Sheik Shack. One of the waitresses thought she was ordering something, but she was only talking to herself about the menu options. Nut-job is right." Becky rolled her eyes all the way around, mocking a crazy person. Elaine smiled.

"Anyway, since you've made the obviously wise decision not to go touring in this less than attractive town, would you like to grab a quick bite at one of the local restaurants?" Elaine asked, as she artfully tucked a few loose strands of hair behind her left ear.

Becky paused before answering. "You know that ordinarily I love getting off the ship for meals. But this is India and stories about all the bacteria in the water here are legendary. I'd prefer to stay aboard and eat something here."

Elaine raised her eyebrow and lowered her voice. In her most seductive Lauren Bacall voice, she asked, "Like what you ate the other night."

Becky squirmed in her seat when Elaine said that. She did not make eye contact with Elaine. She crossed and recrossed her legs and fumbled with the iPhone in her lap.

"Hey, what's up? You look uncomfortable. I was just kidding."

"But were you? Really?"

"Whoa, Becky. I didn't mean anything by it," Elaine defended.

"I know, I know. I'm just edgy. If I told you I've thought about it almost constantly since we were together, would you believe me?"

"Sure. I have too," Elaine acknowledged.

"But not in the way you have."

"How do you know what I was thinking?" Elaine asked.

"Well, let me tell you what *I've* been thinking. That's why I stopped by," Becky said.

Elaine sat back, put her glasses back on her nose, and nodded in the way of inviting further conversation.

"Let me start with the other night. It was amazing. As you know, it's something I've never done before. I'm glad we did it. I have no regrets. But it was odd for me. Uncomfortable even." She squirmed again, afraid the words would come out wrong. "It's nothing against you. Lord knows you made it all so seamless, so smooth, so easy, so wonderful. It's me. Only me." The leg crossing exercise grew more rapid.

"Relax, Becky. I understand. Those nuns at Sacred Heart really made an impact on you I see." They both smiled. "I suspected you weren't enjoying yourself as much as I was, but . . ."

"I was. I was. That's just it. I really enjoyed it," Becky assured her. "You made me feel so special, so desired, so warm. I haven't felt that with Harris for years. But it felt odd. Wrong even. I guess you're right, it was the way I was raised. Catholic school for all those years. Living in a cloistered environment in Jupiter, Florida, I was never exposed to any of that stuff."

Elaine smarted a bit when Becky referred to their intimate encounter as *that stuff*, but she was careful not to display her feelings.

"I love being around you. You're smart, logical, well-informed, and thoughtful. I don't want to lose that connection. But I don't think I want to pursue the other connection, the sexual stuff," Becky said, continuing to display a high level of discomfort with the entire conversation.

"Is that all?" Elaine asked.

"Well, yeah. I guess so. Why, isn't that enough?

"Becky, that's all fine with me. I thought you were going to tell me you didn't want to be friends anymore."

Becky opened her eyes widely and leaned forward.

"Oh, no, nothing like that. Not at all. I absolutely love being around you. You make me laugh and make me so happy. I'd never want to lose your friendship."

"Well, that's a relief. I was scared for a second there." Elaine paused, took a deep breath, and leaned back before continuing. "You know, that's another important thing about being gay that sets us apart from our hetero friends."

"What's that?"

Although she wasn't sure she liked being included in a sentence that referred to her as gay, Becky was curious about where Elaine was going with this.

"We can have sexual interludes and then go right back to being friends with no judgments or hard feelings. Straight people don't do that. I remember when I had boyfriends in high school and college. Things would get hot and heavy, and we would have tremendous sex." Elaine smiled as she reflected on some of her teenage sexual interludes with young men. "Then we would break up and do everything possible to avoid each other. Gay people, women or men, are not like that. Maybe it's because we're part of a community that's discriminated against in so many ways that we feel the need to protect ourselves and each other. Whatever it is, it works. I haven't had one woman as a lover who I couldn't call up today and ask for a favor or take to dinner," she said, proudly, her chin held high.

A smile shimmied across Becky's face. Her eyes lit up.

"So now we're former lesbian lovers who can still be friends? That's really cool," Becky said. She shuddered with excitement at the thought of referring to herself as a lesbian, albeit a former one. "So about that meal you suggested."

"What about it?" Elaine asked.

"Why don't you join me tonight in Schooner's? We can enjoy a nice, safe meal on board together," Becky offered.

"Schooner's? Are you serious? You're the one who's usually so concerned about people seeing us together. People will talk. The Gripers will go crazy."

"Screw them," said Becky. "Screw them all. You're my friend, and I can invite any friend I want to dinner on board this ship."

"You're aware that if I join an owner in one of the owners' dining rooms, I need to wear my uniform?"

"That's fine with me. Wear what you must. But join me for dinner. I insist. I'll make a reservation for 7:00."

"Wow, that's terrific. Aren't you the big and bold one now?" Elaine ribbed.

"That's right. Maybe you've shown me a few things, and I have a better perspective now. Empowered even. I am woman, hear me roar." She started to sing the iconic song but stopped after three lines and a loss of memory about what followed.

Elaine was amused. "OK, Helen Reddy, you've made your point. I'm looking forward to it. See you at seven."

As Becky arose and headed for the door, Elaine added, "There's one more thing you should know."

"What's that?"

"I may have my uniform on, but I won't be wearing any underwear," Elaine said, as she raised her hand to her mouth.

"Stop it," Becky shrieked with laughter. She picked up one of the beanie animals Elaine had on her credenza and threw it at her. "You're incorrigible!"

Chapter 24
Golf Course Tensions

When the itinerary was provided to the staff in advance of each upcoming year, Stephanie Holsson's job got more complicated than most others. She was tasked with identifying and securing reservations at the best golf courses in relative proximity to the ports on the itinerary. Paradise's owners were snobs about many things— food, wine, shopping—but the best of any of those was readily ascertainable through any of a series of guidebooks. Moreover, one didn't need a reservation to wander Rodeo Drive or Worth Avenue. Golf courses, on the other hand, were not so easy. Many of the world's finest courses were private and usually unwilling to accommodate a group of twelve or sixteen nonresident golfers.

Through her years as a certified LPGA teaching professional, Stephanie had amassed an impressive stable of connections. Moreover, many of the suite owners had contacts, in the form of pros at their home clubs, who could make calls to the visiting clubs to help secure tee times. But, still, the process was arduous.

Local complications added to the challenge. By order of Captain Pugliese, the course could not be more than eighty miles from the ship. He was afraid that slow rounds or misdirected bus drivers could delay events aboard the vessel. For that reason, the captain was not at all fond of golf outings scheduled on days the ship was due to depart a particular port. Similarly, Stephanie was concerned about getting to the course in time for the appointed tee times if the outing was schedule for the ship's day of arrival. Language barriers, non-responsive pro shops, and last-minute changes to the ship's itinerary all contributed to the challenges attendant to scheduling tee times around the world.

The suite owners didn't care to know anything about the behind-the-scenes workings of golf scheduling. Or anything else aboard Paradise for that matter. They wanted the best services and employees money had to offer and had no interest in knowing how it all came to pass. They each paid millions of dollars for their luxury suites and coughed up tens of thousands of dollars a month in condo fees. That should get them whatever they wanted, they reasoned. At least most of them.

Cochin, India, was never in danger of being compared with Augusta, Georgia. Nevertheless, it was the first port in a new country and the suite owners expected to play golf. Although she had never been there, Stephanie had come across decent reviews about The Cial Golf & Country Club. Importantly, it was located near the port so transportation concerns could be mitigated.

Stephanie was able to secure two tee times which was just enough to accommodate herself and the seven owners and guests, all men, who had expressed interest in playing that day. To Stephanie's delight, the hired bus actually arrived on time. Such things were both uncommon and unexpected in India.

As was proper ship protocol, Stephanie allowed all the golfers to board the bus first. She assumed an empty seat near the back. No sooner had her fanny hit the seat than Claude Azulai came and stood over her.

"Hey, Steph, I haven't been up to the simulator these last few days because I've been busy. But I've been working on that wrist hinge move you showed me."

"That's great. You'll see how much more power you get out of it."

Secrets never remained secret aboard Paradise, and Claude's interest in Stephanie Holsson was a poorly kept one. After Claude's golf lesson with Stephanie, Eva voiced her displeasure at her boyfriend spending time with a woman who could have passed for a super model. Hell, Stephanie *had* been a model. In Sweden, no less.

Besides being handsome and desirable, Claude was flirtatious. Eva had little tolerance for that sort of behavior. Even in her own suite, Eva ranted about Claude's apparent attraction to the ship's golf pro. On one occasion, when Marc and Karen Romanello stopped by for lunch at Eva's suite, Eva made a few not-so-subtle comments about Claude's affinity for golf on the ship and his seeming obsession with Stephanie Holsson. Consequently, the waiters who delivered and cleared lunch from Eva's suite also heard Eva voice her displeasure with the situation.

Through the infamous rumor mill that traveled at supersonic speed below deck, Stephanie learned that Eva's jealous streak had reared its ugly head. More troubling was that Stephanie was at the tip of Eva's spear. It had taken all Eva's willpower, and some serious cajoling from Marc, for Eva not to fire Stephanie after her Chaweng Beach Club topless incident. If Eva even suspected that Stephanie was a speed bump on her road to a happy life with Claude, Stephanie would be gone, fired immediately.

Stephanie loved her job aboard Paradise, as did almost all members of the crew. It was true they were working in the hospitality business, but this was the highest end hospitality market on the planet. Suite owners sometimes tipped their favorite crew members in excess of $5,000 at Christmas. And collecting those sums, in cash, from a handful of different owners certainly made life more pleasant around the holidays. Stephanie was not intent on doing anything that would jeopardize her job security or cause her to run into Eva's headwind.

The bus started to move and Claude took advantage of the opportunity to plop down right next to Stephanie. For the duration of the ride, he peppered her with questions, not only about golf, but about herself. At times, Stephanie found him engaging, and almost pleasant. But the third time his leg brushed against hers, she remembered how dangerous he could be to her job and reputation.

"Since there are all only eight of us today, I presume you and I'll be in the same foursome," he suggested.

"Actually, it didn't work out that way. Mr. Marshall is new to the ship, and we always try to have the new players play with the pro. That's why you and I were paired together last week," she said, offering a self-serving white lie. Before Claude could ask the next obvious question, Stephanie continued. "And Mr. Gagne and Mr. Varna have been taking lessons with me this week, so I promised we would play together so I could keep an eye on them."

"But I wanted you to keep an eye on me," Claude said with a wink. "Because I'll be keeping an eye on you." That type of comment was exactly why he was *not* scheduled to be playing with Stephanie.

After what seemed like an eternity to Stephanie, the bus arrived at The Cial Golf & Country Club. From the outside, it was no different from any of the other average golf courses Paradise visited throughout the year. The driver pulled the eight bags from the belly of the bus and leaned them against the splintered blue wooden rack in the bag drop area. When Claude went into the pro shop to buy a new glove, Harrison wandered over to Stephanie.

"Is that one of the owners or is that your boyfriend?"

Mortified, Stephanie looked at Harrison with a penetrating glance.

"Boyfriend? What would ever make you say that?" she asked defensively.

"I heard the way he was talking to you the whole ride. Telling you about his favorite shave cream, why he doesn't like tight swim trunks. All that stuff. I'm not saying there's anything wrong with it, I just assumed he's your boyfriend."

"He is most definitely *not* my boyfriend," Stephanie huffed.

If Harrison had heard that conversation, Stephanie had to believe that some of the other suite owners on the bus must have overheard some of it as well. She'd have to take steps to keep her distance from Claude, and to make her detachment painfully obvious before a fatal rumor spread.

"By the way, you and I are playing together today," Stephanie said.

"We are?"

"Yup. I thought I could provide some on course instruction, if you'd like that."

"I'd love that," Harrison said.

"Great. Let me go inside and take care of business with the pro shop. I'll meet you at the driving range in two shakes of a lamb's tail."

"Mia!" Harrison exclaimed. "That was Mia Wallace's line when Vincent picked her up at Marcellus's house."

Stephanie smiled appreciatively. Yet again, she said, "You really do know your *Pulp Fiction*, don't you?"

"I do," he said, simultaneously proud he was able to display that knowledge of the film and excited about his newfound cinematic pal.

Stephanie and Harrison were paired with perhaps two of the most boring owners on Paradise. And that was fine with them. The course was not at all memorable, except for a sign by the seventeenth tee box warning to be alert for incoming aircraft. Indeed, the course was so close to the runway that when large planes landed, the players were affected by the wind from the engines. It wasn't quite as close as the runway in St. Maarten was to the beach there, but damn close nonetheless.

From the time they teed off until the last ball plopped into the cup on the eighteenth green, Harrison and Stephanie were like kids at play. For Stephanie—as was the case for most of the crew on the ship—time away from the ship was a bit of a playdate. Yes, they were working, but they were doing so in a more relaxing environment. After all, how stuffy and formal could one be on a golf course?

After the driver loaded the bags back into the bus, Stephanie spied Claude continuing to look at her.

"Sit next to me," she said to Harrison as they waited to board.

"I was planning to."

"You were?" she asked, optimistic he might have taken more than a professional interest in her.

"I was." After a dramatic pause, he added, "Just to talk *Pulp Fiction*, of course." Harrison nudged his leg against Stephanie's after he saw the glow fade from her smile. Her smile immediately returned.

"I was just kidding. Anyway, it's the least I could do for you. After you told me Claude's not your boyfriend, and you shared those stories about Eva and her jealous tendencies, I intuited that another ride like this morning's might not be in your best interest."

Stephanie looked at Harrison thankfully, almost wistfully. Besides being a fellow *Pulp Fiction* aficionado, he was clever, funny, and insightful.

They rode quietly on the trip back to the port. Without saying so, both realized any conversation could be easily overheard, much as Harrison had heard Claude's conversation with Stephanie that morning. Having spent four hours riding in a cart together, and with Harrison due to be on the ship for the next couple of weeks, nothing really needed to be said where it could be overheard.

Because they were sitting in the last row, they were the last ones off the bus. As they walked towards the ship, Harrison summoned up his innermost *Pulp Fiction* and repeated one of the lesser-known quotes from the iconic film. "I hope you didn't mind the silence."

"Why do we feel it's necessary to yak about bullshit in order to be comfortable?" Stephanie asked, parroting the exact way Vincent Vega had responded to Mia Wallace in the film.

Perfectly on cue, Harrison uttered the next line Mia had spoken to Vincent, "That's when you know you've found someone special. When you can comfortably shut the fuck up for a minute and comfortably enjoy the silence."

"Special?" Stephanie asked, her eyes beaming with enthusiasm.

"Yes, you're very special. You've helped me eliminate my slice in a way no one has so far," he said.

Stephanie feigned a pout. "And I was just beginning to think you liked me."

"You were, eh? Well if you straighten out my drives, I may just love you," he said with a wink.

They went their respective ways, each going to different parts of the ship, Stephanie back to her cabin to change and Harrison to his visitor flat to shower. By the time she got to her office in the simulator twenty minutes later, the message light on her phone was flashing. She tingled with delight when she heard Harrison's voice say, "I'm not gonna get thrown out of a fourth floor window for giving anyone a foot massage, but I'll see you for a lesson tomorrow morning."

Stephanie sat back in her chair and shook her head. The day began with her sitting next to a man she desperately needed to avoid. With whom being linked could result in her immediate firing. And it ended with a man she desperately wanted to know more about. Who knew as much as she did about her favorite film.

Chapter 25
Favors at the Front Desk

"Is today a full moon or something?" Donna Lafat asked Eva the day after Paradise set off from Cochin for the short sail to Mangalore. Eva had stopped by the front desk where Donna was working. Eva often did that just to check on things, but she was doing it more frequently now that Peyton Flynn might be lurking somewhere aboard Paradise.

"Why do you ask?"

"Everyone's asking for special treatment today," Donna said.

"Like who?" Eva asked.

"Like everyone. And after you try to get them what they've asked for, they change their minds. Some of these women change their minds more frequently than Snoop Dogg changes names."

Eva laughed. "How can I help? What kind of stuff are you being asked for?"

"Take Mrs. Tarpley, that wild lady from Birmingham—the one traveling with her mother. She asked me to get her tickets for a cricket match."

"That shouldn't be so difficult. Have you spoken with the concierge staff?"

"Yes. But it's some kind of world championship and India is playing Pakistan," Donna explained.

"Oh, shit," said Eva.

"Shit is right. Apparently, they're the two best teams in the world. Who knew? But then again, who follows professional cricket? As you can imagine, tickets are almost impossible to come by. Why would that old bat want to go to a cricket game anyway?"

A knowing look washed across Eva's face.

"Because she's not who she says she is, that's why," Eva said in a conspiratorial whisper.

"You mean . . ."

"Exactly. Peyton Flynn. I've said it before and I'll say it again. She asks for all kinds of exceptional things and then slams hotels when they don't deliver. It's not fair, but the best properties are able to pull off miracles and deliver." Eva looked around, careful to be sure she wasn't overheard.

"Not fair is right, but I'll see what we can do about those tickets. From what the concierge said, they're about $5,000 - $8,000 a ticket," Donna said.

"She doesn't expect us to *pay* for them. Just to make them available for her to purchase."

"Well, that's a relief," Donna said. "But what about restaurant reservations?"

"What about them?" Eva asked.

"She asked if we could get her a reservation for four at Indian Accent."

"In New Delhi? It's funny you mention that because I just heard of that restaurant yesterday from Claude. He said it's the most famous restaurant in all of India. I told him it's out of the question because the ship's not going anywhere near New Delhi. And Mrs. Tarpley wants to go there?"

"That's what she said. Money can buy tickets to the cricket match, but I've been told that getting those reservations is next to impossible," Donna said.

"I'll talk to Elaine and the team," Eva said. "They need to pull out the stops and get her whatever she needs. As for the cricket match, if you can secure the tickets, get them. Remember that we'll invoice her folio, and she'll actually be buying them. But we'll spring for a car and driver to take her there and back. A gift from Paradise's management," Eva added with a contrived smile.

"Wow, that's nice of you." Donna punched away at her keyboard to memorialize what Eva had just allowed. "I hate to even bring it up, but that Mrs. Bracker is also looking for weird things."

Eva rolled her eyes. Suite owners aboard Paradise often made extravagant requests. When they could be accommodated, they were. And when they couldn't be, they couldn't be. But now that the ship was in India—where Peyton Flynn had posted her last review—everyone was paying extra attention to any special requests made by people staying in the ship's visitor flats. Any one of them could be Peyton Flynn. And getting a superb review on Peyton's Places would be the end of any financial concerns for Eva and the rest of Paradise's suite owners. Condo fees would be fixed at reasonable rates, the note to Mitsubishi Marine could be paid and extinguished, and the owners would have guaranteed financial security deep into the future. But first things first. If Peyton Flynn *was* aboard Paradise, she had to be sure to have the best experience she'd ever encountered or none of that mattered

"You said something about Mrs. Bracker. What is she asking about?" Eva stretched her forearms across the reception desk and clasped her hands.

"She wants to know if it's possible for us to help her rent a dining room in the Taj Mahal," Donna said.

"*In* the Taj Mahal? Not one of the fancy Taj Mahal hotels, but in the Taj itself?" Eva asked.

"Yup, in the Taj itself," Donna affirmed.

"Holy shit. Full moon indeed. What'd you tell her?" Eva asked.

"I said we're looking into it. I didn't think it was possible, but Candy said they have banquet rooms available for weddings, so it might be a thing."

"Well, you know the drill. Pull out all the stops and if we can make it happen, let's do it," Eva said, resigning herself to the eccentricities that seemed to be raining down on the reception desk's parade.

"Anything else I should know about?" she asked, hesitatingly.

"I wasn't going to say anything but . . ."

"Are you serious?" asked Eva. "There's more?"

"There are three other ladies we've been keeping an eye on. When they came aboard, they caught Candy's attention, and she put them in the Peyton Flynn database. Hold on, I'll pull them up." Donna effortlessly hammered what seemed like hundreds of keys on her keyboard before she found what she was looking for. "One's from Australia. She said she was diagnosed with a deep gum infection before she left Sydney and wants to know if we can arrange for her to have root canal," Donna explained.

"In India? Are you fucking serious?" Eva asked. "She was diagnosed with a gum infection in Australia and decided to travel 5,000 miles to spend time on a ship floating in the Arabian Sea? That doesn't sound like Peyton Flynn. That just sounds stupid." Donna smiled appreciatively.

"*If* she's telling the truth, Candy was suspicious that it could be a setup."

"I'm not worried about that one. It just doesn't make sense. Besides, have you ever seen dentists in India? They practice on the streets. I'm serious. People stand in line, and, when it's their turn, they sit on a carpet in front of the dentist. He gives them a bottle of something or other to swig, then reaches into their mouth with a pair of pliers. I've seen it. I'm telling you, it's not a pretty thing. I wouldn't put too much stock in that woman. I mean, if she needs some sort of treatment, let's see if we can get it for her. But don't worry about her being Peyton Flynn. What else ya' got?" Eva asked.

Donna winced at Eva's dentist description before continuing. "There's a lady from New York. Just outside the city, actually. Patricia something or other. She makes bizarre requests of the wellness center almost every day," Donna said.

"Have you heard some of the things Mrs. Perlmutter has asked for? Or Mrs. Rasmussen? What degree of bizarre are we talking about?" Eva inquired.

"The first day, she insisted she wanted two masseuses at the same time—one to focus on her bottom half while the other worked on her head and neck."

"There was nothing sexual involved in that, was there?" Eva asked.

"No, just odd. Everything about her is odd," Donna said.

"And they had to do this at the same time?"

"Yves said the team could manage it, so they did. The next day, she asked if the team had cold banana leaves to wrap her face and neck after a sauna," Donna said.

"Do they?" Eva asked as she rolled her eyes.

"No. But they didn't tell her that. They told her they didn't have any appointments available that day and they contacted Chef Rolando to see what he may have in the kitchen."

"That's brilliant thinking," Eva said. "Who thought of that?"

"Yves."

"There's a reason I love that guy. Good thinking," Eva commended.

"But, wait, there's one other thing. She asked if anyone from the fitness team could observe her SCUBA pool certification test while she's aboard."

"What did you say this lady's name is?" Eva asked.

Donna checked her computer screen before answering, to be sure she got the name right. "Silverman. Patricia Silverman. Why?"

Peter Antonucci

"When you step back and think about it, those requests might just be the type of thing we could expect from Peyton Flynn. They're bizarre, but not unattainable. What did we say about the SCUBA question?"

"I don't know. I'll have to ask someone in the fitness center. They just told me about the request," Donna said.

"Well, if there's any way we can handle it, let's do it," Eva said, her voice dripping with resignation. "This Peyton's Places watch is going to kill me. Everything Elaine has been saying seems to measure up, and, if there's any chance we're going to get reviewed, I want us to get the highest score ever attained. Anything else?"

"Just a couple of weird things, but nothing super demanding," Donna said.

"How weird? Or do I even want to know?" Eva asked.

"There's a lady from Virginia, Ms. Roank. She's been on board three days and she has asked Stephanie Holsson to restring her tennis racquet every day?"

"Every day?"

"Weird, right? I mean, even the pros don't restring their racquets every day. And this woman is no pro."

"Why? How old is she?"

"About seventy," Donna replied. "But why would she do that anyway?"

"I don't care. Whatever floats her boat. I don't care if Stephanie has to restring that racquet three times a day, let her do it. In fact, I'd rather have her do that, then be available for golf lessons," Eva said.

"Really? Why's that?"

Eva rolled her eyes, not knowing if Donna was aware of the extent of her dislike of Stephanie. "Let's just say that Claude seems

207

to have renewed his interest in golf. And Stephanie has already proven she's not someone who can be trusted."

"Oh, you mean that little incident in Ko Samui?"

"Little incident? Are you kidding me? She took her freaking top off in a hotel pool and it ended up all over the Internet," Eva screeched. "I wanted to fire her then and there, but Marc stepped in and defended her. If she did anything like that around Claude, I can tell you termination would be the least of her problems."

Anger flashed in Eva's eyes. Donna knew she was wandering into dangerous territory so she tried to steer the conversation away from Stephanie and back to Peyton Flynn, whichever guest she might be.

"So we'll have her string away," Donna offered in an upbeat voice.

"Morning, noon, and night. I really don't care if her fingers bleed. Let her string Ms. Roank's racquet every waking hour of the day," Eva said. Donna's squinting manifested her confusion about what Eva meant. Eva elaborated.

"Look, I know it sounds catty, and I should probably direct my anger at Claude more than at Stephanie, but I'm a woman. And I don't like my man looking at another woman. I love Claude, and I'm going to give him the benefit of the doubt. But Stephanie has already proven herself to be . . . well, to be less of a woman than you or me.. So I don't like her. I don't like her being around Claude. Heck, I don't even like her being around me anymore, and I used to enjoy her company."

Eva's pressure point was obvious. "So I presume we should not put Stephanie at your table for any upcoming banquets?" Donna asked. Her comment performed the intended consequence of making Eva grin.

"No, Donna, you shouldn't do that. But if you do, have Chef Rolando serve something like mushy peas. If he serves anything that requires the use of a sharp knife and the little Lolita is anywhere near me, things could get dangerous."

Donna smiled and said, "Note to self, no steak knives around Eva and Stephanie. Check. Oh wait, check this out." She nodded in the direction of Caitlin Cappilletti who was passing through the lobby.

As if on cue, and without any apparent concern for her surroundings, Caitlin asked, "Does anyone around here know how to play chess?" before answering herself, "No but I bet there are some backgammon players." She continued, "There are? Do you know where?" And then, "I'm not sure, but let's keep looking."

"What the hell did I just see?" Eva asked.

"That's Caitlin Cappilletti. We call her Crazy Caitlin. She walks around talking to herself. But she doesn't just talk to herself, she asks questions and then answers them right away. It's the weirdest thing."

"I'd say. And with our luck that's Peyton Flynn," Eva chuckled.

"Don't laugh. Elaine already has her on her spreadsheet."

"That Elaine. If anyone can figure this whole thing out, it'll be her." Eva smiled as she headed back up to her suite, relieved her paramour was politely waiting for her, and not in the golf simulator with the buxom Ms. Stephanie Holsson.

Chapter 26
Harrison Takes a Lesson

The morning after the golf outing in Cochin, Harrison Marshall showed up in the golf simulator at 8:05 a.m. He was armed with two coffees from Sheik Shack, both still steaming hot.

"Is that for me?" Stephanie asked in an impish voice, spying the cup with its lid still intact.

"It is. Short pulled espresso with a foam shot."

"How'd you know that's my drink?" she asked.

"I have my sources. Besides, a man never tells his secrets."

"I thought it's women who don't tell their secrets," Stephanie said.

"That's fine with me. You don't tell me yours, and I won't tell you mine."

Stephanie walked over to Harrison, took the cardboard cup, and feigned a curtsey. It was such a tender moment, she thought. She almost wanted to kiss him on the cheek, but the time was not right for that. At least not yet. Moreover, she couldn't afford to make a mistake in that regard, not being under Eva's scrutiny for even the slightest misstep. So instead, she resorted to a line from the opening scene of *Pulp Fiction.*

"I love you, Pumpkin."

"I love you, Honey Bunny," he said, right on cue. "Opening scene. And he follows it with, 'Everybody be cool, this is a robbery.'"

"Then they start shooting up the place." Stephanie reminded him.

They both laughed, once again impressed with their respective abilities to remember so much of the dialogue from their mutually favorite film.

"So who are we going to shoot up here?' Stephanie asked.

"I get the feeling you'd like to shoot that Claude guy. Am I right?"

"I don't have anything against him. He's not crazy aggressive or inappropriate."

"He's not? He sure looked inappropriate to me."

"He's a guy who flirts. I'm used to guys like that. Believe me, I've seen a lot worse. I know how to keep my distance. Especially since he's Eva's boyfriend. Eva would tar and feather me if she thought there was anything between us."

"But you said there isn't," Harrison said.

"There isn't. But there's a history with Eva and me, and, if she even suspected anything, that would be the last straw for me."

"What's the history?" Harrison asked.

Stephanie paused and took a deep breath. She meandered back to her desk and thought for a minute about how she wanted to respond. How much of her previous indiscretion did she want to reveal to Harrison Marshall, a nice enough guy with whom she seemed to be making a connection. She exhaled as she announced her conclusion.

"Are you in a hurry for your lesson, or do you have some time?"

Harrison realized Stephanie could be about to answer his question with more than a dismissive comment. If he wasn't intrigued when he asked the perfunctory question, he was now.

"I'm not in any hurry at all. To be honest, I'm a bit tired from yesterday. If I don't even swing a club once today, it wouldn't bother me."

"Then shut the door," Stephanie said before motioning Harrison to have a seat on the blue suede couch next to the hitting area.

"There's a long version and a short version," she began. "I'll spare you a lot of the details. But one day a few months ago, when the ship was anchored in Vietnam, several crew members went ashore to a fancy resort. A bunch of us got a little wild in the resort pool. Not just the resort pool, but the resort *quiet* pool. Some of the girls started dancing suggestively. They even had a wet tee shirt contest. One thing led to another, and I ended up in the pool, dancing topless." She paused and took a sip from her coffee cup. When she looked up, she caught Harrison staring at her.

"You did *not* just stare at my boobs, Mr. Marshall. Did you?" she squealed in a playful voice.

"Guilty as charged," Harrison confessed. "And please, when we're together, dispense with that Mr. Marshall shit. I'm Harrison."

"But ship rules . . ."

Harrison cut her off. "Ship rules are that you're to make all the guests happy, right? And comply with their requests? So my request is that you call me Harrison. Can you do that?"

"OK, Harrison," Stephanie said in a sarcastic tone. "And I'll also forgive you for staring at my chest. I guess I had to expect that when I told you what happened. Anyway, the board had a meeting, and several people were disciplined. Eva was ready to fire me, but the chairman of our board, Marc Romanello, spoke up on my behalf."

"Is that because he saw you topless? Are they that good?"

"Stop it," Stephanie insisted, feigning a grimace. "Don't be bad. I'm telling you what happened. Marc's an avid golfer and a good friend. For whatever reason, he stood up to Eva. I'm grateful for that, but it's been made abundantly clear that I need to watch every step now."

Harrison looked at Stephanie as he took it all in. He understood the gravity of what had transpired, and how Stephanie's job could be in danger.

"Thanks for sharing. That explains your resistance to Claude yesterday."

"That and other things. Look, I'm here to do a job. I'm a single woman who tries to keep her head down. But let's face it, I have to run around all day in a little golf skort or tennis skirt and, because I'm 5'11, my legs do attract a fair amount of attention. Attention I don't really need these days."

"Not just your legs," Harrison said, dropping his eyes to Stephanie's chest again with a mischievous smile.

"Stop it! Do you want me to just stand up and pull off my shirt? Would that make you happy?"

"No," Harrison said firmly. "Well, maybe. But it would get you fired, and neither of us want that."

Harrison stood up, placed what was left of his coffee on the table at the end of the couch, and grabbed one of the clubs he had used the day before.

"So let's move on to something less controversial. Like my horrible slice yesterday."

"I thought you didn't need a lesson today," Stephanie said.

"I didn't. I was feeling lethargic. But let's just say you aroused me with your story."

"You're incorrigible. But let's go. Warm up and we'll take a look at what's pulling your junk left all the time."

Harris looked down at his crotch. Like schoolchildren sharing an inside joke, they laughed together. Harrison placed five balls on the mat and drove them into the screen on the front of the room.

"You're whippy," Stephanie said. "You're shaft is bending as you complete your backswing. When you bring your hands down against the ball, the head of the club is not lined up straight so the ball shoots left."

Harrison stopped what he was doing, dropped the club to the ground, and placed his hands on his hips. "My shaft is not bending. I can assure you it is perfectly rigid."

"Get over yourself," Stephanie teased. "Are you going to harp on that subject all day, or can we focus on golf?"

"You brought it up," Harrison pleaded. "So what do we do about my bent shaft?"

"I want to see something," Stephanie said as she returned to the side of the simulator containing her desk and a few lockers.

"My bent shaft?"

Stephanie's mind raced with potential responses, all of them fun, but none of them appropriate. She opened one of the lockers and removed a bag of clubs. "You're lucky. The guy who's the best golfer on the ship happens to be a lefty. And you're even more lucky because he's not here right now. He's also one of the nicest guys you'll ever meet. I know he'll have no problem with you using his clubs." She handed Harrison the seven iron from the new bag of cubs.

"Wow, PXGs," he exclaimed. "These are some serious clubs. Definitely out of my price range."

"I'm not selling them to you, silly. I just want to see how the ball reacts if you swing with a stiffer shaft," Stephanie said.

Harrison took a few practice swings before lining up some balls to hit. As if by magic, the balls went appreciably straighter, with better contact than he had enjoyed before.

"You're amazing. You fixed my shaft, and now I'm shooting straight," he said, proud of his clever use of the double entendre.

"Stop that. You're really bad."

"Actually, I'm not. I'm very good. And, if you play your cards right, you might be able to find that out for yourself." Harrison winked and ran his tongue across his lips with the sophomoric cockiness. He hit a couple of more shots into the screen.

"You're a magician. How'd you know that would fix it?" he asked.

"I didn't. But I had a suspicion. See, aren't you glad you stopped ogling me and finally got around to hitting golf balls?"

"It's not all about what we ogle. After all, it's unfortunate that what we find pleasing to the touch and pleasing to the eye is seldom the same."

Stephanie laughed. "I almost forgot about that scene. And that line. That's what Fabienne said to Bruce Willis when they were in bed together before the fight. But I guarantee you, what *you* seem to find pleasing to the eye today would also be pleasing to the touch." Stephanie thrust her breasts forward. "But, alas, my friend, that's not an option for you so you'll just have to stick with ogling. Now that you've got your swing figured out, go enjoy your day. And you might want to start it with a cold shower."

Harrison smiled and snapped off a fake salute. He handed her back the PXG club with which he had found golfing nirvana and returned to his visitor flat to process what had just happened.

Chapter 27
Board Meeting to Discuss Peyton Flynn

Mangalore, India, was a necessary stop for Paradise before reaching the more popular ports of Goa and Mumbai. In Mangalore, the ship onboarded much needed supplies before traveling to the larger, more commercial, and more corrupt ports of India. A voracious reader, Eva had learned that although Mangalore was an interesting city for a variety of societal reasons—the population is 85% Hindu, 10% Christian, and 5% Islam and boasts a 94% literacy rate with over 70% of its inhabitants having at least some amount of postgraduate work—it wasn't exactly a World Heritage tourist destination. As a result, she designated Mangalore the perfect place for the directors to convene a meeting.

Creatures of habit, the directors generally assumed the same seats in the board room whenever they convened. In this instance, however, Becky Hirschfeld was attending her first formal board meeting. She arrived when only three directors had been seated, so she was unsure of her place at the table. She snickered. "Is there assigned seating or do the new kids just sit in the back?" Her giddiness laid bare a nervousness Becky rarely exhibited.

"Come sit here, next to me," Marc suggested, patting the chair to his immediate right.

"Is this where Harris used to sit?" Becky asked about her erstwhile husband, whose seat she was effectively replacing.

"Not at all. He used to sit as far away from me as possible. I kind of liked it that way."

Becky grinned.

As the directors filed into the room, Elaine Dwyer walked around the table placing board materials before each seat and making sure each director had whatever they needed for the meeting.

"This should be a relatively short meeting, Elaine," Eva shot over her shoulder as she entered the room. "You can tell the housekeeping team to plan on refreshing the room in about an hour." Eva looked at Marc and added, "Unless our esteemed chairman has some new business I don't know about."

"No, I think things will be pretty cut and dried today," Marc responded.

Marc made the requisite notations for the minutes about a quorum being assembled and the meeting being duly noticed before he launched into the topics of the day.

"It seems like the major buzz around the ship involves this Peyton Flynn character and a very real possibility she's on our beloved vessel as we speak. Of course, all this is conjecture, but she published a report on the Oberoi Amarvilas in Agra, India, a few weeks ago, and, apparently, she just published a review about another Indian hotel last week. Since Eva has been working with Elaine Dwyer on collecting intelligence about just who this Peyton Flynn might be, I'm going to turn the floor over to Eva for a presentation."

"Thanks, Marc." Eva stood and walked to the front of the room where an eight foot by ten foot map of the world was mounted. She clutched an iPad in her left hand. "Yes, Peyton Flynn has struck again. This time, she visited the iconic Umaid Bhawan Palace Hotel in Jodhpur. For those of you who are not intimately familiar with India's geography, Jodhpur is about a three-hour flight from where we're docked right now," she said, pointing out Jodhpur on the map. "That doesn't mean she's definitely in our neighborhood, but it's a hell of a lot closer than the United States or Europe."

"I've stayed at the Umaid Bhawan Palace," Lorraine Williams volunteered. "It may be the finest hotel in the world. What did this Peyton person have to say about it?" she asked in a voice many would interpret as pretentious if they didn't know her.

"She agrees with you, Lorraine, about the excellence of the property. I won't read the entire review for you. Of course, you're free to read it on your own, but here are the highlights." Eva opened the cover of her iPad, scanned the article, and proceeded to share the highlights of Peyton Flynn's review. "She describes how it took fifteen years to build the incredible property that began as the private residence of the Jodhpur royal family."

"Yes, when there *was* a royal family in Jodhpur," Lorraine interjected.

"Yes, of course, when there *was* a royal family there. Anyway. . ." Eva continued as she swiped across her screen, keen to share the positive attributes of the Umaid Bhawan Palace Hotel Peyton Flynn had identified. "She raves about the Palm Court marble used in the construction of the property and the family museum located within the hotel. She goes on to talk about some of the unique characteristics of the hotel such as its century-old architecture, dancing peacocks, twenty-six acres of lush gardens, amazing restaurants, blah, blah, blah. She praises the physical aspects of the property and declares it a must-see, manmade wonder of the world."

"I'm sure there's a *but* coming up somewhere," Marc said.

"There is. For one type of mistake, she awarded enough demerits to reduce the grade from a ninety-seven to a ninety-one. Ready for this? The front desk staff didn't respond to her requests promptly enough. They responded, just not fast enough."

"Seriously? That cost them six points?" Marc asked, incredulous.

"I don't think ninety-one sounds so bad, personally," Mario Garramone chimed in.

"Well, it is. Kind of. I mean, it's better than an eighty-one, but we're looking for 100, or as close to it as possible," Eva said.

"Tell us more about these requests," Becky asked.

"OK, listen to this." Eva turned her attention back to her iPad and read. *"The front office staff was pleasant, well-dressed, and highly efficient. Whenever I asked for anything out of the ordinary, they complied and found a way to make even the most unusual requests a reality. However, they didn't do it on a timely basis. For example, on the first day I arrived at the property, I was tired and intended to take a nap. I called the front desk and asked for two extra pillows. I specified that I wanted oversized pillows, and they had to be foam, not down. After a while, I couldn't keep my eyes open, and I laid down on the bed. Two hours later, I woke up and showered. As I was dressing for dinner, a handsome, perfectly outfitted bellman rang my door and presented me with two oversized foam pillows, just as I had requested. Ordinarily, I might not have been so quick to let the delay affect my review. But, the next day, when I was having trouble logging onto the Internet in my room, it took an hour after I called downstairs for the technician to come fix the problem. I don't know if the delays were the fault of the bellman, the technician, or the front desk, but they were delays, nevertheless. And when a hotel is seeking a superior review from Peyton's Places, as I presume all properties are, missteps in service are just not acceptable."*

"I can't say I disagree with her conclusions. But that seems kind of harsh, don't you think?" Marc asked, looking around the room for approval.

"Exactly. This is India, not London. Doesn't she know that the culture here doesn't revolve around the strokes of the minute hand on a clock?" Mario added.

Eva closed her iPad cover and walked back to her seat. "Guests at luxury properties don't really care where they are," Eva retorted. "They're paying outrageous amounts of money for their stay, and they expect to receive outrageous service. If India, or any other country, was charging $200 a night for a suite, one would be justified in suggesting that the service might not be best in class. But when they are charging $8,000 a night for a suite, delays are utterly intolerable."

"So it sounds like we need to make sure our front desk people hear this and know they've got to step up their game," Mario said as he stood to help himself to a Diet Coke from the credenza.

"We've been telling them that every day since we learned Peyton Flynn might be in the area," Eva answered. "You'd be amazed at how many bizarre requests they get downstairs every day."

"Like what?" Becky asked.

"One lady from Alabama, Ginger Tarpley I think her name is, wants tickets to the world cricket championship between India and Pakistan. Another wants to rent a dining hall in the Taj Mahal. A lady from Australia thinks we can arrange for her to get a root canal while we're here," Eva explained.

"In India? Is she crazy? Does she want to get her whole face infected?" Mario asked as he returned to his seat.

"Wait, there's more. We've got another American lady who makes bizarre requests of the spa staff every day. And one from France who has asked for three cases of Evian to be delivered to her room every day so she can use it to bathe," Eva added.

"Didn't Michael Jackson use to bathe in bottled water?" Becky asked.

Mario cut her off. "I thought French people don't bathe that frequently anyway."

"You are *definitely* not going to be selected to be our brand ambassador when we visit France, Mario," Eva said.

Lorraine snickered.

"Ready for the last one? There's an Israeli woman who is begging us to allow her to bring her cat aboard for three days of the week she is sailing with us," Eva said.

"And what's she going do with the cat for the other four days? Throw it overboard?" Mario joked.

"Oh, shush you," Eva said, raising her index finger in his direction. "We didn't get around to asking that question. Unfortunately, that one is out of our hands. Indian authorities do not permit transportation of live animals on any vessel docking in their waters. But you can see what I mean. If Peyton Flynn is on Paradise, and, if she's trying to test our staff with bizarre requests, we're having a tough time figuring out who she might be. Frankly, all those requests are complicated and not easy to accommodate, let alone quickly, as the demanding Ms. Flynn seems to require."

"Look, we can only do what we can do." Marc stated, looking directly at Eva. "To the extent we can accommodate any of those requests, we should do it. And we should do it because we are Paradise, not just because we're trying to impress Peyton Flynn. But, if they involve breaking laws, putting our staff at risk, or doing things that are at odds with our mission statement and allowable protocols," Marc continued, his voice rising, "we're not going there."

"I tend to agree with you, at least in principle," Eva said. "But keep in mind that a truly excellent rating from Peyton's Place would go a long way towards solving many of our fiscal concerns. It would buy us at least a dozen years of financial stability."

"So who's going to interface with the front desk staff to go through all this stuff?" Marc asked.

"I'll stay on it," Eva said as she opened her iPad cover and typed a reminder to speak with the front desk personnel. "I'll coordinate with the reception team, especially Donna Lafat. Elaine Dwyer's our overall point person so she'll liaise with the concierge team, bellmen, and anyone else who we suspect might be forward facing with Ms. Flynn. Marc, can I ask you to be in touch with the wellness center, fitness center, and your friend, Stephanie Holsson. One lady seems very focused on wellness already, so you might want to jump on that right away," Eva instructed.

"I can handle those. You do realize it's tough for me to get any time in the golf simulator with Stephanie now that your friend Claude is monopolizing her," Marc teased.

From the way she glared at Marc, straightened her shoulders, and slammed her iPad cover shut, it was clear Eva was not amused.

"If that topless hooker takes as much as one step out of line, I'm asking Captain Pugliese to offload her in the middle of India. I'm still not over that stunt she pulled in Vietnam, and you're well aware of that. Just talk to her and the others and make sure everybody's ready for anything that could come our way," Eva said, her shoulders tensing as she squeezed the life out of a hapless napkin.

"Yes, Eva," Marc said in a voice that did little to hide his awkwardness as a result of Eva's response. In summary fashion, he added, "I think we all know what our priorities are. Unless anyone has any further questions, I think we stand adjourned."

The directors looked around the table at each other. Each one shook their head, indicating there was no new business to be offered. They slowly gathered their papers or iPads and walked towards the exit.

"Marc, would you be a doll and hang back for a sec?" Eva asked.

Marc obliged and they stood aside while the other five directors filed out of the room.

"I'm asking you to be serious with me now. How much time is Claude really spending with her?" Eva asked.

"With Stephanie?"

"Well not with the pastry chef. Yes, with Stephanie."

"Not all that much," Marc said, not wanting to start trouble for either Eva or Stephanie. "I was teasing you. He only goes up there in the mornings. I guess that's the time you go to the gym so you've been giving him a pass to go to the simulator."

A successful litigator, who long ago learned her face should never reveal what she's thinking, Eva remained expressionless. But Marc knew Eva well enough to intuit that what he'd just said surprised Eva. She had no idea that's where Claude was going every morning. Marc couldn't possibly have known that Claude had told Eva he was going to swim, take a walk around the upper decks, or join a Pilates class many of those mornings. But Marc knew something was amiss.

"Thanks, buddy. I appreciate that." Eva took a deep breath which Marc took as a sign she was relaxing just a bit. "I'm going to ask you something as a friend—please take it easy on the Claude and Stephanie jokes in front of others. I'm not sure what's going on, but I don't like to air my personal affairs in public. Of all people, you should know that." She paused before continuing. "And I meant what I said. If that little whore responds to him, even in the slightest, she's gone. Do you understand?"

"Yes, Eva, I think we can agree you've made yourself quite clear on that. I can promise you this—as a friend. If I notice anything going on, I'll let you know. And I'll be sure not to let anyone else know." He thought about telling Eva that any problem she might be having with Claude might be attributable to Claude, and not

Stephanie, but he thought better of it. Marc thought about what an idiot Claude would be to screw up a relationship with Eva. On occasion, and this was one of those occasions, his mind flittered back to the way Eva had introduced him to tantric sex when they vacationed together those years ago. And how Eva was so beautiful, kind, loving, and generous. Only a fool would screw that up.

"I know I can always count on you. By the way, I was going to ask if you and Karen would like to join me and Claude for dinner one night. Check your calendar and let me know your availability, and we can take it from there."

Marc held the door while Eva left the room. As he watched her white pants sashay through the opening, the happily married Marc Romanello let his mind briefly wander to a place he tried not to visit anymore.

Chapter 28
A Party Invitation

While the board was going about its business, Harrison Marshall enjoyed breakfast in Schooner's. Upon returning to his visitor flat, his plan was to change into a swimsuit and spend some time luxuriating at the pool. The seas were calm and the wind robust—the perfect time to bask in the sun without feeling the ill effects of the Indian heat. The red message light on his phone was blinking so he consulted the handy reference card on the desk and figured out how to retrieve his message. He smiled when he heard Stephanie Holsson's voice.

Hey, I'm not sure what you're up to today, but even if you don't feel like practicing, do you mind popping into the simulator for a second? I've got kind of a weird question to ask you.

As instructed, he pushed #2 and the phone rang at Stephanie's desk.

"Hey, did you get my message?"

"Yup. That's why I'm calling. I was just about to hit the pool. Would this be a bad time for me to stop by?"

"No, it's perfect. C'mon up."

"See you in five minutes."

The unbridled enthusiasm in her voice caused Harrison to smile, even more broadly. He changed into his pink whale printed Vineyard Vines swimsuit and slipped his key card, phone, ear buds, and sunscreen into the pockets of his fluffy white Paradise robe. With his sunglasses perched on top of his curly light blond locks, and his feet ensconced in the ship's white flip-flops, he took the elevator to the ninth deck and headed to the simulator. Stephanie took one look at him and laughed.

"You're definitely not here to hit golf balls, are you?"

"I told you. I'm going to the pool to get a little exercise this morning. What's up?"

With a giggle that approximated that of a freshman coed who had just been invited to her first sorority rush, Stephanie left her desk, walked behind Harrison, and shut the door. For his part, Harrison remained fascinated by the length of Stephanie's legs. In fact, every time he saw her, he continued to be amazed that her legs were so much longer than he remembered the time before, even if it had been only hours.

"This is going to sound crazy, but I've got something to ask you. On the last Friday night of every month, the crew has a party below deck in our lounge. Every month, there's a different theme, usually depending on where the ship is. This month's theme is a costume party. But not just a regular costume party. We're each supposed to dress as our favorite character from a movie. And I was thinking . . ."

"I know exactly what you are thinking. Mia Wallace, from *Pulp Fiction*, am I right?"

"Yes, but that's not all. I wanted to know if you'd like to join me. It would be so much better if we could do it together. You know Mia Wallace and Vincent Vega."

"I've never thought of myself as John Travolta, and you certainly don't look like Uma Thurman with black hair." They both laughed at the thought. "But it does sound kinda fun. Am I allowed to be there though? If it's only for crew, how do I get to be invited?"

"I'm working on that. Suite owners and their guests are not permitted to go below deck. Supposedly, that's to avoid any hanky-panky with the crew. If you could see our crew cabins, you'd know that's never going to be an issue. Most of us have bunk beds and some of the boys in engineering share three to a cabin. If someone in the crew was going to fool around with one of the suite owners,

I assure you that would happen in the owner's suite. And it does, between me and you.

"But anyway, since the manifest shows that you came on board alone—not as the guest of an owner—I'm trying to find out if that prohibition applies to you. I just think it would be such fun for us to go as Travolta and Thurman. Are you a good dancer?"

"Slow down a second. I don't want you to get in trouble for doing anything you shouldn't be doing. If there's a rule saying the party should be only crew, don't violate it on my account. I'm not worried about me, I'm worried about you. Especially with everything you've told me about Eva having it out for you."

"I know, I know. But I just want to have fun. It would be such a great idea and I can't imagine why anyone would get their knickers in a bunch over that. I've asked my friend Candy Podeski what the rules are. Have you met her? She's the Sales Manager on board. Really stunning blonde with big boobs."

Harrison smiled at Stephanie and knowingly dropped his gaze to her chest.

"That description seems to fit a lot of people around here."

"No, I mean she's got *great* tits," Stephanie explained, holding her hands out in Dolly Parton fashion. "There are a few other interesting things about Candy too, but nothing you need to worry about. At least not now. The same as Eva gets wonky about Claude hanging around me, I'd do the same if I saw you hanging around Candy. So steer clear of her."

"Then, why'd you tell me about her?" Harrison asked playfully.

"I didn't *tell* you about her. I just said that I asked her if it would be all right for you to come to the party."

Stephanie took a step closer to Harrison, cocked her head sideways, and gave an impish smile.

"I really, really want you to come with me. Will you? Please? Pretty please. Pretty please with sugar on top."

"Hey, that was the Wolf's line when he told Vincent and Jules to clean the blood car. *Pretty please with sugar on top.*" Harrison glowed with pride at remembering yet another *Pulp Fiction* line. "Here's the deal. I'd love to go with you. It sounds like great fun. But only if you promise you won't get in trouble."

Stephanie hopped three times on her toes, clapping her hands, again like a giddy college coed. "I promise I won't get in trouble. At least not for that," she added as she leaned forward and gave Harrison an unexpected kiss on the cheek. "If I'm going to get in trouble, it's going to be for something good. Something worth it." She smiled and although he didn't know precisely what song she was singing, he was confident he knew the melody.

"The only thing is I didn't bring anything aboard that looks remotely like what Travolta wore in that movie."

"Don't worry about that. I'll take care of it. I'll take care of everything. Just promise me you'll come. And that you'll dance with me."

"I promise," Harrison pledged, anxious to get to the pool before his swim trunks exposed the degree of his growing arousal. "You get permission and I'll be there."

If the kiss on the cheek was unexpected, Harrison was totally surprised when Stephanie hugged him tightly and whispered in his ear.

"Thank you, thank you. You have no idea how much this means to me."

It might not have been clear to Harrison how much it meant to Stephanie, but it was unquestionable that Stephanie knew what it meant to Harrison, at least in one regard. When she leaned tightly against him, she felt the extent of his swelling manhood.

Not wanting to make things, awkward, or to accelerate them in a manner Stephanie might not have intended, Harrison took a step back.

"Well, this was an unexpected surprise—in more than ways than one," he confessed. "I need to go to the pool, listen to some music, and process all this. I thought I was coming on board to have some fun and better my golf game. And now . . ."

"And now what?" Stephanie asked.

"And now, let's just say things have taken a pleasant turn for the better."

"Good. I'm glad to hear that. Your golf game isn't so bad anyway. Now get out of here before my next lesson comes in and people start to suspect something between us."

"Is there anything to suspect?"

"I don't know, is there?" Stephanie asked as she tapped him on his butt. Harrison smiled, opened the door, and walked out knowing things were about to get complicated. Very complicated.

Chapter 29
Eva, Claude & Lorraine Have Dinner

Eva Lampedusa was caught in a quagmire. She thought Claude Azulai could be the guy for her. He was everything she dreamed she needed in a man—smart, handsome, rich, gorgeous, fun, and a great lover. He was an accomplished lawyer with impeccable credentials, and she had always enjoyed her jaunts with him. But they had been just that, jaunts. Every time they were together, it was to catch a weekend of passionate lovemaking, wining and dining, and being out and about town. Claude's passage aboard Paradise marked the first time they were spending a protracted amount of time together. As almost always happens in these situations, invisible cracks became visible, and visible ones became wider.

Claude was a flirt. Initially, Eva had found that to be one of his most endearing qualities. It was one of the things that attracted her to him. But when he started flirting with the reception staff, waitresses, maids, and then Stephanie Holsson, Eva didn't know how to handle it. A confident, successful lawyer, who spoke three languages, led a massive firm, was revered by Manhattan's business and legal communities, and knew she had looks and a body that were kryptonite to most men, Eva was not used to sharing the spotlight. It was new for her, and that newness bred discomfort. Intellectually, she was aware it was Claude who was the ill-behaving one, not Stephanie, but emotionally she couldn't bring herself to admit she might have made a mistake. That she might be entrusting her heart to a man who does not deserve it, or who will eventually break hers.

Eva kept a tight circle of confidants in life and an even smaller one aboard Paradise. Outside that circle, she didn't reveal herself to anyone. But within that circle, she sought counsel and advice. At the center of that circle was Lorraine Williams. Perhaps some of their closeness was bred of their commonality. A billionaire paperboard magnate in Canada, Lorraine relished her privacy more than anyone on the ship. She had endured a very public divorce that played out in the Canadian press, complete with salacious allegations about her ex-husband's five-year affair with the editor of a Montreal newspaper. She had also suffered a strained relationship with her daughters, one of whom came aboard Paradise the previous year and had fallen in love with one of the ship's chefs. Aboard the ship, Lorraine had become even more reclusive after she engaged in a relationship with a former Wimbledon champion who died of an overdose in her suite. Although Lorraine had no indication the lothario was into drugs, the entire episode remained the subject of dinner table gossip aboard Paradise for months.

So when Eva became entangled in her internal dilemma, there was no better person for her to consult than Lorraine, her mentor in life experiences. She decided a dinner with Lorraine and Claude would arm Lorraine with a matrix of data points with which Lorraine could guide her.

Dinner at Lucky Seas was usually quiet and that Thursday night was no exception. Long, perfectly polished planks of teak, beckoned diners into the red-hued dining room. Each table was meticulously set with a glass lazy Susan in the middle, chopsticks and a water glass neatly positioned to the right of grey and white chargers, on which darker grey linen napkins were perfectly folded. Several of the suite owners were eating ashore, and others had opted for the ship's other restaurants, Schooners, Leeward, and Shoreline. Lucky Seas had only four reservations that evening, so it was relatively easy for Eva to secure a table where they would be out of everyone else's earshot. When she made the reservation, Eva told

Amon, the maître d', that they would like to have a private table in the aft section of the restaurant against the floor to ceiling windows, and he accommodated.

Although Lorraine had briefly met Claude the morning the board convened in Eva's apartment, they had not been formally introduced. Of course, Eva had spent months sharing bushels of information with her closest friend, but Lorraine wasn't going to let that interfere with her right to cross examine Claude, especially in light of his conduct on the ship. For the next two hours, they drank, dined, and conversed about a constellation of subjects only three well-traveled international executives could navigate. Lorraine was enthralled by Claude's expertise in international politics and equally impressed by the vision he had for overhauling his country's constitution. When Claude excused himself to use the restroom, Lorraine shared her opinion with Eva.

"He's a real darling, Eva. You'd better keep him close or I might just ravage him myself."

"Really? Do you like him? You think he's a keeper?" Eva asked smiling, hopeful for a positive response.

"The man has an unusually high IQ and an unusually low body mass index. What better combination could there be?" Lorraine said as she raised her eyebrows in approval.

"I know. But his obsession with golf is something I need to come to terms with. I like the game as well. And I'm a far better player than he'll ever be. But I don't obsess about it. And I certainly don't spend as much time in that damn simulator as he does," Eva said, her voice sounding nowhere near as cheery as it had been seconds earlier.

Lorraine leaned forward to be certain she couldn't be overheard. "That's because you're not impressed by a Swedish ex-model who could grace the pages of the Sports Illustrated swimsuit edition, or even Playboy."

"And he shouldn't be either. Not when he has me," Eva reproached.

"Honey, even when you put a ring on their finger, that doesn't stop them from looking," Lorraine said, holding her diamond clad hand up for Eva to admire. She had been divorced for over ten years, but she still wore her five-carat ring almost daily. "There's no law against that either. Look but don't touch. Just like we do with the guys in the fitness center."

Eva ignored Lorraine's latter comment. "OK. But other than that, do you really like him?"

"If I tell you *no*, will you promise to deposit him outside my door so I can explore the goods and come to my own conclusion?" Lorraine teased.

"You're evil," Eva shot back, grinning. "I don't share."

"Good, then keep him for yourself and stop being so jealous. And if the jealousy really gets to you, then you need to do something about it."

After he returned from the restroom and finished his second martini, Claude began to hold court, expecting to impress Lorraine further. It worked—until Claude twice addressed the waitress as *sweetheart*. But perhaps his greatest transgression was his repeated references to Stephanie Holsson and the enjoyment he'd been experiencing from his time in the golf simulator.

"Whoever had the idea to install a golf and tennis simulator on the ship is a perfect genius. I mean, what could be better than having a morning tea and going upstairs to take a golf lesson? In fact, your golf pro has been kind enough to offer me coffee cake these past few days."

"Oh, she has, has she?" Eva asked, her tone doing little to hide her indignation. "Has she managed to keep her clothes on, or did she offer you that too?"

"Of course not. What do you mean?"

Eva wondered whether it was possible Claude had not heard about Stephanie's transgression at the Chaweng Beach Resort. But she decided not to go down that path. She loved Claude. Lorraine loved Claude. He was salvageable. Stephanie was not. She had to go.

Chapter 30
Craig and Claude in the Simulator

On occasion, Paradise was forced to alter her itinerary for reasons unforeseen months, weeks, or even days earlier. It's journey through India was one of those times.

Bunkering, or fuel purchasing as they called it at sea, was arranged many months in advance. In fact, on occasion, the ship's management team purchased diesel oil futures a year or two in advance, a standard practice in the maritime and aviation industries. When Paradise left Mangalore, it was set to dock in Goa for two days, primarily to bunker 500 tons of VLSFO, the fuel utilized by Paradise and most other cruise ships. With Paradise averaging twenty tons of fuel per day while cruising at twenty-five knots, that would be enough of the black gold to carry them for nearly a month.

The fuel had been quoted at $480 per ton, but when Captain Pugliese radioed ahead to confirm the arrangements with the port agent in Goa, the agent quoted a price of $690 per ton *due to unforeseen circumstances*. The captain, assisted by Paradise's general manager and board chairman attempted to explain the contractual arrangement with the port agent, to no avail. It remained unclear whether the agent was unwilling to honor the contracted price or was just in the market to extort Paradise out of an excess of $100,000. In any event, Marc Romanello and Eva Lampedusa made the final decision. They instructed Captain Pugliese to bypass Goa and arrange for the acquisition of fuel in Mumbai, a much larger city.

The details of these negotiations were not shared with the suite owners and guests. They were not secretive, but the board tried to spare everyone the gory details of each executive decision. It was not to hide anything, but to avoid the predictable criticism that would come from the Gripers. The board simply directed the front desk team to inform everyone that Paradise would enjoy two more sea days as they traversed the west coast of India, and that tours of Goa had been cancelled.

Lior Perlmutter, Oliver Rasmussen, and a few other malcontents darted to the bridge to make their own inquiries of Captain Pugliese. The bombastic skipper took no issue with their questions or criticisms. He even rather enjoyed reminding them he was the master of the vessel and suggested that skipping Goa was both his decision and his prerogative. Under the laws of the seas, there could be no debating a captain about maritime decisions, so the Gripers would have to just sit down and shut up. In fact, he used almost those exact words.

Word of the fuel extortion trickled down to the crew level, but no one seemed to care much about the details surrounding the decision. All they knew was there would be two additional sea days, and sea days meant all aspects of the ship would become busy. Owners and guests would not be leaving the vessel at all. The teams from the wellness center, fitness center, concierge desks, and food and beverage department all huddled as their managers laid out revised staffing requirements and the hours that would be required. Such staffing changes were not unusual aboard Paradise. The staff actually enjoyed having their routines mixed up now and again. But everyone had to be ready to accommodate the potential new on-board demands. Especially if Peyton Flynn was somewhere aboard Paradise.

Stephanie Holsson was aware that sea days meant more lessons in the simulator and no golf outings on terrestrial fairways. She enjoyed many of the owners who were regulars in the simulator. Not only did she favor the time she spent giving them lessons, she appreciated their senses of humor, political persuasions, and diverse personalities. On the first sea day from Magalore to Mumbai, however, she was faced with a new set of dynamics, one she could definitely have done without.

There was a new name, Craig McDougal, on the roster of golfers who had signed up for lessons that day. Stephanie had never met Craig, but she had heard stories about him from Candy Podeski. Below deck, Candy regaled Stephanie with the story of how Craig had behaved so badly when she took him on a tour of the ship. Since Stephanie was about to endure Craig McDougal for a morning golf lesson, Candy spared no details when warning her friend about all the sexually suggestive comments Craig had made to her.

"When I walked him through the restaurants, he kept telling me he likes his meat juicy and tender, and sizing me up like I was a piece of wagyu beef," Candy had said, scowling with obvious disgust. "He even brushed up against me a few times, just so he could feel my tits, I think. Oh, and you should have seen his teeth. I know the Brits are reputed to have bad teeth, but he took it to a whole new level. Not only were they cragged, but they were also only slightly lighter than a Guinness lager." She shuddered ever so slightly before continuing. "He also made some kind of comment about satin sheets or being in the sheets with me. But by that time, I'd already stopped listening to him."

"Wait, isn't that the guy who raped his niece, or something like that?" Stephanie asked impatiently.

"Exactly. His sister's daughter. And his brother-in-law beat the crap out of him for it."

"Oh, shit," Stephanie remarked as something dawned on her.

"What?" Candy asked.

"He's my first lesson this morning." She rolled her eyes. "Just the way I wanted to start my day."

"You gotta do what you gotta do," Candy said.

"Ugh, this is going to be painful. Maybe he won't be as hard on me as he was on you."

Candy eyed her golfing colleague up and down. She playfully lifted the bottom of Stephanie's golf skort to view her long, tapered legs and then rested her eyes on Stephanie's breasts.

"Oh, he's going to be hard on you. And hard *for* you too, I'm guessing," Candy said, laughing hysterically.

"Well, then it'll be a short lesson," Stephanie promised. "I'm sick of being a male fantasy up there. There's more to me than legs and boobs."

"I know, but they're pretty good too," Candy responded, suggestively looking Stephanie up and down.

"Candy!" Stephanie shrieked.

"I know. I know. I was just kidding," said Candy.

"Ugh, between him and Eva's friend Claude, I'm having all the luck these days. Why can't guys like that take up hiking or something that doesn't involve me?" Stephanie asked sarcastically.

"Because then you wouldn't get all that attention."

"That's attention I can live without, for sure."

"I feel for you Steph, honest I do. But better you than me." Stephanie paused as a smile lit her face. "Remember the guy I met up there, in the simulator. And then golfed with. Harrison—the guy I told you about," Stephanie said, changing the subject. "The one I want to bring to the crew party."

"Oh yeah, I checked about that. There's no reason you can't invite him. And apparently many of the other crewmembers have met him and think he's a doll. So I'm sure there won't be any pushback. But keep going. Do tell."

"There's not much to tell. At least not yet. He's adorable and handsome and everything else. And he knows *Pulp Fiction* as well as

I do. But, more importantly, there's a real connection there. I can't put my finger on it, but it's like we can read each other's minds. And he has a delicious sense of humor," Stephanie said.

"Just how *delicious* is he?" Candy asked, flicking her tongue around her lips.

"Stop it! We're not there yet. Although I did kiss him. Only once. And it was on the cheek. He's too irresistible for me. I can't wait for you to meet him."

Stephanie stood in front of the mirror, flattened her skort, made sure her shirt was tucked in, and gently removed her lipstick.

"What's that about?" Candy asked.

"That's about not looking like a China doll when I meet that McDougal character."

"And you think that's going to turn him off?"

"Well, it's not going to be there to turn him on," Stephanie replied.

"No, but *those* are going to turn him on," Candy said, again looking at Stephanie's chest.

"With the mood I'm in, if he even *thinks* about rubbing up against me, I'll deliver a three wood to his groin."

"He might just like that."

"Not the way I'm going to do it," Stephanie assured her.

"Well, good luck. And remember, don't let these guys get to you."

"Oh, I can assure you. No one is going to *get to* me," Stephanie said as she left the cabin on her way to the simulator.

In the crew elevator to the ninth deck, Stephanie was reminded why she enjoyed her job so much. Her co-workers were pleasant, always friendly, and willing to help each other. As she exited the elevator and walked to the simulator, she was reminded why she enjoyed the suite owners so much. She walked past three of her favorite owners, each of whom said good morning and stopped for a brief personal conversation. This level of interaction didn't occur on land where she saw students once every other week for a lesson, and certainly not on cruise ships where passengers were transient strangers. On Paradise, she saw the golf regulars a few times a week, either in the simulator or on one of the outings she arranged.

When she arrived at the simulator, Craig McDougal was already inside. He had turned on the lights, fetched a couple of clubs off the wall rack, and even managed to turn on Stephanie's desk computer that fired up the simulator on the front of the room. These were things even the suite owners would never do.

Standing in the door frame, Stephanie bore witness to a few of McDougal's horrific swings. She also was treated to a view of him picking his underwear from his ass and rearranging his package. *This is going to be an adventure*, she thought.

"Hi there, I'm Stephanie Holsson," she said in her most cheery morning voice while entering the simulator. He jumped, startled. She cringed when she spied him undressing, and then screwing, her with his eyes.

"I see you've helped yourself to some clubs and balls, which is just fine. We usually don't have people other than crew using the ship's computers, but you wouldn't have known that, I'm sure."

As if he hadn't just been admonished, McDougal offered his hand and introduced himself. "I'm Craig McDougal," he said, his eyes never wavering from Stephanie's body. "I'm a friend of the Hirschfelds. Becky Hirschfeld, I should say. I understand Harris has been dethroned, so to speak, for doing bad things so I shan't identify myself with him. I only do *good* things," he said with an unnatural emphasis on good and a wink to boot. "I might buy one of the luxury suites if I have a good time during this visit."

Stephanie silently hoped McDougal would have anything but a good time if a good time was going to cause him to become a suite owner. And if he was going to have a good time, she certainly was not going to be any part of it.

"Since you seem to have been hitting some balls already, let me take a look at your swing and we can get started."

McDougal took a nine iron and hit four very errant shots that sprayed all over the front of the room. To be fair, the seas were angry and all but the sturdiest seafarers with excellent golfing technique would have had a hard time hitting the ball. An experienced and professional instructor, Stephanie went about applying positive feedback.

"I'm not seeing any consistent faults."

"That's a good thing, right? I've been playing for years, but I thought it a good time to get a little tune up, you know what I mean? That and Candy Podeski told me you'd be very accommodating and anytime I can hook up with an accommodating woman like yourself, I'm not gonna miss that chance," he said with a grin, displaying those same beer-colored teeth Candy had described only minutes earlier.

Stephanie made a mental note to pay Candy back for her suggestion. She ignored his latter comment and tried to revert their focus back to golf.

"You're right. Not having consistent faults is always a good thing. But I noticed that you have your right hand wide open," she said, grabbing a club of her own off the rack and demonstrating what she'd observed. "You'll want to turn that right hand more to the left so your right thumb points straight down your shaft." As the words left her mouth, she was aware of the potential sexual innuendos that could come in response to that comment. She was beyond grateful when McDougal didn't seize that low hanging fruit.

"Like this?" he asked as he rotated his hand in the manner Stephanie had just demonstrated.

"Exactly. And when you make impact . . ." Stephanie was interrupted by an assertive voice entering the simulator.

"Good morning. What's up, Stephanie?" Claude asked as he took a look at McDougal who was caught off guard.

"Good morning, Mr. Azulai. I'm giving a lesson to Mr. McDougal right now. If you'd like to come back in about forty-five minutes, I'll be free then."

"But the other day, I told you I'd stop by first thing in the morning. I presumed you wouldn't forget, and that I'd be the first lesson on your calendar today."

Stephanie hadn't forgotten a thing, and she resented the innuendo that she had. "I recall that you mentioned something about stopping by but we never really confirmed anything. Anyway, how does 9 o'clock sound to you?"

Claude was barely listening to Stephanie. He was sizing up McDougal the same as one would size up an adversary before a duel. Claude's shoulders grew visibly larger and his chest became puffed out as if he had swallowed one of the ship's life vests. He wandered over to the wall rack and pulled a driver off the shelf. He stood next to McDougal, stretched his arms, and prepared to take a practice shot.

"I'm not sure there's enough room in here for two people to hit at the same time without someone getting hurt," Stephanie instructed.

"Well, the driver's going to need some room so it would be best if this guy steps back a bit because you're right, there's not enough room in here for two people to swing clubs at the same time."

The last thing Stephanie wanted to deal with on a Friday morning—or any morning for that matter—was two strutting peacocks both of whom had made sexual overtures towards her. If only it were nine hours later, she could have a cocktail and let all this silliness pass. But it wasn't. It was 8:15 a.m., and she had to deal with it.

Claude walked towards McDougal, extended his hand and said, "Hi, I'm Claude Azulai. I'm on board with Eva Lampedusa. I presume you know who she is. The founder of this ship."

McDougal was flummoxed. He had signed up for a lesson, and Stephanie had begun instructing him before this guy just wandered into the middle of things. However, it was evident this new arrival was not going away easily and that he had some point to prove. McDougal was a blowhard, but he was a cowardly one. He had no interest in challenging anyone, especially if there was any chance he would not emerge victorious. Hitting on defenseless people, such as drunk women or even teenagers, was one thing. But picking an argument with someone who appeared to be toting an oversized chip on his shoulders, was another.

"That's fine. I really just wanted to check out the simulator and see what it's all about. I don't need any formal lessons. Besides, I need to go downstairs and crunch numbers to see which luxury suite I want to purchase," McDougal said as he replaced his club on the wall rack.

Candy had also told Stephanie there was no way Craig was going to buy a suite. For one thing, he lacked the necessary funds. And for another, his entrée to the ship was through Harris Hirschfield, who had been exposed as an embezzler and fraudster. Even if he could somehow overcome those two insurmountable obstacles, there was no way he'd be able to obtain the eighty-five percent vote required to be allowed to buy a suite. In sum, he was a non-issue aboard Paradise. A smarmy and loathsome non-issue, but a non-issue nonetheless.

Once McDougal replaced his nine iron on the wall rack, he strutted towards the door, but not before he helped himself to one last, disgusting visual undressing of Stephanie Holsson. Then he was gone.

"I'm glad that bloke is out of the way. Now, let's talk about me," said the self-assured Claude.

"I'm happy to give you a lesson whenever you'd like one, but I certainly did not have you on my calendar for this morning," Stephanie said, keen to remind Claude that she had not made any error.

"I know that. But you do now," he said, smiling.

"What do you want to work on?" Stephanie asked.

"My rotation. Do you remember the last time I was up here and we did that rotation drill?"

"I do." Stephanie was all too aware of how she had allowed Claude to stand behind her while she innocently demonstrated the proper rotation of her right hip, only to find him pressing his dick into her butt.

"Well, I've been practicing that move. I'd like to try it again, but this time I'll rotate my hips and you just watch how I do it. You can tell me if I'm doing it correctly."

That certainly sounded a lot safer to Stephanie. After jousting with the lecherous Craig McDougal, even for only a few minutes, the last thing she wanted was another man's sexual attention. Claude took three full swings, each time rotating his hips more than he had during their previous lesson, but not finishing his swing completely.

"You've definitely been practicing. I can see that. I can see how you've gotten more limber too. That's fantastic. And, by the way, something I didn't mention and that I always find helpful are the Pilates and stretching classes they have in the fitness center. They would help limber you up. But, anyway, everything looks good, but I'd like to see you finish your rotation more. At the end of your swing, your belt buckle should be facing the target line."

Claude stepped back and took a few more swings, trying to emulate what Stephanie had just described. He still came up short of doing what she wanted. On his last swing, he even lost his balance and fell off to his left. Stephanie explained the logistics of the turn and demonstrated it for him a few times. Perhaps because his attention was locked on Stephanie's adroitly shaped legs, he couldn't complete the swing the way she had done it. Finally, as she did with many of her clients over the years, Stephanie stood behind Claude, put her hands on his hips, and pushed his right hip around to exaggerate the motion she wanted him to experience. She did that a second time and had just stepped back when she looked up and saw Eva standing in the doorway of the simulator. Her mind was flushed with relief that Eva had not come in a few minutes earlier. Had she seen Stephanie standing behind Claude, with her hands on his hips, Eva would have fired Stephanie on the spot.

"Oh, a little early morning golf lesson, eh? I thought you were going to the wellness center," Eva said, her stare focused intently on Claude.

"I was. But I couldn't get this hip rotation thing out of my head. I thought I'd come up here and ask Stephanie to help me straighten it out," he said, nodding towards his statuesque instructor.

"You do remember I'm an eight handicap, don't you? Don't you think I would've been only too happy to help you with your swing. I'm sure Stephanie is more than capable, but it would've been nice if you had asked me. It would also have been nice if you hadn't lied and told me you were going to the wellness center."

Eva was angry. She never lost her temper on the ship the way Marc or Mario did, but the anger was obvious nonetheless. Her radiant smile was gone and the spaces where her once gentle blue eyes had been located were now occupied by blue guided lasers. Thankfully, at least from Stephanie's perspective, those lasers were locked on a male target, and not on her for a change. Stephanie knew she had done nothing wrong, and she knew Eva could see that. Stephanie didn't seek out Claude. Stephanie wasn't the one who had lied about where she was going. She was the innocent, at least on this occasion.

"Finish up your lesson and then come up to the suite. I'd like to talk," Eva demanded of Claude.

Stephanie exhaled with relief, recognizing that Eva's wrath was directed solely at her pupil, and not at her. However, that relief was short lived when Eva added, "Take your time though. I wouldn't want you to miss any time with our resident swimsuit model."

With that, Eva turned and marched out of the simulator, her fury evident to anyone within fifty feet. Stephanie was certain Claude would follow her but to her dismay, he didn't. Instead, he remained in the simulator, another twenty minutes, trying to perfect that element of the golf swing that eluded him.

Near the end of Claude's time there, Caitlin Cappilletti wandered into the room, looking almost dazed. Claude didn't notice her immediately, but Stephanie did and turned to greet her. No sooner did Stephanie open her mouth, than Caitlin asked, "Do you think I could learn to play golf?" And then answered, "No, you don't have enough patience." Stephanie wasn't attuned to Caitlin's propensity for speaking to herself so Stephanie launch into her formal introduction.

"Hi, I'm Stephanie Holsson, the golf pro. How can I assist you?"

Caitlin seemed to snap back to reality, asking, "My, aren't you the prettiest woman on the ship?" Before Stephanie could even blush, Caitlin answered, "I'd vote for the Sales Manager though."

"Excuse me?"

"I'm leaving now," said Caitlin as she turned and walked out of the simulator.

"What the hell was that?" asked Claude, his face scrunched.

"You got me," said Stephanie, her eyes bulging like she'd seen an apparition. "Strangest thing I've seen in quite a while. And around here, I've seen some pretty strange things." She chuckled, grateful for the comedic distraction.

After the morning's misadventures were behind her, Stephanie sat and looked at her computer screen. It was only 9:30 a.m., and she was already drained. At least she had no further lessons scheduled all morning so she had a chance to confirm the golf outing she had arranged for the ship in Mumbai. The owners and guests were scheduled to play at the Bombay Presidency Golf Club, a location that sounded regal but that Stephanie knew approximated a low class public course in the United States. As the face of the golf program, she always suffered the blame when the courses were not up to snuff for the arrogant suite owners aboard Paradise. Stephanie knew they would all be disappointed with the outing in Mumbai, but there was nothing she could do about it. It was not her job to build golf courses. Nothing about her day was going well until her phone rang shortly after noon.

"Hi Steph. It's Harrison Marshall."

Her eyes lit up, and she sat erect in her seat. She knew exactly who it was before he even said anything.

"Oh, hi, Harrison. I was just about to call you," she said, careful not to point out that she knew who was calling when his name displayed on her desk phone.

"So are we on for tonight? Were you able to get permission for me to attend that crew party?"

"I certainly did. I spoke to Candy. I told you it wouldn't be any problem. She's dying to meet you, by the way."

"Oh, she is, is she? And why is that?"

"Let's just say I've told her some things about you."

"Hopefully not that I am an atrocious golfer, and you never want to be seen on a course with me again."

"No, silly. Not that. But what a girl tells her girlfriends in confidence is kind of a big thing. It's a secret. Candy and I have lots of secrets. I thought I told you that."

The breadth of Stephanie's smile was apparent to Harrison even through the phone. There was something about her voice that excited him.

"Anyway the party starts at nine o'clock. Those things always begin late below deck because we have to take care of all you fancy people first," she teased.

"Great. I'm excited. I can't wait to meet Candy and all your other friends. By the way, you said it's a costume party and I'm supposed to go as Vincent Vega. That's great except, like I told you, I don't exactly have a costume like that with me on the ship."

"And like *I told* you, I didn't think you would, so I've taken care of that. I hope you don't mind, but I've taken the liberty of securing a bolo tie, and a cheap looking gangster style jacket for you. Forty long. And black boots, size ten. I hope that's all correct. I presume you travel with a white shirt?"

"I do. And that's perfect? How'd you know my size? And where'd you get that stuff on a ship?"

"A girl knows these things. Did you think you were the only one sizing someone up while you were with me? I noticed a lot about you."

"Like what else?"

"Like I'm not telling. Oh, and don't forget that there'll be dancing at the party tonight. Maybe even a contest. So wear comfortable shoes. Are you up for that?"

"Sure. If I'm coming as John Travolta, I'd better be able to dance, right?"

"Not John Travolta, Vincent Vega. You'd better start getting in character now, kiddo." Stephanie inhaled and channeled her inner Uma Thurman. "I wanna dance. I wanna win. I want that trophy so dance good."

"Yes, Mrs. Wallace. We'll win," he said, chuckling.

"Good. I'll have housekeeping deliver the stuff to you within the hour. Unless you want to come up here and pick it up yourself."

Harrison wanted to run upstairs right away so he could spend time with Stephanie. But he thought better of it. He decided to downplay the feelings he was having for her until he was certain she felt the same way about him.

"You could always bring it to my visitor flat," he suggested.

"What? And get fired? Crew are never allowed in owners' suites or visitor flats," Stephanie explained. "I told you that already."

"Wishful thinking," he ribbed. "I guess I don't understand all these rules. Owners and their guests can't go to the crew bar, but untethered visitors can. That doesn't make much sense to me."

"Nor to me. But that's the way it is. And after all that happened this morning, I can't take any chances."

"What happened this morning?"

"It's a long story. I had to deal with Claude again. He came upstairs for a lesson and Eva walked in."

"So?"

"So I was lucky she didn't come in a minute earlier. I had my hands on Claude's hips and was showing him the proper way to rotate through his golf swing. If she had seen that, she would've taken his club, and slammed me in the head."

"I'm still not sure I understand the problem," Harrison said.

"I don't either. At least not completely. I think there are problems between them, and I just got stuck in the middle, although I'm not really in the middle at all. That and the fact he lied to her. Apparently, he told her he was going to the wellness center, and she found him in the golf simulator. She rarely comes up here when I'm here, so I'm guessing she came on the prowl looking for him. Anyway, it was uncomfortable, and I don't need any more tension with Eva."

"Sounds like a generally crappy morning."

"Oh, and then the oddest thing happened. Some lady wandered into the simulator talking to herself. I didn't know what she was up to at first. She asked me a question and then answered it herself. I introduced myself to her, and she did it again. There's definitely something wrong in her head. It was kind of amusing though. A welcome change from the other stuff."

"Sounds like an all around bizarre day."

"You have no idea. There was another guy before that. A real womanizer. There are some crazy stories about him. I'll tell you tonight after a few drinks."

"Are you sure you wouldn't like to invite one of these guys to the party instead of me?" Harrison trolled.

"I'd rather lick a bus."

"How is it that you attract all the sex starved men on the ship?"

"Like you?" she baited.

"How do you know if I'm sex starved?"

"Well, are you?"

"That's a loaded question. I guess you'll have to find out for yourself."

"Oh really?" she said, drawing out the second word to last nearly three seconds.

"Yup. Now if you'll excuse me, I was on the way to Sheik Shack to get a burger. A big kahuna burger, actually. That's a Hawaiian burger. I ain't never had one myself yet," Harrison said, once again digging deep into his *Pulp Fiction* repertoire.

"Very good. That's Jules, not Vincent. But at least you're in the *Pulp Fiction* state of mind.

"Oh, one last question. Where is this party?"

"Good point. The crew lounge is called Poseidon. We named it that ourselves because we're the gods of the seas around here. Not the rich people who just write checks to pay the bills," she said with more than a hint of disdain in her voice. "It's below the floors you're allowed to visit. I'll tell you what. Meet me outside the fitness center at 9 o'clock. There's a back staircase from there that takes us right down to the crew level."

"I'll be there. With my bolo tie and gangster jacket. Thanks for that, by the way."

While the phone call had been short, the tenor of it changed the entire direction of Stephanie's day. She reverted to her perky, effervescent self, smiling warmly to all those who came her way. She could even deal with Claude Azulai or Craig McDougal, though those were the last people she hoped to run into.

Stephanie's morning seemed long because so much had gone on in such an abbreviated time. Her afternoon was going to seem even longer because there was so little going on. She called her mother, called her grandmother, and even called her college roommate. Although no one questioned her explicitly, they could each sense Stephanie's happiness. She spoke rapidly, took a few breaths, and giggled regularly. Since Stephanie had experienced more than her fair share of heartbreak, every woman in her life was happy for her.

Below deck, word was spreading among the crew that Stephanie had invited the sexy guy from La Jolla to the crew party that night, something that had never been done before.

Chapter 31
Eva Makes Decisions

Eva had had enough. When Claude returned to Eva's luxury suite, the lecture he received was stern and relentless. Wasn't she good enough for him? Didn't she satisfy him sexually? Wasn't she playful enough? Smart enough? Beautiful enough? Why did he have to fixate on that damn golf instructor? The one who took her top off and showed her tits to anyone who wanted to see them? Is that what Claude wanted, a bimbo for a toy?

At the conclusion of her diatribe, and as she observed Claude's nonplussed response to most everything she said, Eva concluded that Claude had to go. She also concluded that Stephanie had to go, but that was not a *right now* issue. She'd have to deal with HR and all the crap that went along with that. That would take time. Dumping Claude wouldn't.

Eva decided she'd tell Claude to get off the ship in Lakshadwep, Paradise's last stop in India before heading off to a three-week dive and snorkeling expedition in the Maldives and Seychelles. It was still two weeks away but hey, why not have two weeks of good hard sex before she cast him off? He'd been her only lover in a few years and she enjoyed the sex immensely.

Stephanie was another story. Eva knew that Stephanie hadn't really done anything blatantly wrong, but she was tired of seeing Stephanie's name in the middle of scandals involving sex. Well, not real scandals, but scandals Eva had ordained in her own mind. She was also just tired of seeing Stephanie. Part of her felt guilty because she appreciated that this was all Claude's doing. In her heart, she knew the golf pro had done nothing wrong. But she had developed an allergy to the young woman and she knew she would be sick as long as Stephanie was on board *her* ship. Eva would have to talk to Marc since he was the chairman of the board. He was also Stephanie's biggest champion among Paradise's management. Eva knew she'd have to build a dossier of offenses to satisfy Marc. In Eva's mind, and from a human resources standpoint, Stephanie's topless dance show in Vietnam was more than enough to merit termination for cause. There were hundreds of competent golf instructors out there, and Eva was sure Paradise would be able to find a new one—one who would remain dressed at all times.

Her main concern the rest of the day centered around Peyton Flynn. It was Friday of the last week of the month, and everyone expected the latest version of Peyton's Places to go live Sunday evening. There were enough signals that Peyton Flynn was in the area that Eva was fairly convinced she was onboard already.

Eva decided to meet with Marc that same afternoon. She wanted to bring him up to speed on where they were with all the potential Peyton Flynn sightings. She rang Marc's suite, and they agreed to meet in Sheik Shack for a coffee.

Marc showed up wearing a flamboyant Hawaiian shirt adorned with baseballs, pineapples, and Yankees logos only he could pull off. Eva hid a smile, still somewhat infatuated with the man who had become her best friend over the years. She briefly considered why she had fixed him up with Karen, rather than keeping him for herself. But she was happy for him, for them.

Marc sat next to Eva, close enough they could speak freely without risk of being overheard by the attentive crew or any passing suite owners.

"What's up, pussycat," he began.

Eva wasn't used to being addressed like that. As a consummate professional, she commanded the respect of her clients and law partners. If anyone else had spoken to her like that, she would have castigated them. But coming from Marc, she considered it endearing.

"I'm glad you're so chipper," Eva began. "I've been killing myself with all this Peyton Flynn nonsense."

"Yeah, so what's the latest?" Marc asked as he perused a menu he already knew by heart.

"You remember Mrs. Tarpley, the lady who wanted tickets for the India versus Pakistan cricket game? Well, the concierges were finally able to procure them for her."

"That's great," said Marc, motioning to Sammie, his favorite waiter, who stood waiting for some sort of signal.

Eva continued. "Not only that, but I authorized a complementary car and driver for her. If she's Peyton Flynn, that should earn us a boatload of bonus points, if you'll pardon the pun."

Marc winced, unimpressed at Eva's attempt at humor.

"Oh, c'mon," Eva said, playfully slapping Marc's forearm with her own menu. "At least I'm working while you're . . . doing whatever the hell you're doing these days.

"Anyway," Eva continued, "there's more. Not only was the staff able to accommodate Ms. Silverman's request for banana leaves after her sauna, but Elaine Dwyer learned that one of the guys on the engineering team is a certified SCUBA instructor, so she arranged for him to give Ms. Silverman the pool certification test she so desperately wanted."

"That's what we're reduced to? Banana leaves and SCUBA lessons?" Marc asked. With Sammie standing behind him, Marc pointed to his favorite item on the snack menu, coconut custard pie. Sammie made a notation and asked Eva if she would be having anything; she declined.

"That's what *I* am reduced to. You're the damn chairman of this thing. You could be doing some of this work, you know?"

Marc smiled. "But you look so cute when you get all wrapped up in this minutia."

Eva glared at him. She was busting her ass to save the enterprise from serious financial concerns, and Marc was cracking jokes. She continued, explaining to Marc that arrangements had been made for the rental of one of the lesser dining rooms in the Taj Mahal to accommodate the lady from New Jersey who had her heart set on hosting an event there, and she was thrilled with the outcome. The only thing Paradise could not coordinate was an oral surgeon to perform root canal on the woman from Australia. The ship's doctor had identified two possibilities but, after the front desk utilized one of the Indian-speaking bellmen to call their respective offices, Eva concluded that neither was safe enough to recommend. The guest in question was very prominent in Australia and had a long history of complaining to the press, and to her lawyers, when things went awry. Eva had decided the ship would rather not recommend a surgeon who didn't check out, rather than risk a procedure gone bad and the attendant attention and negative coverage the lady could visit on the ship.

"With my luck, Mrs. Bad Molars is Peyton Flynn," she said.

"As long as we handle it delicately and explain our rationale, I don't think she'll mind what we're saying. She might even give us a boost in her assessment for being so cautious and protective of our guests," Marc replied.

"I don't know. And I don't know about any of the other requests we've gotten this week," said Eva.

"Like what else? Besides what you shared at the board meeting the other day," Marc asked.

Sammie walked by and Eva waved him down. She pleasantly apologized for not having given him an order when Marc did. She asked for a black iced mocha latte with a double shot of espresso.

"Holy shit," Marc remarked after hearing Eva's caffeine-laden howitzer of an order. "Are you gearing up for battle?"

"That depends," Eva said stone-faced.

"On what?"

"Never mind. Let's finish this stuff and, if we have time, I'll tell you."

"Is this about Claude?" Marc asked, leaning end, even closer to ensure he was not being overheard.

"I said never mind." Eva was all business and Marc knew to stop teasing her. "One lady asked if we would allow her husband and daughters to land on our emergency helipad because they were scheduled to get onboard in Goa and we decided not to stop there."

"We can't do that." Marc said. "The helipad's only for medical evacuations. It really wouldn't bother me personally, but the Gripers would make a big deal of it. As soon as that helicopter takes off, each of them would want to be able to have a helicopter come in and out to ferry them to different cities. That just has to be a hard no."

"I know that. And that's what I told her. But you never know which one of these people is Peyton Flynn," Eva said. "Wait, you'll love this one," she said, softening up a bit. "A guy from London, really well-dressed formal looking guy, went to the front desk late at night and asked if we could get him some *safe female entertainment* when we get to Mumbai."

"I didn't know any women were safe," mocked Marc.

"Very funny, wise guy," Eva said.

"What did they say?"

"Donna Lafat handled it delicately. She told him we were not permitted to engage in any conduct on the ship that was illegal either in the port we are located in at the time, or our home port,

Miami. So, even though prostitution is legal in India, it's not legal in Miami. Of course, she didn't use the word *prostitution*."

"It's legal in India?" Marc asked.

"Yes. Is that something you'd like me to share with Karen on your behalf?"

"Very funny. Anything else?" he asked.

"A couple from New Zealand asked if we can get them drugs. I don't even consider that unusual since the staff gets asked for that at least a couple times a month."

"They do?" asked Marc.

Eva smiled. "I know, right? Well apparently they do. That was news to me too. I can understand people wanting to use drugs. It's a natural thing. But going to the staff on a ship like Paradise and asking them to procure drugs? That's insane. I mean, would they do that if they were staying at a Ritz Carlton or Four Seasons?"

"Especially since some of the countries we're traveling through punish drug possession with long prison terms, or even death. I remember Midnight Express," Marc added.

"Maybe I'm just being super sensitive this week because we know Peyton Flynn is in the area. Hell, I *know* I'm being super sensitive this week. But we've got to do what we've got to do, right?"

"Yes, but not if it involves bringing hookers or heroin onto the ship," Marc said.

Eva laughed. "That sounds like a modern-day version of truth or dare—hookers or heroin." Sammie reappeared with Eva's drink and Marc's pie.

"Oh, and don't forget about Crazy Caitlin," Eva continued.

"Yeah, I've heard some rumblings about her. What's that all about?"

"She asks questions and then answers them herself. Doesn't even wait for an answer," Eva said as she blew on her latte.

Marc shook his head in bemusement. "I'm just glad you're the one handling all this. If I heard about these special requests and oddballs, I have no idea what I'd say to some of these weirdos."

"Oh yes you do. I do too. And that's precisely why you're not handling them."

Marc smiled, amused. Eva was right. Marc would have told some of the women they were entitled aristocrats who needed to get over themselves, or that they were out of their minds—which they were.

"There's one other thing," Eva said as Marc was getting ready to take a bite out of his pie. He lifted his chin, the universal signal that begged for additional details. "Stephanie Holsson. She has to go."

"What's she done now?" Marc asked, bracing for the worst. With the pie in his mouth, he stopped chewing.

"Nothing really. I mean nothing worse than usual."

"Nothing is not a fireable offense, Eva. Even a hotshot lawyer like you must remember something about employment law from law school."

"I don't mean nothing. Well, kind of," Eva said.

Marc began chewing in earnest as Eva continued.

"Let me explain. I went up to the simulator this morning and saw her giving Claude a lesson. A golf lesson."

"She's the golf pro, after all. Unless I'm mistaken, giving golf lessons is the essence of her job description."

"Let me finish. She was standing very near to him, like right behind him. They weren't touching or anything, but she was pretty close. And there were smiles. They were giggling and talking," Eva explained.

"Let me get this right. Our golf pro was standing behind a golf student. And they were actually enjoying themselves? That's terrible. Fired? She should be hanged for something so horrible," Marc said in a mocking voice.

"Shut up and let me finish," Eva barked. One of the other suite owners who was at the counter ordering a sandwich turned suddenly when he heard Eva's strong admonition. She raised her right hand in a pseudo wave and took a tentative sip of her latte.

Eva turned her attention back to Marc and lowered her voice. "How would you feel if that was your wife? What if it was Karen up there, and there was a handsome man standing right behind her and they were laughing together while he was teaching her golf?"

"I'd be angry as hell," Marc said, deadpanned.

"Exactly. Because you'd be suspicious."

"No. Because Karen would be learning to play golf, and she'd eventually want to play with me. That's what would get me angry."

"You're an asshole," Eva snapped, even more loudly than before. The same man turned again and Eva shrugged her shoulders, palms up, as if to say she was sorry.

"I'm being serious, Marc. There's always been something about her that's bothered me. I just can't stand her being here anymore. I'm bringing it to the board on Sunday for a vote. If you're going to vote against me, I respect that. In fact, I expect that. But I wanted to give you the courtesy of a heads up before I bring it up," Eva said, her voice beginning to quake.

"Eva, slow down. I'm not going to go to war with you about this. If you feel so strongly that Stephanie needs to go, then she'll go. We can always get another golf instructor, but I don't like it as a precedent with the staff. Unless Stephanie's done something overtly wrong, we'd be firing her because you don't like the way she smiled at your boyfriend."

"*Done something wrong?*" Eva said, straining to keep her voice to an angry whisper. "Need I remind you about her burlesque show at the Chaweng Beach Resort? We were all over the freaking Internet. And, to make matters worse, that happened at a critical time when we were trying to sell a lot of the available luxury suites."

"You should have done something about it then if it bothered you so much," said Marc.

"Are you being serious? Or just dense? I *tried* to fire her. I directed *you* to fire her. It was in front of the entire board. You sat there and defended her and defended her until I changed my mind. I should never have let you do that to me."

"I'm sure there are a lot of things you wish you'd never have let me done to you," Marc said with a wink.

That caused Eva to react in a way Marc hadn't expected. She lowered her voice and said, "Marc Romanello, I enjoyed everything you did to me that weekend. And I sure enjoyed all the things I did to you. But that's not what this is about. This is about maintaining decorum on this ship, keeping our reputations pure, and making sure this ship never again appears in travel gossip rags."

"We can also thank Harris Hirschfeld for that. I think what he did was far more embarrassing to the ship's ownership than what a rambunctious young woman did after a couple of drinks." Marc held a piece of pie on his fork, inches from the side of his face, while he continued speaking. "He was one of our own, a luxury suite owner, a member of our board. And we caught him embezzling from the ship in three different ways. What does that say about our financial risk controls and assessment? Look, if you want to fire Stephanie, I'm not going to get in your way. Hell, I don't even think you need to convene a board meeting for that if you don't want to, but you're making it personal, and you need to separate that out. Stephanie's done nothing wrong since that day in Vietnam. You and I both know that. This is about you. You and your insecurity about Claude."

"OK, so I admit it. So what? It's about me being pissed about the guy I really thought loved me."

"Exactly. As long as you know that. This is a *you* issue Eva, not a Stephanie issue. Do what you have to do. I'll always support you over any employee. I've always respected your judgment, and this time is no different."

"Thank you. I'm glad you see it that way. And even if you don't, I thank you for allowing me to act on my instincts. They haven't failed me yet."

Chapter 32
The Costume Party

A few minutes before 9:00 p.m., Harrison donned his white shirt, bolo tie, ill-fitting jacket, and black boots and wound his way through the common areas of Paradise. He had even managed to style his hair with some sort of conditioner to approximate John Travolta's coiffed style in *Pulp Fiction*. Although most of the suite owners were still at dinner, or enjoying after dinner cocktails, he did run into a few, who glanced at him askance. He most definitely did not look like a multi-millionaire, or a guest of a multi-millionaire. He looked more like a car service driver who had just completed his eighteen-hour shift. Just as he arrived at the appointed spot, a robed Ms. Rasmussen exited the fitness center and looked at Harrison inquisitively. If utter disdain could be reduced to a single glance, Heidi Rasmussen had just perfected the art.

Rather than being shamed, Harrison rose to the occasion, looked directly into her eyes, and said, "You look so comfortable in that robe. You must not be wearing anything underneath it." But for the two inches of MacCallum he had inhaled before coming downstairs to meet Stephanie, he never would have said such a thing.

Ms. Rasmussen harumphed aggressively and shuffled off to the elevator, almost stumbling over her fitness center slippers. She most definitely did not look back.

Less than a minute after Harrison arrived, Stephanie was there as well. For a split second, he didn't recognize her. Stephanie's gorgeous blonde hair was tucked up in a black wig and she wore a white buttoned-down shirt, complete with silver cufflinks. She even held an unlit cigarette in her hand. She bore a striking resemblance to Mia Wallace, Uma Thurman's character in *Pulp Fiction*, only much warmer. Stephanie could do nothing to hide the sparkle in her eyes, and the glow that surrounded her entire face. She was a gorgeous woman attempting to portray a hard one, but her attempt had fallen short. Her covetousness for Harrison was patently obvious, and he was duly flattered. If anything, she looked even more attractive this way.

"Good evening, Vincent. Glad you could make it," she said.

"Wow, you look . . . fantastic," said Harrison, making no effort to hide his enthusiasm. If he wasn't supposed to find her totally breathtaking, he was failing miserably

"You think so? You really think people will know who I'm supposed to be?" she asked.

"By yourself, maybe. Maybe not. But together, I think we make a pretty convincing Mia and Vincent. By the way, what was the name of the song they danced to while they were at Jack Rabbit Slims in the movie?" Harrison asked.

"Tsk, tsk, I thought you knew everything about the film. It's called *You Never Can Tell* by Chuck Berry. In fact, he wrote it while he was in prison."

"I didn't know that," Harrison confessed. "What are the chances they'll be playing that tonight?"

Stephanie leaned forward, looked both ways to make sure no one was watching, and gently kissed a surprised Harrison on the lips. "They'll be playing it, Harrison. You can be sure of that. I've already taken care of it." Before he could say anything in response, Stephanie took his hand and, with her other hand, pushed firmly on one of the wooden panels that lined the hallway. It slid left, revealing an industrial-looking, concrete grey hallway, something the owners aboard Paradise would never see. She led him inside and slid the panel back into place. As Harrison's eyes adjusted to the bright lighting, he was overwhelmed with the enormity of what he was looking at.

"My God, it's like a little city back here."

"You have no idea. Most people on the ship have no idea. Even the suite owners who've been on board since the ship launched have never been down here. Frankly, we don't want them here."

As Stephanie began walking Harrison through the crew area, she explained what he was looking at. "We have over a hundred and twenty crew members living down here. We've got our own cafeteria, lounge, break rooms, library, pool room, laundry facilities, and all that crap. It's also home to the ship's laundry, wine cellars, meat lockers, food storage, owners' storage rooms, infirmary, jail, and a ton of other stuff. I would take you for a tour, but I only asked Candy about having you come to the lounge for the party. I wouldn't want people to get all excited if they saw you in parts of the ship that are off limits to guests."

"No, that's fine. I totally understand. I'm just amazed at the sheer magnitude of everything. You know what they say about sausage and legislation—we like the results, but we don't want to see how it's made. I guess you can say the same about a cruise ship's operations. But I *do* want to see how it's made, what goes on down here."

"Great, but not today. If you're really interested, it's my understanding you can pay $100 and get a guided tour of all this stuff. Heck, Candy would probably give you the tour for free. I probably don't even know all the nooks and crannies down here myself. But, for now, let's get to the party."

As they walked into the main hallway, Harrison felt himself become unbalanced. "Is it me or are the seas really rough tonight?" he asked.

Stephanie smiled. "Oh that. Well, there's a reason all the crew quarters are below deck. It's definitely rougher down here below the water line. I don't feel it anymore. None of us do. We get used to it after a few days at sea. And, after two or three months, even the most ferocious seas don't really faze us."

It felt totally natural to Harrison to have Stephanie lead him by the hand down the long corridor with the word *Broadway* painted in large white letters against a pale blue wall. Crew members were rushing by, most in uniform, heading to tend to one guest or another. For the first time, Harrison saw a small cadre of Filipino men wearing white jumpsuits, similar to what caddies wear at the Masters.

"Who are those guys?" he asked.

"They're part of the engineering team. They keep us floating and boating, as the saying goes."

"Why are they wearing all white?" Harrison asked as he noticed the dozen or so men wearing white coveralls standing in front of a large bulletin board. "I would think they deal with a lot of dirty machinery. Grease and all that stuff. Won't those uniforms get filthy?"

They kept walking while Stephanie enthusiastically explained the ship's policy. "That's one of the captain's directives. He's maniacal about keeping the engine room clean. Most ships' engine rooms are dirty. That's why their engineering crews wear navy or gray. Captain Pugliese insists on keeping everything immaculate. He's super OCD in that way. So, if one of the guys finishes his shift looking filthy, the chief engineer has to address it. He has to ask the guy what was going on that caused him to become so dirty."

"Sounds logical, but it also sounds like a lot of extra laundry work." Harrison was captivated by the sheer whiteness of his surroundings. The walls were white, the frames around the bulletin boards, safety signs, fire extinguishers, and crew photographs frames, were all white. It was as if they were in a hospital.

"I'm sure it is. But Captain Pugliese doesn't care about that. He's a bit arrogant in that regard. He cares about his ship and his crew. We all like him because of that. People who have worked with him for years would walk through a wall for him. He doesn't care if the owners have to spend more money to have housekeeping do extra shifts of laundry or even have to buy new uniforms for the guys."

"Wow, that's cool. I mean, it's nice to hear that he commands that much respect," Harrison observed.

"He's an amazing guy. Besides being arrogant, he's totally self-absorbed and bombastic. But if you're crew on his ship, you're one of his people. And Captain Pugliese protects his people like no other boss I've ever seen. For example, an owner once questioned why the ship needed a full-time golf instructor and suggested it would be more cost-efficient if I spent some of the evening hours waiting tables. The captain didn't even know me yet, but he called us both to the bridge and ripped the owner apart for insulting one of the crew and doubting my value to the enterprise. He actually made the owner apologize to my face. That was unreal. I can't imagine any other captain doing that."

"How'd that work out."

"I haven't seen that owner since. Not once. And that's fine with me. But more importantly, that story got around—not just with the crew, but with the owners. The bottom line is that, if you fuck with one of the crew, you're going to have to fuck with Captain Pugliese. And, believe me, that's not pretty."

"Well, I hope there are some exceptions to that. I could certainly envision a situation where fucking a crew member might be a wonderful experience, but I'm not so sure I'd feel the same way about being with him," Harrison said, being sure that Stephanie saw the way he was sizing her up and down approvingly.

Stephanie squeezed Harrison's hand twice, as if to give some sort of signal, not even knowing herself what that might be. Harrison snuck his hand around Stephanie's waist, pulled her close, and returned the squeezes. Although neither one actually understood the meaning of the signals they were giving, they both realized the effect of what they were doing.

Stephanie led Harrison down the hall towards Poseidon. A pair of swinging doors were painted to resemble an undersea experience, complete with fish, sharks, ocean turtles, and brightly colored coral. Stephanie pulled open one of the doors, exposing colored lights that were randomly strafing the floor. At least sixty people in costume were already laughing and drinking. Harrison smiled as he took in versions of Elon Musk, Brittney Spears, Stormy Daniels, James Bond, and dozens more. A few hearty souls were already dancing and obeying Pharell's command to clap along like a room without a roof. A few people stole glances in Harrison's direction. It seemed that most were more interested in the partiers' respective costumes than the presence of someone they didn't know. Many of Stephanie's and Candy's friends were aware Harrison would be the flip side of Stephanie's Mia Wallace's costume, but they were much more interested that Stephanie had bucked the trend of never inviting non-crew to a crew party. Perhaps no one had ever thought of it before, but Stephanie was definitely the first one to explore it as an option. It didn't take Demonsthenes' logic to deduce that if Stephanie was bringing a man to the party, there had to be some sort of romance between them. No one, not even the demonstrative Stephanie Holsson, would test the rules by bringing someone who didn't matter to her.

Harrison was amazed. He tried not to stare as he took in the scene unfolding before him. The room was immense, certainly by seagoing standards. It was as big as most rooms in many boutique dance clubs he'd visited ashore. And the technology was beyond anything he expected. There were thick steel bars all around the room securing different types of lighting to the ceiling. It seemed that each track held a unique collection of lights, but they all worked together like a perfectly choreographed dance routine.

The walls were decorated with massive photographs of ocean-going animals ranging from seagulls to radiantly colored fish to breaching whales. Many of the photographs had been taken underwater, lending even more uniqueness to the room's ambiance. Between the photographs, murals of seascapes had been painted on virtually every available inch of wall space. Harrison stood silently as he tried to digest the scene before him. For a moment, he even forgot Stephanie was at his side. He certainly had forgotten he was on a boat somewhere in the middle of the Arabian Sea.

"What do you think?" asked Stephanie, who was enjoying Harrison's incredulity.

"It's breathtaking. I mean truly unreal. This is way better than what the old people have upstairs."

Stephanie laughed. "Shhh, don't say that too loudly or they'll make us take it all apart. We did it ourselves. Or, I should say, they did it themselves. I mean, I did my part, but I didn't take any of the pictures or paint any of the murals. But the crew did all of it. Every photograph you see on the wall was taken by somebody in this room. And the pictures on the walls were painted by a handful of the women in housekeeping who were artists back in the Philippines." Stephanie looked at the ceiling. "The lighting was all installed by our engineers on their time off. Captain Pugliese was immensely supportive. He always ordered extra materials for projects above deck so the guys would have stuff to work with for our spaces. He says he shouldn't get any credit for this, but without him, we never could've done it."

"I'm just in awe. I never expected this. I don't know what I expected, but it wasn't this. Perhaps some kind of a simple tiled floor with fake wood paneled walls like we used to have in my fraternity house. But certainly nothing like this. Not at sea anyway. And definitely not down in the crew area."

Stephanie was proud of her environment and prouder still of her coworkers. She was already beaming with pride when she reached over and kissed Harrison on the cheek. "I'm glad you like it," she said.

"And I'm glad you like me," he replied.

A few of the female servers from the food and beverage department were standing together in the far corner of the room. When Stephanie kissed Harrison, the ladies' giggling and whispering set a fairytale-like spell over the room. Something magical was in the air and whatever it was, Harrison didn't want it to end.

"So this is Vincent Vega?" asked a seductress in tight black, shiny pants, an off the shoulder black sweater and wildly teased blonde hair.

"Candy," Stephanie screamed. "You look outrageous. I love your costume. Harrison, look at her. Doesn't she look just like Olivia Newton-John in *Grease*?"

"She certainly does. And that makes me a lucky guy. I mean if I'm John Travolta, I get my choice of Uma Thurman or Olivia Newton-John tonight."

Stephanie turned towards Harrison and pressed herself straight up against him. She put both arms around him and pulled him in tightly. "*You most certainly do not*," she said. "You are Vincent Vega tonight, and my husband, Marcellus Wiley, told you to take me here to dance. If you don't behave and dance with me—and only me—I'll tell him that you gave me a foot massage. And you remember what happened to the last person who gave me a foot massage."

"I know, I know, he got thrown out of a fourth story window," Harrison said, repeating one of the oft-cited lines from *Pulp Fiction*.

"Exactly. And being thrown from the fourth floor of the ship would put you in a very undesirable situation." Stephanie squeezed Harrison and made the introduction. "Harrison, this is Candy, my very best friend on the ship. And, Candy, this is Vincent Vega, *not* John Travolta. So, if you even think of putting your hands on him, I'll have Samuel L. Jackson blow a hole right through your head."

"Pleased to meet you," Candy said, extending her hand to Harrison. "I know I owe you a phone call and a tour of the ship. I've heard a lot about you. We all have. I'm thrilled Stephanie was able to convince you to come down and join our little party."

"It didn't take that much convincing," Harrison confessed. "When she told me it was going to be a costume party, I couldn't resist. In fact, when I first looked at Stephanie, I couldn't resist." Harrison fixed his gaze on Stephanie as he laid bare his first real articulation of his feelings for her.

"Aw, isn't he sweet?" Stephanie said. "Now, c'mon, let's be cool like three little Fonzies and get something to drink." As they walked to the bar and Harrison leaned over to get their drinks, Candy made the universal OK sign to Stephanie behind Harrison's back. She then ribbed Stephanie by rolling her eyes skyward, licking her lips, and pretending to grab Harrison's butt. Stephanie flashed her a fake scowl, and the two women started laughing.

"What's the matter? What'd I miss?" asked a confused Harrison.

"Nothing, Vincent, nothing. But Candy and I have to go powder our noses. We'll be right back. Just don't get too friendly with any of the other women here. Remember what I told you about that window." Again, she kissed him on the cheek.

As much as Harrison enjoyed those flirtatious kisses, he was ready for something more. Something more passionate, more meaningful.

Candy and Stephanie disappeared, and Harrison slowly made his way over to a table where a dazzling array of food was displayed. At first, he wondered why the crew was being treated to such exceptional delicacies. But then he remembered who cooked them. The crew obviously had access to everything in the kitchens.

Donna Lafat from the front desk had checked Harrison into the ship when he arrived, so she recognized him and stopped by to chat for a few minutes. So did Elaine Dwyer, the ship's Entertainment Director whom Harrison had asked about some of the events on board the day after his arrival. He was starting to feel comfortable even though he was the only outsider at the party.

Before too long, Candy and Stephanie returned, bubbly and expressive. Stephanie grabbed Harrison's hand and led him to the dance area, which had become instantly crowded when Frankie Valli started crooning, *You're Just Too Good to be True*. They held each other as they danced, never even separating for those parts of the song that would have called for it. As the dance evolved, so did their expressions of interest in one another. For the first time, they kissed. Really kissed. Public displays of intimate relations were relatively rare among the crew. And, when they did occur, they usually happened in the shadows. Only a few times before had couples actually made out while attending a party in Poseidon. So the passionate make out session between Stephanie and Harrison had attracted most everyone's attention.

When the song was over, their embrace was not. They continued to hold each other and shuffle their feet slowly, even though the music had segued into ABBA's *Dancing Queen*, a song that most definitely did not invite slow dancing. At the end of the first verse, Stephanie led Harrison off the dance floor and back to the bar. She ordered a second drink and released any inhibitions as she screamed every line of the song, while jumping up and down. Stephanie was glowing with perspiration.

"What got into you?" Harrison asked.

"Never you mind, Daddy-O. When the dance contest begins, I expect to win, remember. But I don't think they're going to play our song for another hour, so we'll just have to keep dancing until then. Kind of warming up, you know. And when he gets ready to play it, Candy and I might just have to pop into the ladies' room and powder our noses again."

Harrison looked around to be sure nobody could hear him. He leaned over as he whispered to Stephanie. "Are you guys really doing the make-up thing in there, or are you doing the kind of lines that messed up Mia in *Pulp Fiction*? You know, where she overdosed."

Stephanie looked at Harrison, not sure how to answer the question. Had they been that obvious? She had checked her nose and upper lip before she left the ladies room to make sure there was no evidence of the Bolivian dancing powder anywhere on her face. But *powder our noses* was the exact line Mia uttered in *Pulp Fiction* before doing enough cocaine to cause her to overdose. She didn't know how to answer him, how receptive he would be if she told him the truth. So she eased into it to judge his reaction.

"What would ever make you think that we would do something so inappropriate?" she asked with a wry smile. She searched his face for any non-verbal clues about his reaction.

"Don't get me wrong. I'm not judging. I'm just asking. You guys went into the bathroom and you came back bouncing like a couple of Mexican jumping beans. We danced and you finally kissed me. Kissed me like I've wanted you to do for days now, I might add. But you didn't do it until you came out of the bathroom. And now you said you want to go *powder your nose* before we dance again. It's just something that popped into my mind, that's all."

"You could have kissed me before now too, you know," she said, clasping her hands and dangling them before her like an innocent schoolgirl.

"I've wanted to. Oh, how I wanted to, but I was trying to sort out all your shit with those guys. First Claude and then Craig. They were all over you. I didn't know if this was something you do with lots of men or if I was special." He looked at her intently before lowering his voice to signal a different message. "I wanted it to be special. I really did. I mean, I do. I still do. I just had to be sure you were alone. Available."

With the same degree of seriousness, Stephanie stared directly back at Harrison. "I am available. Completely available. At least for now. I'm kind of hoping it doesn't stay that way though." She paused before adding, "As long as we are, being honest, yes, Candy and I did snort a line of blow in the bathroom. I hope you won't judge me badly for that."

"I'll only judge you badly if you don't invite me to join you with the next one."

"Really? You'd like that too? That's crazy. Great, I mean. That's great. Sure, of course." Stephanie was relieved. She held his hand and squeezed it tightly. "The only thing is, you're the first invited guest ever to attend a crew party. I wouldn't want to screw up the precedent by having you get caught in the ladies' room with me and Candy doing blow. It wouldn't be a good look for any of us."

"Look, it's not all that important to me. It's just that if you were doing it, sure, I'd like to join you too. I mean, why should you have all the fun?" Harrison said with his lips tucked to the side in a grin.

"Harrison, if I do more lines, I guarantee *you'll* be the one having the fun. You can bet on that." Stephanie waved their clasped hands across Harrison's crotch dexterously enough to have the back of her hand rub slowly across his penis.

Harrison flinched noticeably in response to Stephanie's suggestive maneuver.

"What are you love birds talking about?" Candy/Sandy asked after completing her best Olivia Newton John strut in their direction.

Harrison dropped into character and did his best Vincent Vega. "Lovebirds? There's no love birding going on here. My boss, Mr. Marcellus Wiley, asked me to take care of his wife tonight. And that's all I'm doing here."

Candy's eyes darted from Stephanie to Harrison and back again. She said, "You know, I'm used to being the most talked about woman on the ship, the one everyone thinks is sleeping with all the owners and guests." She was right. Even though Stephanie was the tall Nordic bombshell, she was somewhat sequestered in the golf simulator. Candy, on the other hand, was known all over the ship due to her forward-facing role as Paradise's Sales Manager. It had to be her business to interact with every guest who boarded Paradise. And it was casually known that her interactions with at least a few male guests had been more than platonic. Candy was outgoing, effervescent, five years younger than Stephanie, and radiated an infectious smile and abundant cleavage. The two women together could turn heads anywhere they went. "I should probably thank you guys for shifting the attention away from me. People only surmised, or fantasized, who I was sleeping with. But everyone on the damn ship knows you guys are doing it."

"We're not though," Stephanie protested. "At least not yet," she added in a stage whisper.

"Well, if you don't hurry up and take this man to bed, I just might," Candy said, dramatically thrusting her attention-getting chest in Harrison's direction. "Maybe you just intend to tease the poor guy until he explodes. Besides, if I remember correctly, Vincent Vega never got it on with Mia Wallace in *Pulp Fiction* either," she reminded them. "So maybe you're destined to remain just golf pro and golf student." Candy and Stephanie exchanged playful looks.

"That's only because Mia Wallace overdosed, and he had to drive her somewhere to get her resuscitated. That and he wouldn't have wanted to be killed by Marcellus' people. What are you driving at anyway?" Stephanie asked.

"Well, I was just thinking that even if Mr. Travolta didn't score Uma Thurman, that same Mr. Travolta got busy with Olivia Newton-John in the sand," Candy explained as she sidled up next to Harrison who was thoroughly enjoying the attention.

"Exactly what are you trying to say? Are you trying to pick up my man?" Stephanie said, giggling.

"I thought you said you guys haven't done it yet. If that's the truth, then Harrison here is a ship virgin, available to all. Or maybe he wants to share us," Candy added with a conspiratorial smile. "That could be kind of fun."

"I'm sure you wouldn't mind that at all. But I certainly would. Heck, I haven't even had a test drive yet. So that's definitely not going to happen." Stephanie lowered her voice and put her mouth a little closer to Candy's ear. "Harrison guessed what we were up to in the bathroom before. He wanted to know if he could join our next little party."

Candy took a step back and feigned surprise. "Really? Well, I certainly have enough to go around. But what about the logistics? Where could we do it? We can't all three disappear into the ladies' room together. How obvious would that be?"

"We were just saying the same thing," Stephanie said.

"How about we go back to my cabin? We would be all alone there," Candy suggested.

"Don't you have a roommate?" Harrison piped up, finding his voice again after being the subject of so much arousing conversation.

"See that woman over there? The one dressed like Cher?" Candy asked, nodding in the direction of a dark-skinned woman with black hair that brushed against the top of her ass. The woman was holding court in a corner of the room, single-handedly maintaining the attention of four men. "That's Sarah, my roommate. As long as the party is still going, she'll be in here. And when it's over, she'll end up with one of those four guys, probably the tall guy dressed like Drake. I'm pretty sure she hooked up with him a few weeks ago, although she denies it."

"You're too funny," Stephanie said. "I'm going to get a sparkling water. Do either of you want anything?"

"I'm fine," Harrison said.

"I'll take another vodka tonic," said Candy.

"I know, I know, twist of lime, right?"

"How do you know me so well?"

"That's what friends are for," Stephanie said.

Stephanie pivoted and walked toward the bar in her best Mia Wallace imitation. Harrison was intrigued by what he was seeing. As Harrison turned his attention back to Candy, she boldly reached around and pinched his ass. He looked at her with a combination of surprise and suspicion.

"Stephanie and I are friends. We share everything. Like I said, I've got more lines for us to enjoy, and we can all go back to my cabin and do them together. Sharing, it's what friends do," she added as she ran her tongue over her lips.

Most men might have been overjoyed at the thought of doing sexually stimulating drugs with these two stunning women, both of whom expressed apparent interest in bedding him. But Harrison was not most men. He was not on the ship looking for sex. He wasn't really looking for anything. More importantly, he seemed to have found a special connection with Stephanie Holsson. He didn't want a few lines of coke and a wild night of an ill-advised threesome to interfere with what may become a real connection.

When Stephanie returned from the bar, *Satisfaction* was playing over the eight Bose speakers that were suspended from the room's ceiling. Not content to just stand there and tap her feet to the beat, Candy grabbed one of her friends and headed to the dance floor.

Harrison leaned over and whispered to Stephanie, "What if we don't wait for our song?"

"What do you mean?"

"I mean, would it be so bad if we left now?"

"I don't have the blow, Candy does."

"I don't need blow, do you?"

"No. But why . . ."

Harrison didn't know how close Stephanie and Candy really were. He didn't want to say or do anything that could interfere with their friendship. He had no idea what the future held for him and Stephanie, so it wouldn't have been right for him to rat Candy out for what she'd just suggested. Or for grabbing his ass. He didn't know if she was serious about it anyway. There were only a few things he was certain of. First, he didn't want anything to do with a threesome, second, he had no need for cocaine, and, third, he just wanted to be alone with Stephanie.

"Sure, we can go. I thought you wanted to stay so we could dance. Like in the movie," said Stephanie, concern apparent in her voice. "Was it something I did?"

Harrison again considered whether to tell Stephanie what Candy had said or done. He thought better of it. "Yes, it was most definitely something you did. It's the way you kissed me a few minutes ago. I don't know why we need to wait to do more of that."

Stephanie looked at Harrison, her relief immediately apparent. What was the point he was trying to make? "We don't. I just thought you were having a good time and wanted to stay at the party. And Candy has that really good stuff. I thought would be fun for us to enjoy it together."

"I don't need drugs. I need you. I was having a good time, but I have a feeling we could have a better time in my visitor flat than we could have in your cabin."

"I'm sure of that too, but I can't go there. You know the rules. Crew are not allowed into the visitor flats. You'll have to settle for my cabin. Will that be alright with you? I promise to make it comfy for you," she said, a smile radiating over her entire face.

"Screw the rules. I'm feeling amorous. Not just horny, but amorous. I don't want to have to squeeze into a bunkbed and risk the possibility Cher will walk in on us. Besides, I took the liberty of ordering a bottle of champagne and some flowers for you. They just happen to be sitting on the dining room table in my visitor flat. You wouldn't want all that to go to waste, would you?"

Stephanie hesitated. She thought about the consequences that could befall her if she were caught in someone's visitor flat. She was already on Eva's hit list and any more transgressions would result in her immediate termination. But she was feeling something special too. Something more than a bunkbed hookup.

"Oh screw it, let's do it. I wouldn't want those flowers to go to waste. We'll go back upstairs to the fitness center door where I met you. You can go into the regular hallways from there and I'll take the crew elevator to your deck."

"Great. I'm in 520," Harrison said.

"I know that silly. I checked that out after your first visit to the simulator."

"You did, eh? Why'd you do that?" he asked sarcastically.

"Oh, I don't know. Just in case, someone had a bottle of champagne there one day I needed to come help empty," she said, squeezing Harrison's hand and kissing him gently on the lips.

The plan was set. And overdue, in Harrison's mind. He didn't like the idea of Stephanie having to sneak up some back entrance though, like she was hiding something. But she was hiding something. And if she didn't hide it, they both understood she'd be out of a job.

They said their goodbyes to Candy who was surprised they were leaving so early. She shrugged her shoulders and raised her hands, effectively asking what she should do with the drugs. Stephanie looked around the room, pointed to Indiana Jones, gave Candy a thumbs up, and blew her a kiss. Candy returned the gesture—both to Stephanie and to Harrison. For a fleeting second, Harrison wondered what it would have been like to have been with Stephanie and Candy together. But the thought quickly evaporated as he realized he was about to be intimate with the woman who had suddenly made him happier than he'd ever remembered.

Chapter 33
Room 520

The setting was ideal. Two dozen red roses were nestled in an oversized vase on the dining room table. Next to them, a bottle of Veuve was chilling in a crystal ice bucket. And Harrison's Spotify playlist just happened to be playing *Strangers in the Night* when Harrison and Stephanie entered the flat. Housekeeping had been there sometime over the past hour, so the apartment was immaculate. In fact, it was one of the housekeepers who helped Harrison access the ship's Wi-Fi network, something that had challenged him earlier in the day.

It was the first time Stephanie had been in a visitor flat, and she wanted to make sure she didn't miss anything. She wandered about, taking in all the furnishings and appointments. She was impressed by the glass and chrome dining table, snakeskin looking dining chairs, and beige Ultrasuede sectional. The artwork was calming, featuring mostly nautical scenes, as well as a few abstracts.

In the bedroom, the blanket and top sheet had been perfectly turned down, and there was a piece of Godiva chocolate neatly positioned in the middle of each pillow.

"Did you do all this stuff before you came downstairs?" Stephanie asked.

"What stuff?"

"The flowers, champagne, playlist. You know."

"As opposed to when you were on your way up here?" he asked sarcastically. "I'm fast, but not that fast."

"You know, you've probably sent tongues wagging throughout the housekeeping department."

"I have? How?"

"Are you kidding? It's pretty obvious you didn't put the flowers or the champagne out for yourself. Unless you're some kind of a weirdo. Are you? If you are, I'd like to know right now. I don't do weirdos," she said in a twittering voice.

Harrison didn't answer the question directly. "I'm pretty sure the tongues were wagging as soon as we showed up to the party together. This just gives them a little something extra to wag about."

"But since they've seen us together, and seen this lovely display you've arranged, they don't have to be rocket scientists to figure out that I'm in your visitor flat. And probably not here for a putting lesson."

Stephanie paused for a second as a realization flooded her mind. "How many nights have you been aboard?"

"Five. Why?"

"And on those five nights, how many chocolates did they put on your bed?"

"I don't know. One? Two? Why?"

"Because I think they're supposed to put one piece of chocolate on a pillow for each person sleeping there. The fact they have two on your bed tonight indicates they expected you'd be having company."

"They're not idiots, you know. I assure you I haven't had flowers or champagne sitting out any of the other five nights. Flowers, champagne, my Frank Sinatra playlist. It's not really a reach, you know."

"Sinatra?" she shrieked with laughter. "Are you really that corny?"

Stephanie walked over to Harrison, stretched her arms around his neck and kissed him, their tongues remaining interlocked for more than a few seconds. When their lips parted, she stayed pressed against him and stared into his eyes. "I like Sinatra. I like corny. I like you. I don't know who you are or where you came from, but there's something about you."

"How do I know you don't just say that to all the boys?" Harrison teased.

"Well, I've never been to an owner's suite or a visitor flat, so that should tell you something."

"And below deck?"

"Pure as the driven snow," Stephanie professed, turning her face sideways and winking at him. "Now, since everybody knows I'm in here, it would be a shame not to open this bottle, don't you think?"

"Sure, but there's one thing I'd like to do first," Harrison said.

"What's that?"

He brought Stephanie in closely and reached his hands around her neck into her hair. When she realized he was struggling to remove her black wig, she said, "Wait, let me help you. There are all kinds of bobby pins in it, and I don't want you to get stuck to me."

"I'm afraid it's too late for that," he said, smiling. "I became stuck to you the minute I first walked into the simulator."

Stephanie grinned and shrugged. She unceremoniously unpinned the wig, tossed it onto one of the chairs, and shook her hair loose. She used her long fingers to pull her blonde curls down until they cascaded around her shoulders, where they had been when Harrison had first set eyes on her. They walked towards the table, and Harrison veered off towards the kitchen cabinets. He opened a drawer above the sink, pulled down two champagne glasses, and placed them on the table. He lifted the bottle, removed the foil wrapper, and dexterously twisted the metal cage seven times to the right. Stephanie tried not to stare, but she was fascinated by Harrison's skill and competence. Her passion crackled, the emotion bursting through her blue eyes. Holding the bottle in his left hand, he gently eased the top off. To Stephanie's surprise, it barely made a sound.

"Wow, that was impressive," she said.

"It was?"

"Yes, it was. Usually, champagne makes a loud popping sound. C'mon, you know that."

"Not in the hands of an expert, it doesn't."

"Oh, really? So you've got some kind of magic touch?" Stephanie whispered as she sidled up against Harrison.

"I guess you'll have to be the judge of that." Harrison lifted his hands and gracefully unbuttoned the top two black buttons of Stephanie's white blouse.

"What exactly are you doing?" she asked in an affected and surprised voice.

"If I have to tell you, perhaps we shouldn't be doing this."

"I mean, there's a perfectly full bottle of good champagne sitting in front of us, and we haven't had a sip yet. Isn't that some sort of a crime?"

"Right you are," Harrison said as he dropped his hands and turned to the table to fill both glasses. He raised his glass to chin level and toasted his new friend. "To new friends. And to the good that might come from my time in the simulator."

Stephanie smiled. "And to the good that might come from my time with your *stimulator*."

He smiled. They touched glasses and drank.

"Mmmm, that's good stuff. Aren't you glad we drank it?" she asked.

"I assure you we were going to drink it. It might have been off your stomach, or off your thighs, but I was going to drink it."

"Oh *really*?" Stephanie squealed. "Pretty sure of yourself, aren't you?"

Harrison looked her straight in the eyes. His seriousness was immediately evident by the directness of his stare. "Yes, I am. And, unless I misjudged things, I'm also pretty sure you're feeling the same way. There's a lot more I could tell you about the way I feel, or the way you feel. But I don't think it needs saying. The chemistry between us is magical, Stephanie. We're not teenagers. We've both been around. I don't know about you, but I haven't felt this connection for a long time, if ever."

Stephanie was overwhelmed. She would have made the same speech, if she'd only had the courage to do so. After the first time she'd encountered Harrison in the simulator, Stephanie told Candy all about it at lunch. And then again at dinner the same night. Every day, Candy was forced to endure whatever new feelings Stephanie had to share about her interaction with Harrison that day, and her fantasies for the future. In fact, Harrison Marshall was pretty much all Stephanie had spoken about the past week.

"I want to learn you," Stephanie said.

"I want to love you," Harrison replied.

By now, Harrison had taken Stephanie's hand and led her to the couch that faced the inky ocean that rolled before them endlessly. There was no one to see them there. No one for dozens of miles and even then, they could barely make out the lights from container ships heading south.

"You're right. Everything you just said is right. I'm not going to judge any of this, or judge you, or judge us. This just seems so unbelievable. But no matter how wonderful it is, how wonderful we are, I know I'm going to wake up one morning and it's all going to be gone," she said.

"It doesn't have to be," he said.

"Why?" she asked with a quizzical look. "Are you going to get a job on the ship doing . . . whatever it is you do in real life? Sail around the world with me for the next three years?"

"That's one option. But not the one I had in mind at this moment."

"Oh, exactly what's on your mind?"

"This," he said, as he put down his glass and resumed unbuttoning Stephanie's blouse. This time, she did not stop him. This time, she let herself get carried away by the moment, the passion, the promise.

The seamless removal of Stephanie's shirt and pants was interrupted only by their impassioned kissing. Harrison flung his loose fitting gangster jacket onto one of the dining room chairs. The next day, neither one would be able to remember who had removed the rest of Harrison's clothing. But it was off. All of it. He sat next to her, fully naked and fully aroused. It was only then that Stephanie realized she was still wearing her bra, the same type of black lace crop top bra Uma Thurman had worn in the scene of *Pulp Fiction* when she had been given an adrenaline shot after overdosing. She removed it. Harrison was stunned by the beauty of the woman in front of him. The only breasts he had ever seen more perfect than Stephanie's had staples in them, and were in the centerfold of his favorite January 1998, Playboy magazine. She was indescribably delicious in every way. Her skin was smooth and white everywhere except her arms and legs, which were almost cinnamon from all those days on the golf course. Even her feet were white, right up to the area two inches above her ankles where her golf socks came to rest. Stephanie had never sunbathed topless, Harrison concluded, because her torso appeared ceramic. There was muscle tone throughout her body, something he admired greatly. Many women were blessed with a fortunate gene pool that enabled them to remain slender most of their lives. But that slenderness often morphed into skinniness, something he did not find particularly attractive. On the other hand, Stephanie's body composition bore witness to the fact she worked out regularly and took care to keep her body toned.

Foreplay, if one could even call it that, was shorter than an eight-foot putt. Harrison's heartbeat was palpably elevated as he massaged her breasts with his hands and mouth, the breasts that had beguiled him all week. He wanted to speak but had no idea what to say. Moreover, it took all his effort to simply remember to inhale and exhale, while his mouth was exploring her body. But his desire for carnal satisfaction was mitigated by his genuine tenderness and feeling for this woman. Alas, he surrendered to those emotions and traveled back to her mouth for more passionate kissing while he held her close.

Stephanie felt smothered. She shared the same tingling and sexual desire Harrison seemed to be exhibiting, but she was tightly wrapped, as if in a cocoon. She had never been with a man who held her so closely, other than times when she was being consoled. She wanted to kiss his neck, run her fingers over his nipples, and reach between his legs, but she was unable to do any of that. Harrison was squeezing her so tightly she sometimes wondered where her next breath was coming from. Ultimately, she was able to free herself. Free enough to return some of the manual manipulation his masterful hands had been able to provide to her.

Eventually, they abandoned the couch, retrieved their champagne glasses, and made sure to remove the chocolates from the pillows for fear they would melt under the approaching waterfall of heat that would inevitably cover the sheets. For the next three hours, they were locked into every part of each other's body. Lips, breasts, thighs, and other parts were all kissed and admired, with equal abandon. After Harrison's final thrusts, as Stephanie's fingers dug into the clammy sheets and he exploded one more time with a guttural scream, they simultaneously released, collapsed, and panted—two passionate lovers who'd found their holy grail.

Stephanie turned towards Harrison and spooned him. She raked her fingers through his hair, firmly rubbing the back of his neck between her thumb and forefinger.

"Mmm," he moaned. "My mother used to do that to me when I was sad."

"Well, maybe I should stop. I don't really want to do anything right now to remind you of your mother." She smiled as she looked down at him.

"That's probably a good idea. My mother's probably the furthest thing from my mind. Although I can't wait for her to meet you."

The words seemed clunky. Ordinarily, Stephanie, or any other woman engaging in relations with a man for whom she had such strong emotional feelings, would be thrilled to hear that sentence. But they were naked at the moment. Aroused. And covered with each other's bodily fluids. It was a big bed, but not big enough for three of them. She released her hold on him, albeit only for a few seconds. Harrison sensed Stephanie's momentary retreat. He turned to face her and made his way up to her face. He held her head in his hands.

"What's the matter?"

"Nothing," she said. "It's just that . . . well, I dated a guy once who was transfixed with his mother. A real momma's boy. That's great and all. Except a guy doesn't want to screw his mother. That's when the intimacy ends and the nurturing begins. That's not what I signed up for." Stephanie snuggled tightly against Harrison's chest and ran her hands over his nipples. "That's definitely not what I want from you."

"I'm way ahead of myself. I know I am. But what's happening between us emotionally is way more than what just happened physically. I mean, this was inevitable. We both knew that." He looked into Stephanie's eyes, as if for confirmation. She did not disappoint. Slowly, she nodded.

"But you know what else is inevitable?" Harrison continued. "We are. Look, I'm not some kind of a crazy person who is going to propose to you right now and tell you I want to spend the rest of my life with you. That would be insane. You'd run right out the door. With your clothes on, of course." He smiled. "But I do. I do want to spend the rest of my life with you. I only mentioned my mother because I want her to meet her future daughter-in-law."

Stephanie said nothing. Instead, with a small tear forming in the corner of her left eye, she stared into the eyes of the man whom she longed to wake up next to her for the rest of her life.

Chapter 34
The Morning After

"I gave her more opportunities than she deserved. You know that, Marc. Now it's gone too far. She has to go," Eva yelled at Marc Romanello in her suite the Saturday morning after the crew's costume party.

Marc began speaking but Eva raised her right hand, shoved it forward, and looked to the ground. Marc knew to be quiet.

"She brought a guest to Poseidon. To a costume party. And don't you dare tell me, it was some kind of an accident, that he just stumbled in there. In addition, from what I hear, they were dressed like Uma Thurman and John Travolta from *Pulp Fiction*. Isn't that cute? Well, I'm glad they had their little fun. And there's no doubt they had fun in his visitor flat. Housekeeping reported there were two dozen roses there, as well as a bottle of champagne. From the little I know about this Harrison Marshall fellow, he doesn't seem like the type of guy who's going to wine and romance himself. Oh, and the final point, lest we forget, our own Levi Perlmutter, your nemesis, and the leader of Gripers, just happened to walk into Uma Thurman in the hallway at 6:30 this morning. She's gone. Don't even begin to try to convince me otherwise."

"I'm not so sure she wasn't allowed to bring a guest to the Poseidon party."

"You're not going to go there, are you?" Eva said.

"But you haven't really met him. He's a really nice . . ."

"This isn't about *him*. It's about *her*. He's not responsible for knowing all the crew rules. She is. This isn't her first rodeo, Marc. We both know that," Eva said. "I've got so much shit to worry about around here I don't need to think about our slutty golf pro. Our slutty *former* golf pro, I should say. I've got the ship's bond holders looking for money, Mitsubishi Marine wanting to know if we're going to make our payments next quarter, and this mysterious Peyton Flynn woman lurking somewhere in our midst. The last thing I need to worry about is which one of our next guests or owners is going to have an affair with our golf pro."

"I think you're upset because Claude . . ."

"You're damn right I'm upset. I'm fucking furious," she said, her face flushed. "And don't mention Claude. This has nothing to do with Claude. I don't know if he did anything with that little whore or not, but I know she violated the ship's rules last night with that Harrison Marshall guy and she's going to be terminated for it. I'll deal with Claude. Besides, that's none of your business, so I'll thank you to stay out of it. It's your job, Mr. Chairman of the Board, to tell Captain Pugliese that Stephanie Holsson is terminated effective the moment we dock in Mumbai."

Marc tried think of an appropriate retort. What came out of his mouth fell flat. "But we need a golf pro on board."

Eva looked at him stunned. "That's what you've got to say. *We need a golf pro on board.* You can be the damn golf pro for all I care. Tell Winchester to hire one. That's what we have a general manager for. So what if we don't have somebody in the simulator for a few days until we get a new golf pro? Do you know how many out of work golf pros are in Europe right now. I could probably find 300 from Ireland alone. Of all your pathetic defenses of that woman, that may be the weakest one."

Marc looked down, appreciating the ridiculousness of what he'd just said.

"When do we arrive there?" he asked.

"Monday at 5:00 p.m.. By 5:30, I'd better see that her key card's been disabled and she's no longer on my ship."

Marc had only heard Eva refer to Paradise as *her* ship on three occasions. And each occasion was marked with the utmost solemnity. He knew Eva was serious, that she couldn't be talked out of firing Stephanie this time.

"How would you like me to handle it?" he asked.

"I don't really care. You're the damn chairman of the board. Do it yourself. Have Winchester do it. Have the captain do it. I don't really care. Just as long as I see her walking down the gangway by 5:30 on Monday."

Just like the devil in Charlie Daniel's iconic song, Marc knew that he'd been beat. Although he and Eva had been friends for many years, and even lovers once, he knew he didn't possess the political capital necessary to save Stephanie's job. Eva was right. Stephanie had stepped out of bounds too many times. The topless episode in Vietnam had been bad enough. She should have adamantly rebuffed Claude's inappropriate advances. Maybe even reported him, even if he was Eva's guest. And, finally, she had invited Harrison to the crew floor. Even if she had received permission to invite him to the Poseidon costume party, the optics were not good given Stephanie's past transgressions. But sleeping with Harrison? On an owner/visitor floor? That was just too much. Especially when her walk of shame was witnessed by Levi Perlmutter who would no doubt use the event to argue that Eva's staff cared little for the ship's rules. It was sad, Marc concluded, but a foregone conclusion nonetheless. Stephanie had to go.

He decided he would inform Stephanie himself. Captain Pugliese could be a misogynistic Neanderthal, and Stephanie did not deserve to be treated like anything less than a professional woman. She and Marc had always enjoyed a cordial relationship, a friendship even. He decided that instead of returning to his luxury suite, he would head straight to the simulator to see if he could catch Stephanie alone.

Chapter 35
Marc Confronts Stephanie

Tim Moore was in the golf simulator when Marc arrived. Although the two men despised each other, civility, often reigned supreme between owners aboard Paradise.

"We're just finishing up here, mate," Tim said.

Marc sidled across the room and took a seat on the suede couch. Tim's New Zealand hyena-like voice bothered Marc. It always had. So did his golf. Tim swung his clubs like a maniac, usually causing more of a concern to other players than to the fairways. Tim was always the first to crack open a beer or three on a golf course and was ill-equipped to hold his liquor.

His penchant for stalking and photographing underage girls was not limited to those who journeyed aboard Paradise. Any young girl who crossed Tim's path could reasonably expect to be made the subject of his crude advances, or photographed when she wasn't looking. Many golf courses employed cute, young girls to operate the beverage carts and sell soda, beer, and snacks to golfers. Most golfers were courteous, even if they were a bit flirtatious. Tim was downright crude.

On one occasion, when he was golfing with Marc and two other owners from Paradise and he had consumed a few beers, he made an ass of himself. As was almost always the case, the cart girl asked the golfers, "Is there anything you'd like right now?"

To the embarrassment of his fellow golfers, Tim replied, "A blow job would be nice."

The cart girl showed poise beyond her years as she sat back, crossed her arms, and said to the group, "Sounds interesting. You boys go ahead and I'll watch."

After she drove away, Marc ripped into Tim for blotting the ship's reputation with a stain of dishonor. It was not Tim's first infraction. Nor was the time he gawked at Donna Bickford during that infamous Chaweng Beach Club debacle. Nor were the times he was accused of taking photographs of unaware, underage children and grandchildren of owners when they came to visit their family on the ship.

As Stephanie completed her lesson with Tim, Marc was revolted by the lecherous way Tim undressed Stephanie with his eyes. He wasn't even subtle. When she was facing Tim, trying to make a point, Stephanie's breasts were the subject of Tim's attention. And, when she turned to retrieve a ball or fetch a training aid, his eyes were riveted on her ass.

Finally, the lesson ended, and Tim brayed a goodbye to Stephanie. He nodded in Marc's direction.

"What's up, Mr. Chairman?" Stephanie said with a smile.

"I don't know how you put up with them," Marc said, already feeling somber about the upcoming conversation.

"With who?"

"With guys like that. Guys who come up here more to look at you than to actually learn something about golf."

Stephanie laughed. "I'm used to it by now. I don't mean to sound arrogant, but I've had to deal with it since I was about twelve years old. I was one of the earliest girls in my class to mature. Not only was I taller than most girls, but I was one of the first to have boobs. That attracts the attention of most of the boys, I'm afraid. I knew what it was about, but I kind of liked the attention. As I grew older, there got to be a point where it caught up to me, and it became a burden. And, now, the pendulum's swung back to somewhere in the middle. When guys like Tim or some of your other fellow owners stare, I really don't even notice anymore. I can't. It would distract me." She smiled, as if remembering times the issue had raised itself in her past.

"Besides, there are far worse offenders than Tim Moore. There's a guest traveling right now who would be dangerous, if left to his own devices. Craig McDougal. He's a friend of the Hirschfelds. He came to the simulator one day and was on me like a fat kid on candy. A real pig, if you know what I mean."

Marc knew exactly what Stephanie meant. He had heard the stories about Craig's indiscretions with his young niece, as well as some other rumors he was keen not to remember.

"There's something I need to tell you in confidence," Stephanie said as she walked to the door of the simulator and closed it. Marc knew the conversation he needed to have with Stephanie wasn't going to be an easy one. But if Stephanie had something so confidential to share, he had to let her share it.

Stephanie crossed the room and sat on the couch next to Marc. In a subdued voice, she asked, "You know who else is a piece of work? That Claude Azulai, Eva's boyfriend. I'm only telling you this because I know I can trust you. He's not quite as blatant as Tim or Craig, but I think he's more dangerous, if you ask me."

"Why's that?" Marc asked, almost reflexively.

"Because he's involved with another woman, and he's been hitting on me. When we played golf in Cochin, he sat next to me on the bus and did everything but rub my leg. Then he's been coming to the simulator and making stupidly suggestive comments. All this while he's screwing Eva. At least with McDougal or Tim Moore, everyone knows they're married in name only. Everyone knows they'd bang anyone who'd let them, but Claude is supposed to be such a big shot. A big shot who's involved in a relationship with Eva."

Marc shuddered. He really didn't care about what may or may not have happened with Claude. He was disquieted because he feared Claude's behavior towards Stephanie could pollute the narrative surrounding Stephanie's termination. How could he pivot from Stephanie's comment to telling Stephanie she was being fired? Directly, he concluded. He had always maintained that the best way to share bad news, either with his family or with clients, was to rip off the Band-Aid and say it like it is. He turned his body so his shoulders were square to Stephanie's. The solemnity in his face foreshadowed the fact he was about to deliver a serious message.

"Stephanie, there's something I need to tell you," he began.

"Oh, no, not another one. You're not going to tell me I've got a great ass," she joked. The upward rotation of her smiling eyes fell once she realized he was being serious. Stephanie's chin also firmed up. "What's up, Marc?"

"I'm going to be direct with you because that's how we've always been with one another. Eva is firing you."

Stephanie's entire demeanor changed. Her always stable hands began to tremble albeit imperceptibly.

"Apparently, you went to a visitor flat last night. Harrison Marshall's flat. I got to spend some time with him the other day, and I found him interesting. He stopped me in the hallway and he shot a few questions at me about the operation of the ship, how it all ran, that kind of thing. Anyway, it's been reported that you spent the night with him there. I understand you also brought him to a crew party in Poseidon."

Stephanie started to speak but Marc cut her off.

"That's not really the issue that has Eva upset. I know Candy Podeski may have given you permission to bring him so we're not even going there. But you know the rules about sleeping in owners' suites or visitor flats. We've even joked about it, Steph."

Suddenly, Stephanie stiffened. "Is this about Claude? Did she think I was fooling around with Claude? Is this her idea of retaliation? She came to the simulator the other day when he was here. She never does that. I happened to be standing behind him and . . ."

"It's not that," Marc interjected. "It has nothing to do with that. I know it's not a good look, but you have to believe me. Rules are rules and you know what they are. You broke one. A very important one."

"But . . ."

"There are no *buts*, Steph. You can't possibly sit there and tell me you didn't know what you were doing. Or that you didn't know there would be consequences. You know Eva's had you in her sights ever since the whole Chaweng Beach Club thing. She wanted me to fire you then but I went out on a limb for you. I like you. I always have. I've tried to protect you every chance I've had. But you sealed your own fate with this one, I'm afraid."

"Harrison isn't just anyone. I know it sounds weird, but we've got a connection. A real connection. I don't know how it was when you met Karen. But the moment Harrison first opened his mouth, I knew there was a special chemistry between us."

Marc looked at her sympathetically. "That's nice to hear. I'm happy for you, Stephanie. I really am. But did you have to go to his room on the ship?"

Stephanie dropped her head and began to sob. Marc felt uncomfortable as he saw her shoulders move rhythmically up and down. At first, he wanted to put an arm around her and console her. But because of the sexual allegations involved in Stephanie's termination, he was hesitant to do so. *Fuck it*, he concluded. He scooched over next to Stephanie and held her. Her crying became more intense, her shaking more uncontrollable. He felt horrible for her, a simple enough woman who was subject to unwanted sexual attention just because of her appearance. She had done nothing wrong with Tim, Craig, Claude, or any of the other men who harbored not so secret fantasies of being with her. When she did get in trouble, it was only because she'd acted not unlike any carefree woman her age might act in similar circumstances. Sure she'd gotten rowdy, and even topless, in Vietnam, but she wasn't the first one in the pool to get sloppy and inappropriate. And, when it came to Harrison, who knew what the story was. There were lots of rumors going around the ship about the attraction between the two of them. No one knew much about Harrison, and he seemed like a gregarious, good-natured guy. If Stephanie was attracted to him and they had decided to act on their feelings, it wouldn't have been a problem anywhere else in the world. They did it in private, behind closed doors, whatever it was they did or didn't do. But, on Paradise, she had broken a cardinal rule, and there was nothing she could offer in her own defense.

After Stephanie's sobs decreased enough for her to think and speak coherently, she asked, "How much time is she giving me?"

"Tuesday," Marc said.

"Like *Tuesday*, Tuesday. Like three days from now Tuesday?"

"I'm afraid so."

"That seems pretty harsh. Is there any way Eva could give me at least another week or two, so I can make arrangements?"

Even though he was aware his honesty would be painful, Marc spoke his truth. "I can ask her, but I'm not optimistic. She might cool down a bit, but she was really upset when I spoke to her earlier."

Stephanie shook her head. Marc was unsure whether Stephanie was more upset at Eva's decision, or at her own brazen decision to spend the night in Harrison's visitor flat. Regardless, the damage was done, and the consequences had been meted out. There was nothing he could say to console her. But, still, he tried.

"If there's anything I can do for you, I want you to let me know. I'll write you a glowing reference, speak to anyone on your behalf, and do anything in my power. Good golf instructors are a dime a dozen. But you're a great one. More importantly, you're a really great person. Not only have you been able to interact with some of the biggest jerks on this ship, but you've done it with a smile. You've never let any of this shit get you down, and, if you have, you've never shown it. If I ran a country club at home, I'd hire you to be my golf pro. Hell, I'd have you run the whole thing." He hugged her tightly and said softly, "I love you, kiddo. I'm going to hate to lose you." He admired Stephanie's unblemished radiance even as she looked at Marc with small black tracks following her tears down the outsides of her cheeks.

"I love you too," Stephanie said. They stood together, and Stephanie wiped her face with a golf towel that hung on the wall rack. "I must look a mess."

"You're beautiful, Stephanie, inside and out. Don't ever forget that." He walked towards the door of the simulator, wanting to leave Stephanie alone to settle herself. He vowed to speak to Eva about giving Stephanie an extra few weeks, but he knew that was an unrealistic expectation. Even if Claude had nothing to do with Stephanie's dismissal, the fact he had been so chummy with Stephanie did not inure to her benefit.

As he was preparing to leave the simulator, Marc asked, "Did you really go to the crew party last night as Vincent Vega and Mia Wallace?"

The mention of the previous night's party brought a smirk to her face. They had, and the thought of it made her happy. Probably one of her last happy moments aboard Paradise.

"We did," she confessed.

"You rock," he said appreciatively. "Where'd you get the costumes?"

"A girl can't share her secrets,"

"Did you have a Royale with cheese?" Marc asked with a grin.

Stephanie smiled. "You're no Vincent Vega, funny guy."

Marc left, but at least he had put a smile on Stephanie's face.

Chapter 36
Saturday's Outrageous Requests

Saturday, the front desk staff was deluged with weirdness. At 10:00 a.m., Lori Bracker approached Donna Lafat and asked to speak with her alone. Donna was aware that Elaine Dwyer had targeted Lori Bracker as being the potential Peyton Flynn. Accordingly, Elaine was keen to give Donna her utmost attention. Donna asked Holly Ensign to watch her station, and Donna walked to the far end of the long marble counter so she and Mrs. Bracker could speak without being overheard.

"Do you remember when we checked in and I told you that this Saturday was my daughter's sixteenth birthday?"

"Of course, Mrs. Bracker. The entire crew is excited about it. I know you told us not to make a big deal out of it, but you may just find some balloons in your visitor flat after dinner," Donna shared enthusiastically. To her surprise, Mrs. Bracker did not object.

"That would be lovely. But I have another request. Since we've been aboard, our daughter Hannah has made friends with several of the other kids. I think they're all children of suite owners. Apparently, there are quite a few of them on board."

"Yes, there are. Eighteen to be exact. That's unusual, but we love having the next generation aboard Paradise." That was bullshit. The crew recoiled when the manifest revealed there would be so many youngsters on the ship at one time. They were usually loud, made all kinds of trouble around the pool, misused the equipment in the fitness center, and ran up and down the hall at all hours of the night. Eighteen little tornadoes was no one's idea of fun.

"Well, Hannah has asked if we could have a party for her tonight, inviting all the other youngsters to dinner. Jack and I

301

assured her that would be no problem. So that's what I'm here to talk to you about."

No problem, thought Donna. The ship only had three restaurants open that night and each was almost fully accommodated with reservations. But given the likelihood Mrs. Bracker would be able to elevate—or destroy—the ship's entire image with a stroke of her pen, Donna vowed to see what could be done.

"All of the ship's restaurants are fully committed tonight but let me see what I can come up with. Might Monday night be a possibility? We arrive in Mumbai that day, and most of our suite owners have made dinner reservations ashore."

Mrs. Bracker looked sternly at Donna as a teacher might observe a misbehaving student. "She's turning sixteen. Today. I can't very well tell a sixteen-year-old that her birthday will be celebrated three days later, now can I?"

Well, she could have if the child and her parents weren't ostensible prima donnas, thought Donna. Or if there was no chance Mrs. Bracker could be Peyton Flynn. But those were not the facts with which she was confronted.

"Let me speak with Chef Rolando and see if we can open one of our other dining rooms for such a special occasion. In case it's possible, and I'm not promising anything, what would you like on the menu?"

Mrs. Bracker hesitated as she put her left thumb and forefinger on her chin and looked heavenward. "Well, that's an interesting question. Teenage girls don't want to eat anything for fear they could be perceived as being overweight. On the other hand, teenage boys want to eat everything in sight. I'll tell you what, I'll leave it to your chef . . . what did you say his name is?"

"Chef Rolando."

"Yes, Chef Rolando. I'm sure he's fed hundreds of teenagers. So whatever he says is good for him is good for us."

Donna was taken aback by this woman's unbridled hubris to make such an extraordinary request for a dinner that very night. But that was the type of thing Peyton Flynn always did. Not just to see the result, but to see the way the property managed the request.

"Great. Give me some time, and I'll ring your flat with the details," Donna said.

"Oh, and one more thing. I read about the ship having some stabilizers or something that stop the ship from shaking. My husband said the weather is supposed to get sketchy tonight. Would you mind having the captain do whatever he does with those stabilizer things to prevent the ship from rocking?"

Donna was aghast. Not only did she want a restaurant opened specifically for her precious daughter Hannah, she wanted a party thrown a few hours hence, and she wanted the captain to effectively stop the seas from doing what seas do. But again, the Peyton Flynn threat loomed large.

"I'll speak with the captain to see what he can do."

"Thank you very much, Ms. Lafat," Lori Bracker said, taking obvious visual note of the name tag on Donna's chest.

Donna returned to her desk and called Elaine Dwyer, who told Donna to call Chef Rolando immediately. At almost the same time, Ginger Tarpley presented herself at the opposite end of the front desk. In her loud and proud Alabama twang, she inquired of no one in particular, "Who do I see about getting an evening gown and some jewelry for tonight?" Wanting to avoid a scene, and cognizant that Ms. Tarpley was another prime candidate to be the author of Peyton's Places, Donna slid to the far side of the desk and addressed Ms. Tarpley. Donna spoke in a subdued voice, hoping it would have the subliminal effect of convincing Ms. Tarpley she did not need to announce her needs at a decibel level that could summon porpoises.

"How can I help you, Ms. Tarpley?"

"Well, I just learned that there's some big hoe down going on tonight, and it calls for formal attire. Mother did all the planning for this trip, and she packed herself a lovely gown. Of course, she didn't tell me anything about these formal events, bless her heart. So here I am, naked for the big ball."

The thought of Ms. Tarpley naked caused some bile to form in Donna's throat. She had a momentary flash of this buxom, naked, Southern megaphone prancing among the ship's glitterati. She did her best to contain her smile, but obviously failed.

"What's so funny? Do you want me to humiliate myself in front of the whole ship?" Ms. Tarpley said in the same thunderous voice.

Donna reminded herself of the potential alter-identity of the woman before her. She could just imagine making a sarcastic comment to Ms. Tarpley that would result in the ship receiving an horrific review. That could not be allowed to happen. No matter what.

"Ordinarily, we don't have a supply of formalwear to be loaned for events. But since you've traveled such a long way, and we value the fact you've chosen Paradise for your vacation, I can speak to Simone and see if I can get you something from our bespoke boutique."

"Where's that at?"

"It's on the fourth deck. Directly across from the conference center."

"I haven't had any reason to conference with anyone, so I haven't been down there yet," Ms. Tarpley said, attempting humor. "What's in the bespoke place?"

"That's where we sell suits, jackets, dresses, skirts, blouses, and jewelry in case someone forgets something, or wants to pick up a little something to remember their journey aboard Paradise."

"You mean, in case someone's as stupid as me and forgets to bring the right clothes?"

Donna laughed in an effort to make Ms. Tarpley feel comfortable. "No, not at all. Many people just like to pick up an extra little something here and there. In any event, let me have Simone open the boutique and you can go down and see what's there."

At that precise moment, Simone happened to be walking across the ship's main lobby with an arm full of clothes. Donna spotted him and trained her head in his direction. "That's Simone right there. It looks like he's in a hurry, but I'll call his radio in a moment and tell him you'll be coming down. I'm sure you'll be able to find something to your liking."

"*Simone* is to my liking. Can I have him for the big party?" Ms. Tarpley asked.

"We'll be happy to make arrangements for you to have the proper clothing for the party, Ms. Tarpley, but I'm afraid we can't rent out our personnel," she said with a smile.

"I just knew you'd say that. Do they have jewelry there too? I always like to have something extravagant around my neck so the men don't all just stare at my girls," she said, looking down at her more than ample chest.

Donna thought she deserved combat pay for having to deal with this level of ridiculousness. Who were these people thinking they could reserve an entire restaurant on eight hours' notice? Or help themselves to an evening gown and necklace because they were too irresponsible to pack properly?

"Simone has quite a remarkable array of jewelry in the boutique. I have to confess I haven't been there in quite a while. But we always rotate stock and I'm sure you'll find something that will suit you perfectly."

"You're so sweet, dear. And how much will it cost me to get outfitted for a party I didn't even know about?"

"There'll be no charge, Ms. Tarpley. Anything we can do to accommodate our guests, we're happy to do. All you need to do is find something you enjoy and have a great time at the party."

Ms. Tarpley was stunned. "And these are new clothes? Or are they things lots of other people have worn and returned?"

"They're new. All new. We don't carry anything used. You'll be quite impressed, I think."

"I'm already impressed," announced Ms. Tarpley. "I'm impressed by you, your delicious smile, and your accommodating attitude. You're just a sweetheart. If you ever come to Alabama, I'd love you to meet my son Brooks. But he's another story. I don't have time to go into all that today. Well, Donna Lafat," Ms. Tarpley said, straining to read Donna's name tag, "you've certainly been sweeter than a hive full of bee honey."

"Thank you, Ms. Tarpley. I hope you find exactly what you're looking for and that you have a terrific time tonight."

Once Ms. Tarpley had cleared away from the reception desk, Donna radioed Simone and told him the situation. "We don't know if she is or if she isn't, but Elaine wants us to treat her like she might be Peyton Flynn. Give her whatever she needs." Simone gladly agreed and prepared to meet Ms. Whoever she was.

Chapter 37
The Last Saturday

While the ship's owners and guests gathered for the ship's weekly Saturday evening formal, Stephanie Holsson was not in a party mood. After a year and a half as a treasured member of Paradise's crew—a member of the original staff—she was seventy-two hours away from the last day of her employment.

Like almost all crew members, Stephanie didn't have an abundance of personal material on board the ship. Most crew traveled with a few pairs of jeans, some workout clothes, lots of shorts and tops, sneakers, and one or two nice outfits for when the crew arranged dinners in port. Stephanie was a bit unique because of her position.

First, she traveled with her golf clubs, a necessary weapon in the arsenal of any golf pro. But also, when the ship visited the world's finest golf courses, Stephanie usually treated herself to a golf shirt or a visor as a remembrance of the occasion. As a result, she had three entire shelves of those souvenirs in her cabin. As she removed and folded them for packing, each one brought back a distinct memory. And each brought a new tear to her eyes.

Since she had nothing to do with the food and beverage service on Paradise, Stephanie was preparing for her own special dinner that evening, thanks to an invitation Harrison had extended to her earlier in the day.

After her conversation with Marc Romanello that morning, Stephanie telephoned Harrison in his visitor flat. When he heard the consternation in her voice, he immediately went to the golf simulator to see what was up. Stephanie closed and locked the door behind him. She didn't really care if she wasn't supposed to have the door locked during the day. She really didn't care about anything else at that moment. She told Harrison everything Marc had said to her, and she discharged all her emotions into his embrace. Harrison listened attentively, allowing Stephanie to prattle on about her prior indiscretion, the warning she had received, and her ultimate termination.

"I feel terrible. If I hadn't come on board, none of this would've happened. You wouldn't have come to my flat and you'd be sailing along as a happy golf pro, fighting off all your potential suitors." He added the predicate of that sentence as an attempt at humor.

"I would *not* have been happy. I wouldn't have met you." After a few sobs, she added, "Last night was the best night I've had since I've been on the ship. No, it's the best night I've had in all the years I can remember. I wouldn't trade it for the world, not even for my job. When I disembark the ship, I'm going to miss you. I'm going to miss Candy and my friends on the ship, but I'm going to miss you most of all."

"Didn't you say Marc is going to talk to Eva? That you might get a bit of a reprieve?" Harrison asked.

"Yeah, he said that. But he also said he didn't feel optimistic about it."

"Well, let's not attend the funeral until we know the body is cold," Harrison said.

"What's that supposed to mean?"

"It means that you still have your job until Tuesday. And maybe beyond that. Listen, I had a nice conversation with Marc a few days ago. He seems like a fairly reasonable guy. I'm happy to talk to him and see what I can do. Maybe put all the blame on me."

Stephanie's crying abated a bit, but her eyes maintained the glum glaze that had befallen them the minute Marc delivered Eva's directive. "That's kind of you, but I don't really think it'll make a difference. It wasn't Marc's decision. It was Eva's. Besides, the blame isn't yours, it's mine. You weren't constrained by the ship's rules, I was. I knew the rules, and I flaunted them just to be with you."

Harrison was silent. He didn't know which way to steer the conversation. He felt horrible for Stephanie. And he felt horrible for his role in her termination. But he didn't feel horrible he had met her and that they had made such an amazing connection.

"I have no idea how all this whole job thing on the ship is going to turn out, but I know *we* are not ending in three days. I've been blessed that you came into my life, and I'm not going to let you go."

"Really? You're not just saying that to make me feel better?" Stephanie asked.

"Really. This allure we seem to be sharing is real. I meant everything I said to you last night. The way you make me feel is utterly other worldly. Stephanie, I'm all in."

"All in until when? When do you get off the ship anyway?"

"If you're getting off in Mumbai, I'm getting off in Mumbai," Harrison said. "I'm not going to let you be pitched into India alone, with no plan or agenda. I could never forgive myself if anything happened to you."

"You would do that for me?"

"I would and I will." Harrison took some solace seeing a subtle smile begin to creep over Stephanie's face. He continued. "Now, instead of moping, I think we should have an incredibly special dinner tonight. I want you to come to my visitor flat and . . ."

"Do you really think that's a good idea?" Stephanie asked.

"Probably not, but I don't give a shit. If the strike against you is that you came to my room, I don't really think it matters if you came once or a dozen times. I'd like to call room service and order whatever you like—your absolute favorite dish. Anything in the world. I've heard this Chef Rolando is world class and that Paradise carries all sorts of foods and ingredients. Let's see if he can make you the best meal you've ever had. I'll say it's for me if I have to."

A broad smile overtook Stephanie's face. She threw her arms around Harrison and kissed him. "Are you real? I'm serious, are you real?"

"I'm real. And I'm real hungry right now. But I'm going only to grab a light bite for lunch, so my appetite is ready for a big meal tonight. So, what would you like for dinner, my princess?"

Princess? Had he called her his princess? Stephanie hesitated as she pondered the culinary possibilities. "Anything I want?"

"Anything you want," he said eagerly.

"You realize that if we order a fancy meal for two, not only will Chef Rolando know what we're up to, but the entire food and beverage team will as well. Not to mention the housekeeping people who have to come set the table, and the wait staff who have to come clear it afterwards."

Harrison shrugged and smirked. "I don't really care, do you?"

"I guess not."

Stephanie released her grip on Harrison and thought about what she might like for a feast. A final feast, so to speak. For a second, she felt like a death row inmate being asked by the warden what she would like for her last meal.

"You know, when I was a little girl, my mother used to make oxtail for us on special occasions. It's kind of like ossobuco. I haven't had it in about twenty years, but it's the best thing I've ever eaten. One day, about three months ago, one of the suite owners I was golfing with said Chef Rolando had made it for him the night before. I can't imagine they have it on board all the time because it's such a rarity, but, if you're asking what my favorite food would be, I'm going to say oxtail. The only thing is, I know it takes several days to cook. I think you have to do it in a slow cooker or a crockpot or something like that. I wouldn't even know how to make it."

"Don't worry about the details. That's the ship's problem. If you want oxtail, I'm going to ask for oxtail." He paused before continuing. "I presume ossobuco would be a second choice? Unless I'm mistaken, they're fairly similar."

"Mmmm, yes. Either would be great, honestly." Stephanie was growing more animated by the second. "Maybe served on a bed of polenta?"

"Let me speak with the sommelier and see what she'd pair with that."

"Oh, Harrison, you can't be real. You just can't."

"But I am. Shining armor and white horse and all that stuff," he said proudly. "What time do you finish working today?"

"I'm supposed to be here until 5 o'clock," she said, glancing at her wristwatch.

"So if I suggest we meet in my visitor flat at 6 o'clock, that should give you enough time to shower and change, shouldn't it?" Harrison asked in a sonorous voice, evincing the seriousness around his offer.

"Sure. But I'm going to ask you one last time, are you sure you want to do this?" Stephanie asked.

"Not only do I *want* to do this, but there is also nothing else in the world I'd rather do. I do have one requirement of you tonight though. Not a request, a requirement."

Stephanie braced herself, somewhere between curious and mystified. Would it be special underwear? A unique sexual position? Would he turn out to be a weirdo after all?

"Sure, what is it?"

"Do you promise you'll do it?" he asked.

"Now it's my turn to be like Vincent Vega. In that scene in the restaurant where Mia made him promise not to be offended. He said, 'I can't promise something like that. I have no idea what you're going to ask me. If you ask me something that offends me, then through no fault of my own, I will have broken my promise,'" Stephanie quoted.

"You really know your *Pulp Fiction*. I bet there's not a line in the movie you don't remember. So anyway, will you promise to do me one favor?"

Stephanie's mindset morphed from humorous to serious, although she was confident he wouldn't ask her to do anything she wasn't comfortable doing.

"I want you to get dressed however you like, as if we were going to a lovely restaurant for dinner. But I want you to take the owners' elevator and walk down the main hall on my floor with your head up. No back stairs. No crew elevator. No sneaking around. I'm proud to be with you, and I hope you're proud to be with me. Let's not cower or feel we have to hide our relationship."

Stephanie glowed with excitement. "Is that what we're in? A relationship?"

Harrison looked at Stephanie the way no one had looked at her for years. "We are. And we will be. Now clean yourself up a bit, muddle through your day, and I'll see you at 6 o'clock."

It took every bit of willpower in Stephanie's body not to say *I love you* at that moment, but she did love him. She adored him. And more than anything else, she trusted him.

At 6:00 p.m. exactly, a radiant and confident Stephanie Holsson rang Harrison Marshall's door. And at exactly 7:00 a.m. Sunday morning, she left his visitor flat, walking even more confidently down the main hall of his floor to the owners' elevator.

She was in love and so was he. They had both shared that emotion in words, action and orgasms many times throughout the evening.

Chapter 38
Sunday Morning

The Saturday evening ball was a massive success. The festivities were held in Leeward, the ship's formal restaurant. Most of the suite owners attended as did five of the ship's guests including Craig McDougal, Lori Bracker, Ginger Tarpley, Patricia Silverman, and Crazy Caitlin Cappilletti. Elaine Dwyer was taking no chances. Any of them could have been Peyton Flynn, so they were each treated with distinction.

With the Saturday evening ball scheduled as the highlight of the week, Chef Rolando was less than thrilled when Elaine Dwyer insisted he accommodate Lori Bracker's presumptuous request. But his ego was such that he would never refuse a challenge, and Chef Rolando rose to the task admirably. Chef Rolando went above and beyond, opening Pasture for Ms. Bracker's bratty sixteen-year-old daughter Hannah and the other adolescent invitees to the last-minute birthday party. Although Pasture was the ship's designated vegetarian restaurant, it would have been almost impossible to find anything remotely vegetarian on the menu that evening. Cheeseburgers, sausages, and fried chicken highlighted the menu, and the teenagers were delighted with such anti-epicurean fare. Steve Draper, the ship's security officer, made sure two of his deputies took turns passing by the restaurant every few minutes. To most everyone's surprise and delight, there were no incidents, save for Hannah making out with two different boys an hour apart.

Little hussie, Draper thought as he smirked and continued his rounds.

Candy Podeski was invited to the ball because of her role as the ship's Sales Manager. She looked striking in her black sequin mini dress with stiletto heels, no small feat on a ship cutting through the ocean's not insignificant waves that evening. Craig McDougal's lust for Candy had never wavered, and he made a complete ass of himself several times throughout the evening. Barely able to contain his liquor, he propositioned her to dance on three occasions. After Candy politely declined, he propositioned her in another way on two occasions. Candy was itching to tell her best friend Stephanie what was happening, but she was happily aware that Stephanie was enjoying a special dinner with Harrison Marshall in his visitor flat.

As Paradise's Entertainment Director, Elaine Dwyer was the coordinator of the event. In that capacity, she was present for most of the evening. Also present for most of the evening was Becky Hirschfeld. While most of the couples attending the gala were so busy drinking and bragging, none noticed the overly familiar glances and repartee between Elaine and Becky. With Becky's express consent, Elaine had arranged the seating plan so she and Becky were at the same table. With Becky's implicit consent, Elaine rubbed her left thigh against Becky's right thigh much of the evening.

For a while Becky entertained tingling sensations around about how fun it would be for Elaine to visit her in her owner's suite again once the party wound down, but she knew that could be disastrous. Now that she was one of the ship's directors, Becky had been apprised of Eva's decision to terminate Stephanie as a result of Stephanie visiting Harrison's visitor flat. As much as she wouldn't have minded another evening of flirtatious fun—and more with Elaine—Becky could not stomach the idea of her friend losing her job because of Becky's selfishness.

Crazy Caitlin was seated at a table with the Gripers. Elaine didn't know where else to put her, and it was a bit of sweet revenge on the people who had made life so difficult for so many.

Not long after she claimed her seat next to Lior Perlmutter, Caitlin said, "How are you doing?" After only a second, she answered,

"I'm good. Maybe a bit tired." Lior looked at her askance. Caitlin made polite conversation with the other diners but reverted to her self-talk a few times every hour. One of the more amusing anecdotes occurred when she needed a second glass of wine. "May I have some wine please? Do you want red or white?" And then, in a stern and not so understated voice, "Can't you see I've been drinking white? Are you a freaking moron?" Those seated around her were rendered speechless. Some thought it comical, but Danielle Perlmutter was frightened. She whispered to Lior that perhaps they should contact someone. Maybe the ship's doctor. Maybe security. They didn't. And Crazy Caitlin continued throughout the evening.

Ginger Tarpley was the belle of the ball. Simone had outfitted her in an ankle length Carolina Herrera silver chiffon dress with complementing Dior shoes. She had also convinced him to loan her a choker length strand of Mikimoto pearls with matching earrings. She and her mother had each coaxed Captain Pugliese to dance with them, something he was expected to do with VIP guests and legitimate purchasing prospects. The captain didn't mind dancing with women at these events. The quintessential flirt, Captain Pugliese greatly preferred dancing with the thirty-or forty-year-old women, even if they were married. But he didn't always have that option. VIP guests came in all shapes and sizes and he knew what was expected of him. Whereas Ginger Tarpley talked his ear off, Captain Pugliese found the elder Mrs. Tarpley quite enchanting.

A bit of a buzz occurred when someone on the ship staff said that Mrs. Tarpley's passport information revealed she had been in India longer than she had represented before boarded the ship. Immediately, Eva, Lorraine, and others started to focus on Mrs. Tarpley as being the most likely candidate to be Peyton Flynn's alter ego. Elaine Dwyer promised to run that rumor to ground the next morning, the last Sunday of the month.

A small crisis intervened the next morning, however, when Mrs. Tarpley returned the goods to the boutique. Simone inventoried everything that was returned and was unable to locate the pearl necklace. He searched the garment bag that contained the clothing, the small velvet bag containing the shoes, and the jewelry box that contained only the earrings, with an absence in the slot allocated for the necklace. He immediately informed the Donna Lafat at the front desk, who in turn notified Elaine Dwyer.

"Are you sure Simone searched everywhere?" Elaine asked.

"I asked him several times. He swore he went through everything three times and couldn't find the necklace anywhere. Would you like me to confirm with Mrs. Tarpley that she returned the necklace?"

"Maybe I should do that," Elaine said. She didn't mean to insult Donna, but if Mrs. Tarpley was really Peyton Flynn, perhaps this was another test. If so, Elaine wanted to be certain the inquiry was handled with the requisite level of care, and from someone with a higher rank on the ship. Donna understood Elaine's point and took no offense. But after Elaine checked with Mrs. Tarpley, and Mrs. Tarpley swore she returned the necklace, Elaine had to elevate the situation to Eva in a late morning phone call.

"How much did we pay for the necklace?"

"Simone says our cost was $850, but it retails for $1495."

"So let me get this straight," Eva said. "We loaned her a designer, dress and shoes, and a necklace and earrings. We got everything back except for the necklace that cost us $850. Is that right?"

"Precisely," Elaine answered.

"And you asked her if she returned the necklace?

"Yup."

"And she said she had?"

"Yup."

Eva hesitated as she briefly pondered the options were available to her. Obviously, a *he said—she said* game of accusations would not result in the necklace mysteriously materializing. The way she saw it, there were two options. She could either charge Mrs. Tarpley's visitor folio $850 or the ship could eat the expense, identifying the loss as a marketing cost in the event Mrs. Tarpley turned out to be Peyton Flynn. She concluded she didn't need to make a decision on the spot. The next issue of Peyton's Places was due tomorrow, Sunday evening, and Mrs. Tarpley and her mother were not scheduled to leave the ship for another six days. She had some time to think about how to account for the missing necklace, in the event it did not reappear before they left.

"Let me think on it. We don't need to make a decision right now."

As the sun rose Sunday morning, a patina of sadness clouded Harrison Marshall's visitor flat. He and Stephanie had spent an amazing evening together. Dinner and wine had been beyond perfect, but they paled in comparison to the adoration and lovemaking that ensued throughout the evening. She offered to call in sick for the day so she could spend time with Harrison. But he told her he had work to do, and they would spend a good deal of time together in Mumbai, before jetting off to Cape Town, where he was planning a surprise for her. Although she was thrilled about leaving the ship with Harrison, and the fact he had planned something special for them, she was despondent at the idea of leaving him in the morning. Nevertheless, as she had promised to do, Stephanie left and walked down the owners' hallway with her head held high. Back in her cabin, she quickly changed into her golf attire and retreated to the simulator where she awaited whatever misfits the day would bring her way.

For most owners and guests, Sunday afternoon was a slow slog aboard Paradise. The generous flow of alcohol Saturday evening diminished the speed with which anyone was moving on Sunday. The ship's passengers were fortunate the seas had bucked the forecast and turned calm the night before. To be extra cautious, Captain Pugliese had deployed the ship's retractable stabilizers before the events of the evening began. The stabilizers, as their name suggests, reduced the amount of rocking the ship had to endure. He did not favor deploying them on a regular basis because they slowed the ship's momentum and resulted in a costly fuel drag. But with the gala scheduled for the evening, he decided that a few hundred extra gallons of fuel was worth it in exchange for a smoother dinner and dancing experience. He did that of his own volition, never even hearing of Ms. Bracker's request that he do so.

Harrison Marshall telephoned Marc Romanello and left a message that he was keen to speak to Marc. He had promised Stephanie he would try to intervene on her behalf, to try to get her an extra week or two before she had to leave the ship, and he planned to fulfill that promise. He realized that Eva was the ultimate decision maker, but Harrison had never met Eva, so he wanted to lay out his case for Marc. After a short game of telephone tag without Harrison sharing his agenda, it was agreed they would meet in Harrison's visitor flat at 7:00 p.m.

Chapter 39
Sunday Afternoon
Peyton's Reveal

Elaine Dwyer invited Eva Lampedusa, Lorraine Williams, Becky Hirschfeld, Donna Lafat, and Candy Podeski to her office at 6:00 Sunday evening to await the latest version of Peyton's Places. At the ball the night before, when Captain Pugliese was appraised of the whole Peyton Flynn situation, he too was fascinated. So even the jolly captain stopped by Elaine's office to mingle with six women and await Peyton Flynn's most recent missive.

The anxiety among the assembled was palpable. Facile jokes and absurd predictions abounded. Elaine even started a pool, inviting everyone to pitch in $5.00 to guess the identity of Peyton Flynn, if, indeed, Peyton Flynn was anywhere to be found aboard Paradise. Lori Bracker was the top vote getter, with Ginger Tarpley and Crazy Caitlin Cappilletti tied for second. Patricia Silverman (who wanted to be wrapped in banana leaves) and Catherine Roank (who wanted her tennis racquet restrung every day) finished tied for last position. All reasoned the crazy Australian lady who wanted her teeth pulled in India was just that, crazy.

The digital clock in the top right corner of Elaine's computer seemed to slow down once it hit 5:50 p.m. The next ten minutes ticked by like an eternity. On not less than eight occasions, Captain Pugliese lifted his fat left arm to check the sweeping second hand on his Rolex Submariner. Three times Elaine refreshed her email to ensure all incoming traffic was open and loading. Finally, at 6:00 p.m. exactly, her screen pinged and an email appeared with a subject line that read, *Peyton's Places*. For the next minute, no sound could be heard except Elaine's voice as she slowly and deliberately read the text of the long-awaited post.

This week, I experienced the finest and most unusual hospitality stay of my career. Those who have been following me for months or even years, are aware that I have never awarded a perfect score to any property I've visited. Until this week.

Those assembled could almost feel the oxygen getting sucked out of the room. Even though Elaine had only read three sentences, perspiration was forming on every forehead in the room.

This visit was made special in two distinct ways. First, I got real visibility into the behind the scenes operation of a property, something most properties hide from their guests, and usually with good reason. And, second, this was not any property. It was a floating paradise, aptly named . . . Paradise.

The yells that emanated from Elaine's office were enough to make people wonder if the entire pool staff had been pitched into the ocean with hundreds of observers screaming for help. Eva jumped up and down and grabbed Lorraine as if they had just won the Wimbledon doubles competition. It was Candy's misfortune to be most closely positioned to Captain Pugliese so she was the recipient of his embrace. Until he let her go so he could hug Donna Lafat as well. Elaine pushed her chair back, stood straight, and hugged Becky tightly. On any other day, the closeness of their embrace might have suggested the sexual relationship they enjoyed. But today, all hugging and squeezing was directly attributable to what they were just reading. And well deserved.

"Shh, keep reading," Eva entreated.

When I first boarded this magnificent vessel, I was greeted by a polite, attractive, and incredibly efficient staff. Even more impressively, it all appeared to work effortlessly. The teamwork, camaraderie, and proficiency was excellent, to be sure. The women running the reception desk were flawless in every way, that day and throughout my visit. Their manager, Donna Lafat, gave a masterclass in grace, politeness, and usefulness.

Donna's smile grew wide as she looked around the room and got winks and golf clap level applause from everyone present.

For the entirety of the week I spent aboard Paradise, I was overwhelmed by the grace and effectiveness of everything the ship's staff had to deliver. The housekeeping staff was prompt and efficient. They tended to my accommodations twice a day— once for morning clean up, and again before bedtime for turn down service. Moreover, anytime I needed an additional service, they were available to clean my room up to four times a day. (Incidentally, the guest rooms aboard Paradise have been given the unique title of Visitor Flats, a delightful moniker.) In fact, on one occasion, a member of the housekeeping staff was kind enough to go the extra mile and helped me accomplish a task that was clearly outside her remit.

The assembled management and owners looked curiously at one another. Elaine shrugged her shoulders and lifted her palms upwards, the universal signal for *I have no idea what she's talking about.*

Elaine continued reading aloud.

I have been on two cruise ships but let me assure you that Paradise is no cruise ship. It is the private, floating enclave of the uber wealth. Some may take issue with the exclusiveness and even arrogance of a residential community that requires applicants to tender a $25,000 application fee, show proof of a minimum net worth of $50 million, pay $20 million to purchase an apartment, and then shell out between $35,000 and $100,000 per month in condo fees. I must say I found that aspect of things unreal, but my role aboard Paradise was not to pass judgment about the owners or the enterprise, but to review the hospitality side of the operation.

"Arrogance?" Becky said.

"Shhh. She's right. But let's hear the rest of it. Keep reading Elaine," said Eva.

A traveler's stomach is the way to his heart, the old adage goes. And aboard a ship, that truism is more accurate than anywhere. The food aboard Paradise rivaled anything I've had anywhere on land. This is not a typical cruise ship scenario with long lines of high caloric slop available at all hours of the day. No, this is some of the highest quality food and exquisite presentation available on the planet, on land, or at sea.

One of the conditions for receipt of a Michelin star is that the restaurant be open to the public. Without that requirement, dozens of private country clubs and enclaves of the rich and famous might apply or even qualify. But let me assure you that not only would Paradise's glorious Chef Rolando qualify for a Michelin star, he might even earn all three.

Being at sea a few days (and unable to taste some of the fine Indian cuisine I'm looking forward to sampling once we get to Mumbai), I had the opportunity to explore a broad sample of the kitchen staff's ability. The menu items were all exceptional, but one of the factors that earned Paradise, a perfect score, was Chef Rolando's ability to improvise. One day when I was itching to test the limits of the kitchen, I called room service and asked for a specialty item I was certain they would not be able to accommodate—something no chef could properly prepare in that time. To my utter shock, six hours later, room service delivered the most wonderful oxtail dish to my visitor flat. I have no idea how they were able to achieve such fall-off-the- bone tenderness in a dish that usually has to be slow cooked for days, but it was the best oxtail I've tasted anywhere in the world. In addition, the chef concocted a red wine reduction sauce featuring lima beans, tomato paste, beef broth, and soy sauce, all served over a perfectly cooked bed of polenta.

Elaine looked up from her computer. Everyone was either shaking their head or making faces that attested to their surprise. Eventually, Eva said, "Oxtails? I never knew we had oxtails aboard. That was one of my favorite dishes when I was a little girl. It's never been on the menu. How the hell did Peyton Flynn get it?"

"Sounds like she just asked for it," Captain Pugliese added.

Eva turned up her mouth as she tried to hide her disdain for his brutish ways.

Becky verbalized what everyone was thinking, "So which one of them looks like the oxtail type?"

"It *has* to be Mrs. Tarpley. I knew it was her. She's the only one who eats everything they put in front of her. Not only is she a foodie, but I think she's a foodaholic," Candy answered.

"Keep going," Eva implored. "Let's hear more so we can see if we can figure out who it is."

Elaine turned back to her screen. "Where was I? Oh yeah, here."

There is far more to life aboard Paradise than housekeeping and food. A lot more. One of the most amazing features aboard Paradise is the fact one can do almost anything one can do on land—and then some. Paradise's fitness center is second to none and the wellness center offers a host of treatments I've never even seen in a terrestrial facility."

"It's Mrs. Silverman," Elaine screamed. "I just knew it. She's the one who wanted to be wrapped in banana leaves in the wellness center. And we got her that damn SCUBA certification test in the pool. I told you we should make that happen," she directed towards Eva.

"And we did," Eva said. "You were right."

Glowing with pride, Elaine continued reading.

As I wrote above, Paradise is a collection of floating luxury suites that would be called apartments in New York. Gorgeous apartments, at that. Wherever there are apartments, there are sales agents and Paradise is no exception. However, the Director of Sales aboard Paradise is quite an exception. Candy Podeski's job is to sell apartments, but she does it with charm, respect, and class. Every potential visitor is treated like a potential purchaser, but only as much as they would like. My interactions with Ms. Podeski were among the most memorable and impressive experiences I enjoyed while on the vessel.

"'Impressive experiences?' Who the hell did you impress like that?" Captain Pugliese asked.

Candy shrugged, lifted her hands, and rolled her eyes. "Hey, I just do my job every day. As Eva said, give them everything they want. That's what I've been doing. We've certainly had some crazies aboard recently so I couldn't begin to tell you, which one of them she is."

I referenced the fact I got visibility into the property's back of the house operations, something that is a real treat for a hospitality geek like me. I was fortunate to meet with several of the suite owners, including members of the board of directors, and even made a nice connection with their chairman. They were all down to earth and lovely.

"You met with her?" Eva yelped. "Who the hell did you meet with?"

Marc's brain raced, shuffling the various candidates around in his head.

Before he could say anything, Elaine continued. *One of my favorite pastimes is golf. 'What does golf have to do with an ocean liner?' you might ask. On Paradise, one can become immersed in golf. There is an incredible golf simulator that also doubles as a tennis simulator. For golf, one can bang balls into a wall and the highly technical lasers, radar, and computer provide immediate visual feedback about club-head speed, ball speed, spin rate, swing path, launch angle, and distance. As a tennis simulator, the wall is rigid and one can literally play a game of tennis against oneself. Under the expert tutelage of the ship's golf professional, Stephanie Holsson, I may have actually lowered my handicap while sailing through the Arabian Sea.*

"I'm not so sure about Mrs. Tarpley," Donna Lafat piped up. "I can't see her banging tennis balls or golf balls."

"Shhh. Keep reading," Eva said nervously.

I also got invited to a special interaction with the crew. It is apparently unusual for visitors to be invited to parties below deck on Paradise, but I was a lucky invitee.

For the second time in fifteen minutes, total silence befell the room. Ironically, Elaine Dwyer was perhaps the only person in the room who didn't know about the crew party crash, so she continued to read. But as she did, pangs of nausea started to envelop Candy and Eva. They hoped and wished they could be wrong. But they weren't.

Not only was I invited to the party, but I was solicited to sport something outrageous because it was a costume party. Of course, I hadn't planned on such a thing, so I had nothing outrageous with me. But the person who invited me shared my affinity for Pulp Fiction. To my absolute delight, she was able to secure a costume that enabled me to go as Vincent Vega, a character I've always wanted to emulate, although without the violence of course.

"Wait, so it's a guy?" Elaine asked abruptly. "Peyton Flynn is a guy?"

"I definitely did not have this on today's bingo card," said Captain Pugliese.

No one in the room looked as crestfallen as Eva. The mention of golf, and the accolades about the pro had given her a clue, but the invitation to the costume party sealed her suspicion. Peyton Flynn was Harrison Marshall, the man who was having a fling with the employee she had directed Marc to fire tomorrow. "Keep going," she urged the anxiety in her voice and face becoming apparent. "Just keep reading."

Normally, my reviews are full of compliments and platitudes, highlighting only the most positive aspects of a property. On this occasion, however, the review would not be complete without mentioning a situation I would not ordinarily accent. During my stay aboard Paradise, it became necessary for the board to terminate one of their long-standing employees. Ordinarily, such an event would pass without comment. But the way the chairman of Paradise's board handled the situation was exemplary of everything about the ship. The crew member in question, the golf pro as a matter of fact, was justly terminated. For cause. For good cause. She had committed several conduct violations aboard the ship, and one could even argue that her termination was long overdue. But the way the chairman personally handled the situation, speaking to her in the most delicate, caring, humane way, spoke volumes about the management of the ship, and the way it feels about its employees.

I could write an entire book about the wonderful experience I enjoyed during my time aboard Paradise. In some ways, the voyage has been life-changing—I know my life shall truly never be the same. But that's the subject for another day. I'm sure the Internet will sleuth out that story when the time is right.

For anyone considering a voyage at sea—or looking for a place to spend a few million extra dollars—I cannot recommend Paradise highly enough. In sum, it is the finest, most impressive, most hospitable, travel experience I have encountered anywhere around the world.

Eva lunged for the phone on Elaine's desk and punched in the numbers of Marc's suite. The second he answered, she demanded, "What are you doing right now? Have you seen it?"

"Seen what?" I just got out of the shower Eva. I'm supposed to meet that Harrison Marshall guy in fifteen minutes.

Eva was blind with fury and tension. "Peyton's Places this week. It just went live. It's us. She reviewed us. Except it's not a *she*, it's a *he*. The *he* is Harrison Marshall. He gave us a perfect score, the first one ever. And he specifically writes about Stephanie Holsson and the fact she's being fired." Eva was speaking so quickly Marc was having a tough time processing everything she was saying.

"Slow down. I've got to unpack all this. You say this Peyton woman you've been following for months is actually a man? And he gave us a perfect score? Is that right?"

"Yes, but Stephanie . . ."

"Wait. I'm trying to catch up to you. You say he wrote about you firing Stephanie?"

"Well actually, he wrote about *you* firing Stephanie. But he did it in a flattering way," Eva explained.

"Whoa. I'm so confused. A minute ago I was in the shower getting ready for a nice dinner with Karen, and now I'm listening to you not make any sense."

"Just get down here. I'm in Elaine Dwyer's office. Can you come down here right away?" she demanded more than asked.

"Let me put some clothes on and I'll be there in ten minutes."

"Make it five. We're all here. Hurry."

"Who's we all?" Marc asked.
"Never mind. Just get down here."

Chapter 40
Sunday Afternoon
Harrison and Stephanie

At the same time the ship's brain trust was assembled in Elaine Dwyer's office, Stephanie Holsson was sitting on Harrison Marshall's couch, sipping a glass of champagne and trying to make sense of all of it. She was alit like a child who had just been given the best Christmas present ever. Her eyes kept darting from Harrison's computer screen to his face, her jaw extending downward a bit more with every paragraph.

"I'm speechless. Totally speechless. You mean these past weeks when everybody on our management team has been trying to figure out which guest is Peyton Flynn, it was you? The whole time?"

Harrison may just as well have eaten a flock of canaries for the smile on his face. "The one and only," he said, his smile as wide as the horizon outside his glass doors.

"What about Mrs. Tarpley?" Stephanie asked.

"What about her?"

"You mean she isn't Peyton Flynn?"

"Honey, I don't even know who Mrs. Tarpley is," Harrison said.

"And all the others?" Stephanie continued.

"What about them?"

"We had it narrowed down to five women."

"Ah, that's the problem. It's often the problem. Almost every hotel I visit operates under the presumption that Peyton Flynn is a woman. Of course, I've never said or written anything to correct that. It's made my job a lot easier."

"You bastard," Stephanie teased. "You really screwed up our team, I can assure you of that. I can only imagine the tongues wagging down below."

"What did you mean when you wrote, *I know my life shall truly never be the same. But that's the subject for another day?*" Stephanie asked.

"It's true. Meeting you has changed my life forever. I don't want to be without you anymore. I'm done traveling alone. When I travel, you'll be with me. And if you're not, I won't travel."

Stephanie smiled sweetly, cocking her head to the side and tossing back her platinum mane.

"Wait, what? And you're not going to travel without me? How are you going to do reviews?"

Harrison ignored Stephanie's question and continued. "You know what's funny? Your friend Marc Romanello called this afternoon and wants to meet with me today at 7 o'clock." Harrison looked at his watch. "That's in about twenty minutes. Obviously, he knew nothing about this week's Peyton's Places article, or my identity, when he called me. I wonder if he cancels. I kind of hope not. It would be kind of fun to sit with him and see what he does, what he looks like after reading my review. I bet he grovels and says the board has decided to let you keep your job."

That was the first time Stephanie had considered the potential ramifications of Harrison's alter ego. What effect would his reveal have on the board's decision to terminate her? Would they be even angrier at her, surmising she must've known it all along? Then she relaxed a bit. What else could they do to her? They'd already fired her.

"Oh my gosh, this is crazy. Where are you supposed to meet him?"

"Right here. He'll probably sit on that very couch you're

occupying right now," Harrison said, pleased with himself.

Stephanie jumped up and lifted her glass of champagne. She wiped the ring of condensation from the coffee table and headed towards the kitchen.

"Where do you think you're going?" Harrison asked.

"Ummm. Upstairs. To the simulator. Or maybe down to my cabin." Obviously nervous and in a hurry to get out of his visitor flat, Stephanie said, "Anywhere but here, that's for sure. I can't be here when Marc gets here."

"Why not. I thought you'd find it quite fun," Harrison offered.

"Fun? What part of it would be fun. He fired me. And then you wrote in a worldwide syndication about my being fired. How fun do you think that sounds for me?"

"I never mentioned your name. Well, not in a bad way," Harrison said, as if that was going to provide any consolation to Stephanie. "Besides, you don't need these people or this ship. I've got everything planned already."

"Oh you do, do you? Would you care to let me in on it? Or are you just going to keep my future a secret for yourself?" she said as she stretched one arm across the kitchen counter and rested the other hand on her upraised hip. She made sure to lean way over so Harrison would get an unobstructed view of her marvelous cleavage.

"Do you want the short-term plan or the long-term one?" he asked cockily.

"You're too funny. You think you've planned my whole life out? Without even consulting me? Do you think I'm just a pretty face and a pair of great boobs who'll do whatever you want?"

"Pretty much," Harrison answered, moving out of the way to avoid being hit by the ice cube his new love had just launched at him. He walked towards Stephanie and embraced her. She allowed herself to be held but gave Harrison a pouty look.

"OK, go ahead. Let's hear it."

"First stop is Mumbai, obviously. I thought we'd spend a couple of days there and then go up to Agra to visit the Taj Mahal."

Stephanie's eyebrows raised with obvious approval.

"Next, we'll shoot down to Cape Town. I'm trying to arrange a safari at Shamwari, one of my favorite game reserves. Peyton Flynn visited them last year and gave them a glowing review. They said they'd love to have Peyton back. Perhaps I'll call in that favor."

Stephanie smiled at the notion that Peyton Flynn, the supposed woman who traveled the world visiting all these glamorous resorts, was none other than the man she was holding in her arms.

"Shall I keep going?" he asked.

"Please do."

"Well, what woman doesn't like Paris?" Stephanie made a purring sound and rubbed the side of her face against Harrison's neck. "So I thought we might visit Paris. Then hit London before heading back to the States."

"Oh, so you're not letting me go home to Sweden?" she asked, glowing. "Will I ever get to see my family again. Pick up any of my things?" She gave him a playful look of concern.

"Of course you are. We're going to fly your parents and your sister over to have an extended visit with us, maybe for a few weeks or so."

Stephanie was tickled and captivated by everything Harrison was saying. "You're too funny. And exactly where will that be?"

"At our house," he replied, grinning even wider.

"We're going to live together? Is that your plan? I don't even know where you really live, or what you even do for a living." Stephanie checked herself before saying, "Well, I guess I do now.

I just never took you for a luxury travel review lady." She laughed, pleased with herself. "Go on now, this is great fun."

Harrison pulled back and locked his eyes on hers in a way that presaged a more serious side of the conversation. "Do you remember the day I told you to call me when you get to La Jolla? That I can get you on Torrey Pines anytime you like?"

"I didn't think you were being serious," Stephanie replied. "Do you live near there?"

"I do. And, if you'd like, I have a job waiting for you in La Jolla," he continued, not so subtly suppressing a grin.

"I'm dying to hear this," she said. "What would I be doing, waiting tables or renting surfboards?"

"Very funny. I thought you might enjoy a job in the golf industry. Ever heard of it."

"Yes, smarty pants. I think I've heard of it. Do tell."

"Do you remember when I first came up here to take a lesson, and you gave me those TaylorMade M6 irons? I wasn't able to hit them well and then you got me those PXGs, do you remember that?"

"Sure, but what does that have to do . . ."

"There was something wrong with those TaylorMades. I called someone at the company and explained everything. Everything about the clubs, about the ship, and about you, in fact."

"About me? Why would you tell them about me? And what did you say?"

Harrison ignored her questions and kept going. "They'll be sending three new sets of clubs to the ship next week." He paused before remembering, "But you won't be here to receive them."

"Wait a second. Do that again. You didn't like the golf clubs so you called somebody at TaylorMade headquarters and they're sending three new sets of clubs? That doesn't sound quite real."

"Bags too. New red and white bags. They just came out this month." Harrison was glowing, and Stephanie was dying to know what was going on.

"The guy I called there . . . well, he's my brother. He's the CEO of TaylorMade. I worked there for eighteen years before I got into the whole luxury travel game. My two nephews still work there. As well as my brother, obviously."

Stephanie was aghast. If one looked up the word *speechless* in the dictionary, Stephanie Holsson's unbelieving face would be the image presented.

"So if you'd like to work at TaylorMade, I'm pretty sure we can make that happen. You might want to work in testing, club development, marketing, or sales. Whatever you want. Or, with that wonderful smile and perfect body you're always bragging about, you could be one of the models."

Stephanie was too excited to be upset by that last comment.

"Are you serious? Are you fucking serious?" She threw her arms around him, her eyes watering in a half-smiling, half-crying exercise. "Oh my God. I love you, Harrison Marshall, I just love you."

Stephanie jumped up and down, releasing Harrison and pumping her fists in the air. She finally stopped for a second and realized she was out of breath. "A week ago, I was teaching golf to a bunch of skirt chasers on a floating tin can, getting love from the top end of a piece of silicone, and now I've met the man of my dreams who's going to whisk me away to Southern California and get me a job with my favorite golf club company in the world. This can't be happening. Pinch me and let me wake up."

They embraced and kissed, passion pulsating between them. The revelation about his true identity, excitement about the new opportunity, and comfort in knowing she found a man who loved her made Stephanie a very happy woman. She headed back to the kitchen to refill their glasses of champagne, having forgot anything about Marc and his 7 o'clock appointment with Harrison. Until the phone rang. Stephanie and Harrison looked at each other like two miscreants who had been caught doing something untoward.

Harrison looked at the desk phone and saw Elaine Dwyer's name displayed. That was confusing.

"Harrison Marshall here."

"Harrison. It's Marc Romanello. Are we still on for 7 o'clock?"

Harrison glanced at the clock on the phone; it was 6:55. "Sure. That works for me."

"Listen, do you mind if I bring Eva Lampedusa with me?" Harrison was surprised at the mention of Eva's name but didn't let on. "No, that would be fine. We'll see you in a few minutes."

When he hung up, Stephanie immediately said, "You said *we'll* see you in a few minutes. Do you really want me to stay here? I'm not sure I feel comfortable being around for this discussion."

"Why not?"

"Oh, let me think," she said, sarcasm dripping off every word. "Maybe because you'll all be talking about me. And talking about the fact I got fired. Oh yes, the fact I got fired because I was sleeping with *you*," she said, her voice slowly elevating. "Right here, in this apartment. Maybe that's why I wouldn't be comfortable."

"Hey, it's up to you. No one's holding you prisoner. You're free to leave if you like. But you might get the last laugh out of this. Instead of being a golf pro working for a cruise ship, making whatever it is you're making here and living on a bunk bed, you'll be in the golf capital of the world living with me on my estate overlooking the shores of the Pacific Ocean and listening to seals every morning. The other thing to remember is that those guys are probably shellshocked right now. They've been kowtowing to all these women they thought would be Peyton Flynn. And it turned out to be me. On the other hand, they got a perfect score, the only one I've ever awarded. Either way, I can't wait to see their faces."

Stephanie considered her options. She knew she didn't have long to think about it. They had obviously called from Elaine's office, and the trek from there to Harrison's visitor flat was less than three minutes. She made an instantaneous decision. She completed the mundane task she had begun, namely filling their champagne glasses. Harrison smiled as he saw the tack Stephanie was taking.

"Good. I'm glad you're staying. This should be kind of fun, after all. You know, this is the first time I've ever launched a review of a property while I was still on premises."

"Why'd you do it this time?"

"Why not? First of all, I gave them a perfect score, so they have to be absolutely elated. The fact I wrote about your termination will understandably cause some angst. They'll have to balance how they deal with everything now. It'll be fun to watch how they do it, especially with Eva coming up here too. Maybe it's my little bit of revenge. Either way, I'll be curious to see their faces since I've aired some of the ship's dirty laundry. Frankly, it would give me the greatest pleasure if you were sitting here."

"You know what, you're right," Stephanie said with emphasis. "I felt like hell when Marc told me Eva wanted me fired. It was the worst day I've experienced since I joined the ship. I've had to put up with all those gawkers and grabbers all this time. Then, I get fired because I fall in love with a great guy and spend time with him. You and I didn't flaunt it. We didn't do anything horrible. We just spent the night together."

Harrison sat back and crossed his arms. He inhaled deeply before speaking. "Steph, you know I'm in your corner, but let's not rewrite history. You've already told me about what you did before I ever met you. You could have been fired for the beach party charade. Marc stood up for you. And we *did* break the rules. I'm not saying I regret any of it for a minute, but it's not like there wasn't a basis for them firing you."

Because she didn't have a good response for Harrison's excellent logic, Stephanie chose to remain silent. Although she only had one button of her blouse open, she fastened that one too, cinching the shirt all the way up to the neck.

"What's that about?" Harrison asked.

"I don't want them to think I'm a slut," she said, her lips pursed.

Harrison grinned. "You think having one button open makes you a slut? You can't be serious. I love your body, Stephanie. I can't get enough of it." His gaze dropped to Stephanie's long legs, most of which extended way below the hem of her short skirt.

The moment Stephanie noticed the way Harrison was looking at her legs, she crossed them self-consciously and attempted to pull down the skirt. That movement frustrated her because no matter what she did, the tiny blue skirt remained at least eight inches above her knees.

"Stop looking at me like that."

"Like what?" he grinned.

"Like you just want to devour me."

"But I do," he guffawed loudly.

"Cut it out or I'm leaving. I don't want to be thought of as the little whore in the room."

Sensing that Stephanie's frustration was real, Harrison put his left arm around her shoulder. Looking into her blue eyes, he struggled for something to say. No clever response or witty retort was sufficient to address the situation. Instead, his heart took charge of his voice, and he simply said, "I love you."

"I love you too," Stephanie said, leaning forward to give Harrison a warm kiss. Just as their tongues became entwined, there was a knock at the door. They each recoiled. When he looked down at Stephanie, she was unbuttoning the top button of her blouse once again.

"What's that about?" he asked.

"If you love my body, I want you to see it and think about it as much as you like. I don't really care what they think of me anymore. Why should I? They've already fired me. I'm done being nervous around this place."

"You're the best," Harrison said, full of joy and pride.

Harrison opened the door and welcomed Marc who immediately introduced Eva.

Chapter 41
Sunday
Eva, Marc, Harrison and Stephanie

"Stephanie's told me a lot about you," Harrison said as Eva entered Harrison's visitor flat. Eva raised her eyebrows suspiciously. Not wanting her to get the wrong impression, Harrison added, "She says you play to around an eight or nine handicap. That's quite impressive."

Eva's facial muscles relaxed. "Well, I've been playing since I was a little girl, so that explains it. Lord knows I haven't had time to play nearly as much golf as I would have liked these past few years."

Eva was not there to talk about her golf game. And she especially wasn't there to talk about the ship's soon-to-be-former golf pro. But then she looked across the room and spied Stephanie sitting comfortably cross-legged on the couch, champagne in hand, looking relaxed and beautiful. This was most definitely not the look of a woman who felt destroyed.

Before the Chaweng Beach Club incident, Eva had enjoyed being around Stephanie, as did virtually everyone else on the ship. They had even gone shopping together twice. Then, as time went on and Claude showed such a blatant interest in Stephanie, Eva's disdain for her grew appreciably. In her heart, Eva knew Stephanie hadn't done anything wrong with Claude or in any other respect after Chaweng. Even after it was reported that Stephanie spent the night with Harrison in his visitor flat—the very same visitor flat Eva was standing in at the moment—Eva had contemplated letting that transgression pass. So what if Eva and Harrison's courtship had been shorter than a Kardashian marriage? They hadn't been obscene or obvious about what they'd done. It was the complaints from the Gripers the previous morning that really forced her to order Stephanie's firing. If Eva was going to be honest, she resented Stephanie for Claude's attention. If not for that, she probably would not have directed Marc to fire Stephanie. But she had, and that made this moment all the more intolerable.

Eva found herself in an uncomfortable position, something she wasn't used to. In all her years as a commercial litigator, deal maker, or the founder of this incredible venture, Eva was always in charge. Groveling, foundering, or being uneasy was not in her repertoire. She was there to thank Harrison, or Peyton, or whatever she was going to call him, for his over-the-top review of her esteemed Paradise. And to smooth over any issues concerning his apparent new love interest.

"Mr. Marshall, on behalf of all of Paradise's suite owners, and the entire management team, I can't thank you enough for the incredible review you just posted on Peyton's Places."

"I did?" he asked, feigning surprise. "I thought Peyton Flynn was a woman. Maybe a jocular woman from Alabama? Tarpley, wasn't it? At least that's what all the gossip around the ship seems to have been all week." Harrison laughed and winked at a visibly uncomfortable Marc.

Eva became more relaxed at Harrison's attempt at humor. "Yes, we certainly did believe that to be the case. In fact, a few women received some extraordinarily special care on account of you."

"I'm sure your wonderful staff would have accommodated their requests regardless," Harrison answered.

"Well, perhaps. But I assure you that everyone in our operation stepped up their game a bit."

"You run a great vessel here, Ms. Lampedusa. I meant every word of what I wrote in my review. In fact, I've meant every word of what I've written about any property since I've been doing this travel gig. As beautiful as your ship is, and as wonderful as are its services and food, any property is only as good as its employees. And you simply have the best."

Eva smiled, graciously, accepting accolades from the man whose glowing review was about to turn around the financial fortunes of the ship. Just a few minutes ago, on the way up the stairs from Elaine Dwyer's office, Eva had excitedly commented to Marc that luxury suite sales would probably skyrocket over the next couple of weeks. Any concerns about making bank payments, or paying the note to Mitsubishi Marine, would soon evaporate. All thanks to this guy. The guy who happened to be having an affair with the one employee Eva ordered fired two days earlier. But still, that act had not adversely affected the review. This guy was a real pro, Eva had concluded.

"Of course, you're losing one of your star employees this Tuesday. One of the few I specifically identified in my review. That's a real shame," Harrison said.

Ouch. Eva wasn't expecting that gut punch. Not so directly, anyway. In Elaine Dwyer's office, Eva, Marc and Elaine had engaged in a brief discussion about whether they should rescind Stephanie's termination. Ironically, it was Eva who proposed downgrading Stephanie's discharge to a warning. Marc concluded it would make the ship's management look weak, reversing its position only in the face of external influence. The grounds for termination were justified and the decision was meritorious.

Before Eva or Marc could say anything, Harrison continued.

"Your mistake is my good fortune." He walked over to the couch where Stephanie was seated and extended his hand, inviting her to stand next to him. They continued to hold hands as he said to Eva, "I have to tell you that I was very conflicted as I wrote my review. As I said, I love everything about Paradise, and it truly deserves all the accolades I bestowed on it. But once Stephanie told me she was being fired, I did wince a bit. Some reviewers might even have retaliated and delivered an undeservedly critical review. Obviously, I didn't. My experiences with Stephanie, on the golf courses, in the simulator, and at the crew party in Poseidon, all comprised important parts of my time aboard Paradise. Through those events, I gained critical insight into the operations of your enterprise. And on a more personal level, I found a woman and a love I never knew existed. Stephanie and I are both thrilled she'll be leaving on Tuesday. I don't mean to speak for Stephanie, but I know she'll miss her many friends from the ship," he said as he turned and faced her. As he continued to speak to Eva and Marc, he remained focused on Stephanie. "I had planned to be on board for another week, but I'm going to disembark with Stephanie."

"If you were planning to sail with us for another week, it would be our pleasure to have Stephanie stay aboard as well," Eva interrupted. "After all, we don't have another golf pro lined up yet and we have a few outings coming up this week. We could even make an exception, and she could stay in your visitor flat, if you'd like."

The offer seemed patronizing, even if genuine. Harrison looked at Stephanie and then back at Eva. "That's very kind of you, but no. We've already made plans. Steph and I are headed north to see the Taj and then going on safari before hitting Paris and a few other towns."

"Are you sure?" Eva asked, silently grateful they were both leaving. It would be untenable to have a member of the crew living in a visitor flat.

"Quite sure. It's all planned out. We'll be traveling for six weeks before heading back to La Jolla. That's where I'm from, by the way. I know my travel folio says Fresno, but that's just the city where I was born."

"Are you sure? We'd love for you to stay," Eva lied.

"Quite sure. It's all going to be great fun. And Paris is such a romantic city." He squeezed Stephanie's hand as he looked at her. "One never knows what could happen there." She squeezed back even harder. "Eva, you run a hell of a great ship. I'd love to return as a real guest one day, if that's OK with you."

"Of course it's OK. Come back anytime you like. And bring Stephanie, of course. In fact, you'll be our guests. Your accommodations and food and beverage will be comped by Paradise's management the whole time you're aboard." Eva looked at Stephanie and smiled. "I might just ask for a few pointers on my short game, if that's all right."

For the first time since Eva and Marc had entered the visitor flat, Stephanie spoke. "I'd love to help you out, Eva. Anytime. You've been very kind to me. And I've learned a great deal about management through you, albeit from afar. I've seen close up why everyone says you're such a great female leader. Heck, a great leader, regardless of your gender." She was surprised when her voice started to crack. "You've been wonderful to me since I've been here. Everyone has. I've learned so much from all of you. Any discipline that came my way was entirely justified. I stepped out of bounds a few times and broke some rules. We can't do that on a ship. I understand that. If everyone did the things I did, this would be a circus, not a luxury ship."

Eva was impressed and humbled by Stephanie's candor. She walked the few paces across the living room towards Stephanie. Stephanie placed her champagne glass on the table and welcomed a hug from Eva. Stephanie could no longer restrain her tears as Eva embraced her.

As she held Stephanie, Eva said to Harrison, "You've got a good woman here, Harrison. Our entire crew is losing a great friend.

I know I am." Then, looking back at Stephanie, she said, "You can get a bit crazy sometimes, but I admire that about you. You've got spirit and you're not afraid to show it. I can't tell you how healthy that is."

The emotion in the room was palpable. Everyone shared a fondness for Stephanie. Eva and Marc were thrilled about the superlative review they had just received. Harrison was elated he had found a partner with whom he planned to spend many years. And Stephanie knew that besides having Harrison by her side, she was leaving Eva and Marc on good terms.

Harrison pulled down two more glasses and emptied the rest of the champagne bottle into them. He handed them to Marc and Eva. Harrison lifted his glass and said, "To Stephanie, and to bright futures for all of us."

They all took a sip before Eva retorted, "To Peyton Flynn, the only woman on the ship who had to shave every day this week." They clicked glasses and all laughed.

After a few more minutes of conversation and laughs, Eva and Marc excused themselves. Marc was preparing to have dinner with Karen and Eva was preparing to tell Claude to go to hell. As soon as they left Harrison's visitor flat, Eva turned to Marc and said, "Call Elaine Dwyer and have her tell Ginger Tarpley she owes us $850 for that necklace."

Made in United States
Orlando, FL
18 August 2024

50502788R00192